Hurting *with* God

Hurting *with* God
Learning to Lament
with the Psalms

GLENN PEMBERTON

Abilene Christian University Press

HURTING WITH GOD

Learning to Lament with the Psalms

Copyright 2012 by Glenn Pemberton

ISBN 978-0-89112-400-9

LCCN 2011051906

Printed in the United States of America

LIBRARY OF CONGRESS CATALOGING-IN-PUBLICATION DATA

Pemberton, Glenn.

Hurting with God : learning to lament with the Psalms / Glenn Pemberton.

p. cm.

ISBN 978-0-89112-400-9

1. Suffering--Religious aspects--Christianity. 2. Suffering--Biblical teaching. 3. Laments. 4. Bible. O.T. Psalms--Criticism, interpretation, etc. 5. Bible--Criticism, interpretation, etc. I. Title.

BV4909.P46 2012

248.8'6--dc23

2011051906

Cover design by Nicole Wilson, Zeal Studios and Thinkpen Design, Inc.

Interior text design by Sandy Armstrong

For information contact:

Abilene Christian University Press | 1626 Campus Court | Abilene, Texas 79601

1-877-816-4455 | www.acupressbooks.com

12 13 14 15 16 17 / 8 7 6 5 4 3 2

For Dana

Remember . . .

You have turned my mourning into dancing;
You have taken off my sackcloth
And clothed me with joy.
—PSALM 30:11

Table of Contents

Acknowledgments

Initial work on this book began while I was teaching at Oklahoma Christian University and preaching most weekends at churches in Oklahoma and surrounding states. I am grateful to those who allowed me to preach, teach, and discuss the Psalms—especially the laments; many of the ideas exchanged in those days have found their way into these pages. Since coming to Abilene Christian University (ACU) in 2005, I have been fortunate to teach classes that included something about the Psalms almost every semester. In my early years here, I was able to accept invitations from churches that enabled me to keep thinking about the laments, try out new ideas, and receive valuable feedback. I am particularly grateful for programs that gave me the opportunity to work with church leaders on this material: Oklahoma Christian University Bible Lectureship, National Conference on Youth Ministry, Christian Education Association Conference, Ray Evans Seminar (hosted by the Alameda Church of Christ, Norman, Oklahoma), Advanced Bible Study Seminar (Gemünden, Germany), and ElderLink and Summit (both hosted by ACU).

In the final stages of this book I was privileged to supervise research undertaken by Austin Holt through a grant funded by ACU for undergraduate research. The analysis of hymnals and contemporary Christian music in Chapter Two is the top layer of Mr. Holt's research (his complete study should find publication soon). Other students have also made direct contributions, especially in formulating discussion questions for early drafts of Chapters Two through Four.

As the book will explain, I have spent much of the past five years at sea. That I am still moving, much less able to complete this book, is a tribute to many people who surrounded me, talked me through days when my pain was high and my morale low. My colleagues in the Department of Bible, Missions and Ministry have been gracious in every way, especially Dr. Rodney Ashlock, chair of the department. To my support team and small group—thank you seems far too little to say: Curt and Deborah Niccum, Lesa Breeding, Dawne Swearingen, and Mollie and Wade Spaulding. I must also express special gratitude to Larry Henderson and Charles Siburt for their counsel and support.

Medical professionals have become an important part of my life— some of whom I cannot imagine getting to this point of my journey without. I want to thank Dr. Corey Brown and his staff at the Abilene Diagnostic Clinic, as well as Timothy Clark, PhD, Mindy Vujovich, PhD, Norma Clarke, and all the staff at the Comprehensive Pain Management Program, Baylor University Medical Center. May you find the blessings of Psalm 41:1–3.

Sometimes the most wonderful and unexpected things happen in the middle of awful pain. It is to the surprise of my life that I dedicate this book.

Preface

Research on biblical lament has been steadily expanding over the past thirty years—even if the practical translation of this work has yet to take much hold among our churches. The form-critical research of H. Gunkel, *An Introduction to the Psalms: The Genres of the Religious Lyric of Israel* (German original in 1933) and S. Mowinckel, *The Psalms in Israel's Worship* (German original in 1962) laid the foundation for contemporary study of lament by identifying different types or genres of psalms—including the lament. On this foundation, a number of scholars have examined the psalms of lament, while at the same time drawing our attention to the near complete absence of this type of prayer from the worship of churches across the denominational spectrum. The most influential of this work has been that by Walter Brueggemann, *The Message of the Psalms* (1984), a theological commentary on the Psalms, and his collected essays in *The Psalms and the Life of Faith* (1995), Kathleen Billman and Daniel Migliore, *Rachel's Cry: Prayer of Lament and Rebirth of Hope* (1999), and Michael Jinkins, *In the House of the Lord: Inhabiting the Psalms of Lament* (1998). More recently, Sally Brown and Patrick Miller have contributed an edited collection that considers lament from a variety of perspectives entitled *Lament: Reclaiming Practices in Pulpit, Pew, and Public Square* (2005). In addition, excellent short monographs on praying the Psalms from Brueggemann, *Praying the Psalms: Engaging Scripture and the Life of the Spirit* (2nd ed., 2007) and Eugene Peterson, *Answering God: The Psalms as Tools for Prayer* (1989) have drawn special attention to the psalms of lament.

My study builds on the work of these and other scholars who have explored the psalms of lament and brought back field reports to us. They have already mapped much of the terrain that lies before us in this book, but, with the exception of the monographs by Billman and Migliore, Jinkins, and Ellington, their maps have been limited to short essays and single chapters that by necessity are fragmentary and only suggestive. Here, I try to assimilate these partial maps into a larger cohesive whole. Though I hope to contribute a few new observations to the ongoing research on lament psalms, my primary objective is not to further research. My aim in these pages is twofold: 1) to make a complete and persuasive case for the restoration of the language of lament in the life of the church and in the lives of believers (especially in Chapters One through Three and Twelve through Thirteen), and 2) to teach the language of lament by careful examination of the lament psalms (Chapters Four through Eleven). To these ends, I have tried to address the text to the faith community and its leaders, limiting academic jargon and references to a minimum. For the sake of this audience, I have also limited my recommendations for further reading to books widely available in bookstores and through online vendors (Appendix III).

The chapters are designed for personal reading as well as for use in church Bible classes and small groups (with discussion questions in Appendix II). Secondarily, some may find this volume to be a worthwhile text for undergraduate courses on the wisdom and devotional literature of the Old Testament or perhaps even a supplementary text for seminary courses on the book of Psalms. Regardless of the venue, I hope this volume brings further attention to the loss of lament in our churches, exposes what this loss is costing us, and stirs our minds to imagine what might happen if we spoke and prayed the full spectrum of biblical faith languages.

CHAPTER ONE

Life on the Sea

While on the sea hear the terrible roaring;
see how the boat of my life rolls with me.
In fear of death and in deepest of anguish,
Lord, hear my prayer; watch my soul on the sea.
—UKRAINIAN POEM (TRANS. STEPHEN BILAK)

The earth was a formless void
and darkness covered the face of the deep,
while a wind from God swept over the face of the waters.
—GENESIS 1:2

We share a common story. What separates us—gender, education, wealth, and social status—are minor details; we are the same. We want a good life, a life that satisfies our hunger for relationships, security, well-being, and purpose. In short, we want a life that works. We don't expect to live forever, but we would like to be healthy. We don't need money to burn, but we do hope for enough to get by (or just a little more). We don't want a dozen best friends, just a few meaningful relationships that last. And our shared hopes unite us against a common fear: What if? What if my health fails? What if drought wipes out the crops or my salary doesn't pay the bills? What if my best friends abandon me when I most need them? And most of all, what if God seems far away when I most need God to be near? Your story is mine, my story is yours, and our story is everyone's story.

Sometime in the winter of 2006, I injured my left foot. It was nothing serious; I couldn't even say when it happened or when I noticed the first twinge of pain. I had been exercising regularly, walking and even jogging the nearly two-mile Lundsford Trail that encircles the university where I teach. All I know is that, over a period of weeks, the intermittent twinges evolved into a constant dull ache. Perhaps because I suffer from a hereditary condition of maleness, I calculated that I must have strained a muscle. So I rested for a while. And, when rest didn't help, I tried stretching and went back to walking, logically deducing that I needed more exercise. Well trained in American values, the voices in my head urged me to walk it off—work through the pain.

In midspring, I sat in a medical exam room feeling stupid for wasting time going to the doctor over a sore foot. Then when the doctor came in, put the x-ray film up on the light box, and pointed to a fine line in the middle of my foot, I felt really stupid. By his estimation, I had been walking on a stress fracture for three months, possibly longer. The diagnosis made perfect sense of my symptoms, though I had to admit to using less than good sense for the past three months. Even so, it was still nothing serious: wear a walking boot and I should be back on the track in eight to twelve weeks.

As I write five years later, both feet are elevated, propped up with soft pillows. I was in and out of my first walking boot within six months. My first surgery was the next summer in July 2007; my fifth was in November 2009. I've worked with podiatrists, orthopedists, neurologists, neurosurgeons, pain management specialists, physical therapists, and psychologists—so many health professionals that I've lost count. Today I'm learning how to live with pain and dysfunction for which there is no medical cure. Since the beginning of this journey in 2006 I have experienced the joy of my two children's weddings and the devastation of my own divorce. I've been the recipient of powerful words of blessing and received counsel that would make Job's friends blush. And while before this life-season I've had my share of struggles with God, the past five years has felt like one intensely long wrestling match with God at the Jabbok. Like Jacob turned

Israel ("one who struggles with God" or "God struggler"), I now walk with a perpetual limp—and with unexpected blessings (Gen. 32:22–32). But all of this is getting ahead of our story.

We do share a story, though sometimes we forget. I'm fortunate that each semester the students who pass through my classes remind me of our common hopes, fears, and struggles. One semester early in my teaching career, I discovered that sitting in the first two rows of one class were a student who had lost a close friend, another his mother and then his father within the previous two years, and another her son. In a more recent class, my students wrote of their own Jacobian struggles with divorce, food addiction, anorexia, Crohn's disease, the death of friends, academic failure, and faith itself. And beyond these self-confessed battles, I know from research about this generation that many of them are silently trying to cope with experiences of sexual abuse, alcoholism, pornography, and inner demons I cannot imagine.

These two classes represent what I've found everywhere I teach, at least if I take a little time and pay attention. In classes on the book of Psalms when I ask (okay, require) students to write their own psalms, 60 percent or more will write a lament, some of which are near-impossible to grade. How do you assign a grade to a psalm about abuse? But again, this is getting ahead of our story.

Seas and Storms

No one escapes life unscathed. Even if we were Enoch and mysteriously walked with God and then "was no more, because God took him" (Gen. 5:24), the years we spend here are "only toil and trouble; they are soon gone, and we fly away" (Ps. 90:10). In the beginning, as Genesis 1 describes creation, God initiated the task of bringing order out of a chaotic mass of waters, separating and dividing—restraining and holding back chaos in order to establish life (Gen. 1:1–10). And as a result of God's work, life flourished as a paradise on earth, at least for a time. But when those made in God's own image made a misguided attempt to be gods, taking control of our lives instead of trusting God, chaotic boundaries began encroaching back on life. We traded paradise for fear, mistrust, guilt, and hard lives (Gen. 3). And when our wickedness grew to epidemic proportions and "every inclination of the thoughts of their hearts was only evil continually" (Gen. 6:5), God regretted making us (Gen. 6:6–7) and did what had to be done. The Lord unleashed the chaotic waters to reverse creation: "all the fountains of the great deep burst forth, and the windows of the heavens were opened" (Gen. 7:11). The waters the Lord separated and divided in Genesis 1 now "swelled so mightily on the earth that all the high mountains under the whole heaven were covered" (Gen. 7:19) and everything God made at creation was erased (Gen. 7:21–23).

God started over with Noah, his family, and all that was with them in the ark. As in Genesis 1, God's wind (or "spirit") blew over the waters (Gen. 8:1). God closed the "fountains of the deep and the windows of the heavens" and restrained the rain (Gen. 8:2) so that the water receded and life re-emerged. As at the first creation (Gen. 1:28), God blessed the new world: "Be fruitful and multiply, and fill the earth" (Gen. 9:1). But life had changed. Paradise was not only barred to human access by cherubim and a flaming sword (Gen. 3:24) but had been wiped off the face of the earth. Though restrained by God (Gen. 9:11), the seas and storms became an ever-present reality and threat to our lives.

If we take Job and the book of Psalms to be representative of Israelite thought, we learn that, in their worldview, water and the deep sea stood for much more than H_2O. Under control, water represents life: "there is a river whose streams make glad the city of God, the holy habitation of the Most High" (Ps. 46:4). But, like other ancient civilizations, the unpredictable, unstable, and life-threatening seas and storms came to symbolize all the chaotic forces that stand against human life and well-being. So Psalm 69 describes false accusations and attempts to destroy the psalmist in terms of water:

> Save me, O God,
>> for the waters have come up to my neck.
> I sink in deep mire,

> where there is no foothold;
>> I have come into deep waters,
>>> and the flood sweeps over me. (vv. 1–2)

The poet is not literally drowning, but to him his enemies are nothing less than chaotic waters threatening to undo his life: "let me be delivered from my enemies, and from the deep waters" (Ps. 69:14b). Other psalmists ask God for refuge under his wings "until the destroying storms pass by" (57:1b) or for God to rescue them from "the mighty waters, from the hand of aliens" (144:7). Sometimes the poets describe the consequences of God's anger in terms of a violent storm at sea.

> Your wrath lies heavy upon me,
>> and you overwhelm me with all your waves. (88:7)

> Your wrath has swept over me;
>> your dread assaults destroy me.
> They surround me like a flood all day long;
>> from all sides they close in on me. (vv. 16–17)

So it is from "out of the depths" (130:1) that the psalmists cry out to the One who alone has the power to tame the chaos that threatens life. Reminiscent of Genesis 1, Psalm 74 celebrates the Creator as the One who

> divided the sea by your might;
>> you broke the heads of the dragons in the waters.
> You crushed the heads of Leviathan,
>> you gave him as food for the creatures of the wilderness.
> You cut openings for springs and torrents,
>> you dried up ever-flowing streams. (vv. 13–15)

Psalm 104 mixes aquatic imagery from the first creation (Gen. 1) with the new creation after the flood (Gen. 8) to praise the power of God.

> You set the earth on its foundations,
>> so that it shall never be shaken.

> You cover it with the deep as with a garment;
>> the waters stood above the mountains.
> At your rebuke they flee;
>> at the sound of your thunder they take to flight.
> They rose up to the mountains, ran down to the valleys
>> to the place that you appointed for them.
> You set a boundary that they may not pass,
>> so that they might not again cover the earth. (vv. 5–9)

Recalling the exodus, Psalm 77 also describes the Lord in terms of one who conquers the seas.

> When the waters saw you, O God,
>> when the waters saw you, they were afraid;
>> the very deep trembled. . . .
> Your way was through the sea,
>> your path, through the mighty waters;
>> yet your footprints were unseen.
> You led your people like a flock
>> by the hand of Moses and Aaron. (vv. 16, 19–20)

So while the sea and storms are a frightening reality to the poets, they know and proclaim a God who sits enthroned over the waters and above the flood (Ps. 29:10).

Set within a worldview in which the sea embodies chaos, Job's complaints and God's response gain clarity. Like the psalmists, Job acknowledges that God alone has the power of creation, the power to control the chaotic sea. Job confesses that God is the One

> who alone stretched out the heavens
>> and trampled the waves of the Sea;
> who made the Bear and Orion,
>> the Pleiades and the chambers of the south;
> who does great things beyond understanding,
>> and marvelous things without number. (Job 9:8–10)

> By his power he stilled the Sea;
>> by his understanding he struck down Rahab.
> By his wind the heavens were made fair;
>> his hand pierced the fleeing serpent.
> These are indeed but the outskirts of his ways;
>> and how small a whisper do we hear of him!
> But the thunder of his power who can understand?
> (26:12–14)

Job also knows that God possesses both wisdom and strength so that

> If he tears down, no one can rebuild;
>> if he shuts someone in, no one can open up.
> If he withholds the waters, they dry up;
>> if he sends them out, they overwhelm the land.
> (12:14–15)

But what Job doesn't understand and openly questions is why God is treating him as if he were a dangerous enemy: "Am I the Sea, or the Dragon, that you set a guard over me?" (Job 7:12), when he is only a mortal who could not possibly be a threat to God (7:20–21). And yet, all Job can see is that God "has kindled his wrath against me, and counts me as his adversary" (19:11).

Consequently, God begins his reply to Job with reference to creation (38:4–7) and discussion about the sea:

> Or who shut in the sea with doors
>> when it burst out from the womb?—
> when I made the clouds its garment,
>> and thick darkness its swaddling band,
> and prescribed bounds for it,
>> and set bars and doors,
> and said, "Thus far shall you come, and no farther,
>> and here shall your proud waves be stopped?" (38:8–11)

The good news for Job (and us) in God's reply is that the sea/chaos does not have free reign in this world. Rather, God has set boundaries and limits to how far the sea may trespass on life (38:11). Even more, from God's perspective the powerful and proud sea is nothing more than a newborn baby that needs swaddling (38:8–9). While the sea frightens and undoes human life, God is stronger and controls the sea with solid bars and doors (38:10). That's the good news. The bad news is that the sea still exists and works its chaos in our world. God has trampled on the sea and conquers it at his pleasure and for his purposes. But just as the generations after Noah learned and the psalmists knew, as long as the sea exists it remains a threat to our lives.

This ancient view of the sea also brings new perspective to stories from the Gospels. Demon-possessed pigs run headlong into the sea (Matt. 8:32) because, like our sins (Mic. 7:14), that is the place they belong. Twice the Gospels retell stories about Jesus and his disciples in storms at sea. In the first, Jesus is sleeping when the frightened disciples wake him asking whether he just doesn't care if they all die. Jesus "rebuked the winds and the sea" with the result of immediate calm (Matt. 8:26). Understanding their worldview, it is little wonder that the disciples are awe struck and ask, "What sort of man is this, that even the winds and sea obey him?" (Matt. 8:27). In the second story, the disciples are alone in the boat, rowing futilely against strong winds, when Jesus comes walking across the sea (Matt. 14:24–25). They are terrified. If they remembered their Scriptures, they knew that no one is able to trample on the waves of the sea except God (Job 9:8). So this time when Jesus gets in the boat and the wind immediately stops blowing, the disciples make the connection, worshipping him and saying, "'Truly you are the Son of God'" (Matt. 14:33).

The book of Revelation also draws on the sea as an image of all that stands against life as it depicts the final epic battle between the Lamb and his enemies. Early in the story, the wind and sea are restrained until the servants of God are identified and marked (Rev. 7:1–3). Later John sees a dragon reminiscent of the dragon Leviathan from the Old Testament (another image embodying chaos—see Ps. 74:13–15; Job 26:13; and Job

41:1–34) and a great beast rising out of the sea (13:1) as well as another great beast rising from the earth that "spoke like a dragon" (13:11). It is only after the defeat of these forces that John sees "a new heaven and a new earth; for the first heaven and the first earth had passed away, *and the sea was no more*" (21:1, emphasis mine). No more sea, no more of the chaos that stands against life. Now God will again live with his people and wipe away every remaining tear. And, with no sea, "death will be no more; mourning and crying and pain will be no more, for the first things have passed away" (21:4). *Maranatha!* Come Lord Jesus.

The extinction of the sea is good news to seasick and battle-fatigued people—all of us. The downside is that John's vision is just that—a vision of what is to come but is not yet. John's hopeful words remind us in the same way God once reminded Job. As long as we live, the sea will always be a threat, a reality with which we will have to contend. Like it or not, we are not living in Eden but in a world of hurricanes, tornadoes, and tsunamis. And no one escapes the hellish reality of the sea—not the prophets, the psalmists, the early church, or even the Son of God. The unstable, unpredictable, and unknown has been part of our world since the beginning and will continue until the end. And so, we not only share the same struggle and the same story but also the same need to find a way to live out our faith in the storm. How do we live with and relate to God when the waters pound and choke us? What do we say to the God who has the power to restrain the storm but chooses instead to let it pour?

Charting a Path through the Storm

Most studies of grief or pain come as the result of a personal experience that sent the author on a quest for answers. C. S. Lewis wrote *A Grief Observed* in response to his wife's death (see also his earlier work, *The Problem of Pain*). Both Harold Kushner and Nicholas Wolterstorff wrote, out of grief for their sons, *When Bad Things Happen to Good People* and *Lament for a Son*, respectively. Few people choose to write about grief or pain unless their own lives have captured and held them hostage. As I have mentioned, this study also emerges from my own struggles with pain—physical, emotional, and spiritual. But while others are especially interested in the problem of theodicy—why innocent people suffer or bad things happen to good people in a world over which the Lord reigns–I'm not looking for answers to this set of questions. It's not that I am uninterested in the philosophical or theological problem or think the answers unimportant; it's just that my path has led to a different set of concerns.

Our response to storms, literal or metaphoric, reveals much about us. In the fall of 2000, after losing a house to a wildfire, my objective was clear: rebuild quickly, replace our losses, and get life back to normal as soon as possible. This response is typical of our culture. When a problem or crisis erupts, we want an immediate fix. We speak of "getting through it," "getting past it," and "seeing the light at the end of the tunnel" from which we will emerge stronger and better for the experience. So we pray for healing (now) and respond to those who are ill by asking if they are feeling better (yet). We share the American dream of being able to triumph over any obstacle and live above every circumstance. And all this self-talk is fine as long as we really do get better or find a happy resolution.

But what if we or those we love don't get better? What if the storm never lets up? What if the issue is not about how to "get through it" or "getting to the light at end of the tunnel" because this tunnel has no end point short of death? What if God chooses not to answer our prayers for healing, for a better marriage, for a way to pay the bills, or for a way out of the mess that is my life? What then? In my experience, when there is no end to the pain or the loss, we simply do not know how to respond to ourselves, to others, or to God. And, in these cases, even the most well-intentioned and sound theological-philosophical explanations about why bad things happen in God's world don't matter because they do nothing to help me live now; they do not stop my pain or teach me how to live within circumstances that do not change. At least for now, I don't care why this storm is flooding my life. I just need someone to teach me how to swim.

I do wonder whether our drive to find answers for why something has happened is symptomatic of our deeper desire for security. We want a world that is predictable—that has rational explanations for everything that happens and therefore is manageable. Explanations give an illusion of control, as if, by understanding why a thing has happened, I will be able to stop it from happening again. Maybe. But, for most of us, life is not so simple and certainly not under our control. Accidents happen, storms break out, diseases erupt, and irreversible damage occurs to our bodies, our relationships, and our plans. Even Job does not live happily ever after. To be sure, after he loses everything, he gets twice his wealth back but not his first seven sons and three daughters. He gets new children, but children are hardly replaceable or interchangeable parts. Job never returns to normal; instead he lives the rest of his life with grief for ten children and the realization that he could lose everything again, including his new children and their children. And now he knows that he is powerless to control what may or may not happen in his life and in the lives of those he loves. Job has to learn to live with that reality.

So at least for now, I'm indifferent to explanations for the chaos that surrounds our lives. I'm also not looking for anyone's sympathy; that's not helpful to me. Nor is it worth our time to try to figure out who is carrying the heaviest load, as if comparisons to one another are going to help anyone. Here's all that matters: *everyone* is living on the sea—it is our human condition. And, sooner or later, our shared journey leads us beyond questions of *why* to questions of *how*. We live in a world that is beyond our control, and life is in a constant flux of change. So we have a decision to make: keep trying to control a storm that is not going to go away or start learning how to live within the rain.

I'm not suggesting that we shouldn't pursue every avenue to help ourselves, including prayer. The faith response to a world beyond our control is not to roll over and play dead. But, at least for me, after years of trying to find a cure that will reverse the irreversible, what I want to know now is how to live with God when things don't get better—how to live out faith in the midst of the downpour. How do I live in an authentic relationship with the sovereign who holds the universe together when my world has been shaken and rearranged? What do I say to this God? To be blunt, if you are looking for answers to why bad things are happening in your life or if you are looking for some spiritual way to improve your circumstances (e.g., to get God to work in your favor), you've got the wrong book. I'm at a different place on my journey. So when you come to realize that there are no complete answers and what answers you discover are not going to change your circumstances, nor is anything else going to undo what has blindsided you—then I invite you to come back and join me on my journey.

I'm interested in how we, as people of faith, live with God in less than ideal circumstances (and that means I'm interested in all of us). I'm also interested in how the community of believers responds to and supports its members living in storms. How may Christians bear one another's burdens and so live out the law of Christ (Gal. 6:2)? How can churches help believers maintain their faith and relationship with God while they are hurting—not just until they get better or until the crisis is over, but when the storm continues or leaves irreparable damage in its wake? And if my story is in fact our story, and I am convinced it is, then our churches are filled with believers who are hurting, to one degree or another, whether visible or unseen. Some come every Sunday clinging to a thread of hope that somehow the church will be the body of Christ that supports them, offers a word of hope, and helps them find a way to walk through the storm with God instead of without God.

I'm concerned for well-intended churches whose assemblies of praise and triumph only know how to pray for and celebrate healing but ignore the chaos raging all around them. Must it be that, because we affirm that God reigns, we have to pretend that everything must be okay or will soon be? I acknowledge a certain value in continuing to hurl our songs of praise against prevailing winds. We do celebrate a God who reigns over and through the storm. But as Walter Brueggemann observes, our contemporary praise assemblies are less likely due to courageous faith and more about fear and acquiescence to an American culture

> that does not want to acknowledge or experience the disorientation of life. The reason for such relentless affirmation of orientation seems to come, not from faith, but from the wishful

optimism of our culture. Such a denial and cover-up, which I take it to be, is an odd inclination for passionate Bible users, given the large number of psalms that are songs of lament, protest, and complaint about the incoherence that is experienced in the world. At least it is clear that a church that goes on singing "happy songs" in the face of raw reality is doing something very different from what the Bible itself does. (*The Message of the Psalms*, 51)

I share Brueggemann's alarm for what passes these days as worship, that a faithful relationship with God requires endless platitudes and songs of joy when our world and our lives are in chaos. I grieve over our loss of the faith language of lament and am concerned for how our practice of praise and worship is shaping us as individual believers and communities of faith.

But more than just raising an alarm, I want to explore another way to live and relate to our God. I believe we are ready to hear and restore the ancient biblical language of lament and in the process provide a much-needed resource for believers living in rising waters. If what I have found in university classrooms and churches is a reliable indicator, believers are aching for words to express the realities of their lives, to speak the truth to God instead of putting on a charade of repetitive and empty praise clichés that ignore or deny the relentless storms. Christians are ready to learn a new, more faithful and authentic language. But again, I'm getting far ahead of our story.

At this point, it is enough to plot a curriculum for learning a new language. To begin, we need to investigate the concept of lament and its presence in the Old Testament, especially the book of Psalms. And, because our interests are not merely historical, our examination of this ancient hymnal of faith will lead us to a survey of our own hymnals and music to see how our songs and prayers compare. What we will discover and document is the near extinction of a once vibrant language of faith (Chapter Two). This dramatic shift requires some explanation. When did lament vanish? Did the early church practice lament, or was lament confined to the era of the

Old Testament? What about Jesus? (Chapter Three). Next, we will put the language of lament under the microscope to examine and describe its tone, texture, and content. At close range, we will see lament to be a distinct faith language with its own vocabulary and grammar for intimate and difficult conversation with God (Chapter Four). Then, we will launch into a series of investigations that plot the underlying causes or problems that led psalmists to use the language of lament: the problem of sin (Chapter Five), discouragement (Chapter Six), health and mortality (Chapter Seven), the presence of opponents or enemies (Chapters Eight and Nine—there are many enemies in the Psalms!), and, most difficult, when God is the problem (Chapters Ten and Eleven).

In each chapter, we will look at examples from the book of Psalms and work to understand their language—what they say, how they say it, and why—with the hope that, in the process of reading and lingering over these prayers and songs, we can learn to speak their language. After this study of lament, we will take note of another type of psalm closely connected to lament: thanksgiving psalms (Chapter Twelve). Thanksgiving and lament not only grow from the same soil of faith but are part of the same organism. The practice of thanksgiving grows out of the prior practice of lament, so the loss of lament actually threatens a second type of faith talk: thanksgiving. We will observe, despite all our praise songs, how authentic thanksgiving is becoming an endangered species in our generation. Finally, while each chapter will include practical reflection, in Chapter Thirteen we will consider specific ways in which we as individuals and churches may implement the practice of lament and live out faithful relationships with God, not above but in the middle of the storm.

CHAPTER TWO

The Book of Praises

Praise the LORD!
Praise God in his sanctuary;
praise him in his mighty firmament!

❧

Let everything that breathes praise the LORD!
Praise the LORD!
—PSALM 150:1, 6

This is not a "word of praise" slapped onto whatever mess we are
in at the moment. This crafted conclusion for the Psalms tells us
that our prayers are going to end in praise, but that it is also
going to take awhile. Don't rush it.
—EUGENE PETERSON (*Answering God*, 127)

In Hebrew, the book of Psalms is entitled *Sepher Tehillim,* the "Book of Praises," a fitting title for a book that proclaims the Lord is "enthroned on the praises of Israel" (Ps. 22:3) and so extends invitations for everyone to join the enthronement procession of praise: the psalmists (39:1–2; 89:1–2; 103:1; 146:1–2), the servants of the temple (134:1–2; 135:1–4), God's people (33:1; 113:1; 147:12; 149:1–4), and all the earth (98:4; 100:1; 148). The psalms encourage us to erupt into "joyous song" (98:4) and "come into his [God's] presence with singing" (100:2)—to "Praise the LORD!" (106:1; 146:1; 147:1, 20, etc.). From these calls to praise come refrains that soar from the pages:

O LORD, our Sovereign,
>   how majestic is your name in all the earth! (8:1)

Great are the works of the LORD,
>   studied by all who delight in them.
Full of honor and majesty is his work,
>   and his righteousness endures forever. (111:2–3)

I will extol you, my God and King,
>   and bless your name forever and ever.
Every day I will bless you,
>   and praise your name forever and ever.
Great is the LORD, and greatly to be praised;
>   his greatness is unsearchable. (145:1–3)

Through the language of *tehillim* (praises) Israel proclaims the fundamental nature of her God and celebrates the joys of a life lived in relationship to the Lord. In praise Israel asserts the unlimited sovereignty of her God: "The LORD is king! The world is firmly established; it shall never be moved" (96:10). And in praise the psalmists testify to God's unfailing love: "his steadfast love endures forever" (106:1). Even creation joins the chorus of praise by "telling the glory of God; and the firmament proclaims his handiwork" (19:1). Indeed, the Book of Praises envisions no person, place, or time that should be devoid of praise to the Lord:

Blessed be the name of the LORD
>   from this time on and forevermore.
From the rising of the sun to its setting
>   the name of the LORD is to be praised.
The LORD is high above all nations,
>   and his glory above the heavens. (113:2–4)

The book of Psalms is the Book of Praises. And yet, it takes only a few minutes of reading this book to realize that Israel's understanding of praise extends beyond our own limited definitions. Israel's Book of

Praises includes a diverse assortment of psalms, some well known and others hardly recognizable. For example, under the heading of Praises, the book not only includes hymns of praise and songs of thanksgiving but also psalms of confidence in the Lord, such as the shepherd's psalm (Ps. 23) or Psalm 46:

> God is our refuge and strength,
>> a very present help in trouble.
> Therefore we will not fear,
>> though the earth should change,
>> though the mountains shake in the heart of the sea;
>> though its waters roar and foam,
>> though the mountains tremble with its tumult.
>>> (46:1–3; cf. Pss. 11, 16, 20, 27, 121)

Another common type of psalm that we might not initially regard as praise is the teaching psalm, i.e. a psalm that conveys or encourages a lesson or value. Psalm 133, a good example of this type, extols the value of community "How very good and pleasant it is when kindred live together in unity!" (v. 1), while Psalm 127 reminds the reader, "unless the LORD builds the house, those who build it labor in vain" (127:1; see also 49, 50, 78). A few other psalms function in particular moments or movements in a worship assembly. For instance, Psalm 15 is as an entrance liturgy, a song for the beginning of an assembly that reminds those gathering of the kind of worship God desires from them:

> O LORD, who may abide in your tent?
> Who may dwell on your holy hill?
> Those who walk blamelessly, and do what is right,
>> and speak the truth from their heart. . . .
> Those who do these things shall never be moved.
>> (15:1–2, 5b; cf. James 1:26–27)

Other psalms were composed for still other occasions in worship and life; for example, a prayer for the king and his troops going into battle (20), a song for a royal wedding (45), and even a psalm for the coronation of a new king ("Long may he live!" Ps. 72:15a).

Taken seriously then, the title Book of Praises is not, as Peterson suggests, an inaccurate title or only accurate because it describes "the finished product. All prayer, pursued far enough, becomes praise" (*Answering God*, 121–22). *Tehillim* has a broader reach than just those psalms that specifically address the Lord in adoration or praise—an important initial insight for our worship and praise generation. In the Psalter, praise includes not only hymns of praise and thanksgiving but also teaching psalms, songs of confidence, liturgical songs, and many other types and subtypes: wisdom psalms (14, 49, 112, 128), pilgrimage songs (84, 122), royal psalms (2, 20, 45, 72, 110), historical reviews (78, 105, 136), songs of Zion (46, 48, 84, 122), and—more numerous than any of these—lament psalms.

The Language of Lament

Lament is a complex language of complaint, protest, and appeal directed to God. At times, lament may be subdued in tone as a poet wrestles with trouble; at other times, lament may be as loud and vigorous as any praise song. In the Book of Praises, the language of lament ranges from mild concerns (4, 26, 61, 120) to desperation for overwhelming difficulties (39, 79) and life-threatening disease (6, 38), from a tone of confident assurance that God will hear and respond (62, 63, 64) to despair over God's inaction or delay (10, 22, 88), from confession of sin (25, 51, 130) to protests of innocence (7, 26), and from nagging questions about God's presence (13, 108) to accusations that God has broken his promises (44, 88, 89). These diverse laments share one commonality: deep faith in God in the midst of pain. Though to some readers it may appear that these poets are weak in faith or having a breakdown of faith, as we will see, they have not lost their faith at all—far from it. Rather, these poets bring to God the life outside of the peace and calm of the sanctuary, life with all of its confusion and pain, life on the sea. And brought to God, nothing is out of bounds.

As long as the language is honest, the book of Psalms does not exclude, deny, or cover up the hardships present in the lives of believers. We are mortal, with bodies that are prone to weakness (38:10; 71:9, 18; 142:3), disease (6:2–5), and pain (38:17). As believers we experience disappointments in life (13:2) and the darkness of depression (38:6, 8, 10; 88:3–7). We have people in our lives who by no fault of our own have become our enemies (69:3; 109:4–5); they lie about us (5:9), take us to court (7, 17), scheme to cause us trouble (28:3) or shame us (4:2), and try to take advantage of us at our weakest moments (71:9–11). We have lifelong friends who abandon us at our time of greatest need (88:8), who turn on us (55:12–14, 20–21), and who return trouble for all the good that we have done for them (109:4–5). And sometimes even God confuses us: a God who all too often seems absent and unresponsive when we most need him (13; 88:13–14; 90), who does not intervene in the world or in our lives as we expect (10; 42:9–10; 60), or is far slower to act than we would hope (74:11; 80; 85), and, on occasion, a God who behaves in such bizarre ways we are left wondering about God's faithfulness (44, 77, 88, 89). All of these struggles and more are at the heart of lament. Nothing is out of bounds, nothing held back, nothing taboo. These psalms teach us that there is nothing a believer may not say to God in lament as long as the lament matches the honesty of our praise. And it is this language in all its diversity that fills the Book of Praises, which outspeaks every other type of psalm and is, as Michael Jinkins points out, "an essential form of worship" (*In the House of the Lord*, 33).

Lament and the Book of Psalms

The book of Psalms consists of five subbooks, corresponding to the five books of Torah (the Pentateuch). Brief doxologies conclude the first four of these books (41:14; 72:18–20; 89:52; 106:48) while Psalm 150 provides a grand finale to the fifth book and to the Psalter as a whole. In the first three books of psalms are forty-seven laments, over half of the total number (eighty-nine): these three books of psalms have only ten psalms of praise and eighteen psalms of thanksgiving and trust. Books 4 and 5 include more psalms of praise, thanksgiving, and trust, bringing their grand total to sixty-nine out of the one hundred fifty. But it takes these three groups combined to outnumber the sixty psalms within the single category of lament (the other twenty-one psalms consist of other types, e.g., wisdom, royal, and liturgical; see Appendix IV for a complete analysis). To the surprise of most first-time and even a few longtime readers, the Book of Praises is in fact a book of lament.

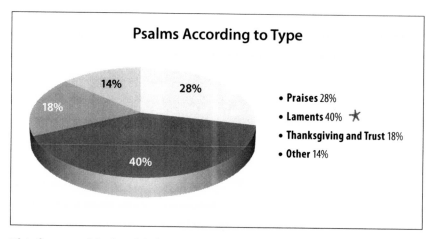

Psalms According to Type

- **Praises** 28%
- **Laments** 40%
- **Thanksgiving and Trust** 18%
- **Other** 14%

This feature of the book left its imprint on me several years ago when I was working through a translation of the Psalms on behalf of the World Bible Translation Center (WBTC). For several weeks I read a draft of Psalms 1–89 (the first three books) against the Hebrew, checking for accuracy and writing suggestions for the editors to consider. The process itself tends to leave one cross-eyed and in a state of lament for eyes that "grow dim" (69:3). That aside, well into the project, Ken Berry, the lead editor at WBTC for this particular translation, asked how I was coming along. I spoke before thinking, not an unusual thing for me to do. But this time my response confused *me*; while the work was going well I was finding it discouraging, even depressing. That didn't make any sense to me. I was, after all, working on the Book of Praises. Ken responded with affirmation for my despair and simply said, "It's the Psalms. It's lament."

Today many Christians view lament with skepticism if not outright revolt, asserting that such language is not faith filled but a dangerous strain of doubt. They argue that people of faith should not complain about their problems, question God's presence, or dispute God's actions, not even in the worst storms. Christians should certainly not accuse God of impropriety! While people of faith are not exempt from problems, they should know that God always has a plan or that "all things work together for good for those who love God" (Rom. 8:28, taken out of context), and they should never question Jesus' promise that "I am with you always" (Matt. 28:20). After all, "faith is the assurance of things hoped for, the conviction of things not seen" (Heb. 11:1); if faith does anything, it removes the need for lament from a believer's life—or so some claim.

Israel did not think about lament as we do. The overwhelming presence of the language of complaint, questioning, and protest in the Psalms suggests that Israel had a different view of the nexus among lament, faith, and praise. The headings of the book of Psalms place lament on the lips of God's most faithful followers—Moses (once in Ps. 90), David (thirty-eight times, e.g., 22, 38), and various temple leaders (Ethan [89], Korah [42–43], Heman [88], Asaph [77, 79])—and assigns lament for occasions ordained by God (e.g., the memorial offering [38, 70]). In the Psalms, it is not those who lack faith who lament but those recognized for strong faith who bring their most honest and passionate feelings to God. Moreover, by the sheer number of laments in the Psalms, it would appear that one major message of the book is this very point: God invites his people to speak the truth of their lives, their pain, and their confusion to the One who can do something about it.

This same understanding of the connection between lament and faith extends beyond the Book of Praises into the lives of other faith heroes in the Old Testament such as Jeremiah, Job, and Habakkuk. Jeremiah laments in six rather famous passages (11:18–23; 12:1–6; 15:10–21; 17:14–18; 18:18–23; 20:7–18). He asks God, "Why does the way of the guilty prosper?" (12:1) as well as why his own pain is unceasing (15:18). He begs for healing (17:14) and for God to deal with his opponents (18:19–23). At a low moment, Jeremiah curses the day of his birth (20:14–18); and at his lowest, Jeremiah brings charges against God's reliability: "Truly, you are to me like a deceitful brook; like waters that fail" (15:18) and accuses God of misusing power: "O LORD, you have enticed me, and I was enticed; you have overpowered me, and you have prevailed" (20:7).

Like Jeremiah, Job also asks God about the prosperity of the wicked (21:7–15) and for God's intervention regarding his friends and enemies (13:1–12; 30:1–15). Job curses the day of his birth (3:1–19) and, far more than Jeremiah, Job calls God to account for his actions (7:11–21; 16:18–22; 24:1–12, 21–25). To be sure, such language runs the risk of going too far, a countercharge that God brings against Jeremiah (15:19–20) and Job (38:1–3; 40:1–2, 6–8). But most of the time God seems to understand not only the pain and confusion these men experienced but the need for them to speak plainly and honestly about it to God.

Such was certainly the case for Habakkuk's complaint. Habakkuk could not understand how God could look at what was happening in his Judean society and do nothing about it (Hab. 1:1–4). Then after God explained his plans to Habakkuk (1:5–11), Habakkuk questioned how God could do such a thing, use a terrible nation to punish his (bad) people (1:12–2:1). So the conversation goes between Habakkuk and God until, at the end of the book, Habakkuk decides to wait for what God has told him will come: a massive invasion that will destroy Judah, Judah's enemies, and maybe even Habakkuk in the process. He has spoken honestly and raised difficult questions about God's ways, and in response God has replied with tough answers. A lack of faith is not Habakkuk's problem—quite the opposite. I want to have just a little of the tenacity Habakkuk expresses in his final words:

> though the fig tree does not blossom,
>> and no fruit is on the vines;
> though the produce of the olive fails,
>> and the fields yield no food;
> though the flock is cut off from the fold,
>> and there is no herd in the stalls,
> yet I will rejoice in the LORD;
>> I will exult in the God of my salvation.
> God, the LORD, is my strength. (3:17–19)

Habakkuk's complaints do not stem from a lack of faith but from an abundance of faith. It is because he believes in the sovereignty of God that his world confuses him and because of his faith in a God of justice that he must take his concerns to God. The same is true for Jeremiah, Job, the sixty lament psalms, and passages in the Old Testament (e.g., Lamentations) that speak to God from the deep seas of life. Faith leads a person to bring praise and pain, thanksgiving and confusion, confidence and questions—all of life—to God. ✘

Lament and Contemporary Hymnals

Apart from a few groups who exclusively use the Psalms as their book of song and prayer, for most Protestants, our hymnals are the functional equivalent of the Psalms for Israel and the early church. Consequently, careful examination of our hymnals provides reliable data regarding the role of lament in our communal life and enables us to compare our practice of song and prayer to the book of Psalms. In this section, I share the results of one such study conducted by T. Austin Holt IV, my undergraduate research assistant at Abilene Christian University during the summer of 2011. Holt examines hymnals from three mainline Protestant denominations (Churches of Christ, Baptist, and Presbyterian). Using the same criteria I use above to sort psalms according to type, he categorizes the songs in each hymnal into equivalent major categories: praise, thanksgiving and trust, teaching and encouragement, and lament. In addition, he identifies categories of contemporary songs with few or no parallels in the book of Psalms: invitation or altar calls, passion laments, and patriotic songs.

As a representative hymnal, Holt first examines *Songs of Faith and Praise* (*SOFP*), a common hymnal among Churches of Christ, which includes 885 songs plus readings and suggestions for medleys. Of the 885 songs, thanksgiving and trust constitute the largest single category (44 percent, 392 songs). In this group Holt includes songs that give thanks for Christ's redeeming work, celebrate the hope of heaven, give thanks for salvation, and express confidence in God's presence and provision. The next strongest category is praise (30 percent, 264 songs). This group includes songs that praise God as Creator, King, and the One who sustains the well-being of life. The third most common type of hymn is lament (13 percent, 111 songs), though, as I will demonstrate below, this large percentage is misleading. The final major category in Holt's analysis is teaching and encouragement, songs that encourage others (or oneself) to live faithfully, proclaim the gospel, or enact some other virtue (8 percent, 73 songs). The remaining hymns in *SOFP* (5 percent, 45 songs) fall into three groups: invitation or altar call songs (32 songs, without parallel in Psalms), liturgical songs for specific moments in worship such as communion (10 songs, similar to liturgical psalms), and patriotic songs (3 songs, somewhat similar to the psalms of Zion).

Analysis of *The Presbyterian Hymnal* (*PH*) and *The Baptist Hymnal* (*BH*) shows the same prevalence of thanksgiving and praise. *The Presbyterian Hymnal* (1990) contains 605 hymns: 30 percent praise (184 hymns), 29 percent thanksgiving and trust (173 hymns), 19 percent lament (116 hymns), 12 percent liturgical (70 hymns), 9 percent teaching and encouragement (56 hymns), and 1 percent altar call and patriotic (6 hymns). *The Baptist Hymnal* contains 674 hymns: 29 percent praise (197 hymns), 41 percent thanksgiving and trust (273 hymns), 13 percent lament (89 hymns), 11 percent teaching and encouragement (72 hymns), 4 percent liturgical (24 hymns), and 2

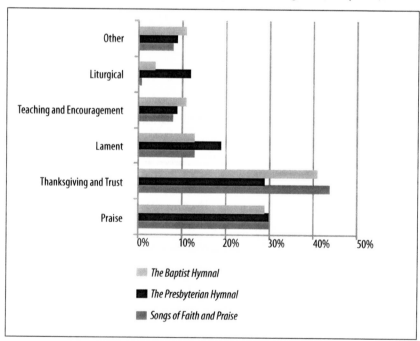

percent altar call and patriotic (19 hymns). Despite the differences among our denominations, we sing and pray the same faith languages.

Comparison of Holt's analysis of our hymnals to the book of Psalms is revealing—and alarming. In the book of Psalms, praise accounts for 28 percent of all psalms (42 psalms), roughly the same percentage as in our song books: *SOFP* 30 percent, *PH* 30 percent, *BH* 29 percent. Similarly, wisdom psalms that teach a lesson or encourage virtue comprise 10 percent of the Psalter (15 psalms), generally the same percentage of teaching and encouragement songs in our hymnals: *SOFP* 8 percent, *PH* 9 percent, and *BH* 11 percent.

The close correspondence between the Psalms and our hymnals, however, ends with these groups. Comparison of the other major categories reveals two significant differences. First, while thanksgiving and trust comprise 18 percent of the Psalms (27 psalms), in our hymnals, this group is significantly larger: *SOFP* 44 percent, *PH* 29 percent, *BH* 41 percent. It is striking to note that, taken together, our positive songs of praise and thanksgiving comprise 59 percent to 75 percent of our hymnals, whereas these two groups constitute only 46 percent of the Psalter. Second, the disparity is even greater between the laments in the Psalms and those in our books of worship. In the Psalms, lament constitutes 40 percent of all psalms (60 psalms), but, in our hymnals, lament comprises less than 20 percent: *SOFP* 13 percent, *PH* 19 percent, *BH* 13 percent. We have replaced biblical lament with songs of thanksgiving and trust. The percentage of songs of thanksgiving and trust in comparison to songs of lament (of all types) in our hymnals is reversed from what we find in the Psalms. In our song books, thanksgiving comprises 29–44 percent and lament 13–19 percent. In the Psalms, lament comprises 40 percent and thanksgiving 18 percent. Other studies of hymnals and worship resources have reached similar conclusions (see recommendations for further reading). My own experience in churches affirms the data. The prayers and songs in most churches today consist almost exclusively of praise and thanksgiving, whether they are the older hymns or the newer "Praise Songs" (a self-revealing title).

Closer analysis, however, reveals an even greater disproportion. Our songs of lament express:

1. an intense but vague desire for a closer relationship with God (61 percent of lament hymns in *SOFP*, 48 percent in *PH*, 70 percent in *BH*);

2. sorrow for our sin—penitential laments (11 percent of lament hymns in *SOFP*, 12 percent in *PH*, 7 percent in *BH*);

3. sorrow for the suffering of Christ—passion laments (10 percent of lament hymns in *SOFP*, 10 percent in *PH*, 10 percent in *BH*);

4. the need for comfort, guidance, rest, and strength (16 percent of lament hymns in *SOFP*, 26 percent in *PH*, 10 percent in *BH*); and

5. the problem of an enemy or lament for the second coming (2 percent of lament hymns in *SOFP*, 4 percent in *PH*, 3 percent in *BH*).

Three of these subcategories correspond to subcategories of lament in the Psalms: subcategory 2—penitential psalms (e.g., Ps. 51, see Chapter Five), subcategory 4—laments for comfort or guidance based on personal weakness and need (e.g., Pss. 42–43, see Chapter Six), and subcategory 5—the problem of enemies, though not lament for the second coming (see Chapters Eight and Nine). However, the other two subtypes have few or no parallels in the Psalms. Subcategory 1, the desire for a closer relationship to God is present in some psalms, but, unlike our hymns, these psalms accuse God, other people, or both of disrupting the relationship. The Psalms do not sing refrains of how they long to be closer to God without directly addressing what or who is causing them not to be close to God. The closest parallel to subcategory 3 (passion laments) are the royal laments (laments for the suffering of a king), but here the correspondence depends on reading the Psalms from a Christological perspective (e.g., Psalm 22 as the cry from the cross). Within their own historical context, however, royal laments are not the same type or genre as the passion laments in our hymnals.

This comparison of our hymnals to the Psalms reveals two significant and alarming results. First, we have almost completely lost the biblical language of lament. Though lament songs comprise a small percentage of our hymnals (13–19 percent), more than 70 percent of these songs are unlike what we find in the book of Psalms. Few of our lament songs correspond to the kind of lament in the Psalms: what constitutes 40 percent of the book of Psalms (60 laments out of 150 psalms) comprises only 3 percent of *SOFP* (30 out of 885 songs), 2 percent of *BH* (15 out of 674 songs), and 7 percent of *PH* (45 out of 605 songs). In other words, absent from our laments are the themes most prevalent in the laments of the Psalter: the problem of enemies, unmerited suffering, and God's failures to act or respond. We may lament, but in most cases we lament in such ways that our practice would be unrecognizable to the ancient psalmists. The vibrant language of lament is dead to us; old texts may remain and a few rather odd people may read what was once a living language, but, for most of us, it has become a curious museum piece in our Bibles. Expressions of unresolved pain, confusion, desperation, and sorrow—in other words, lament— are nearly extinct.

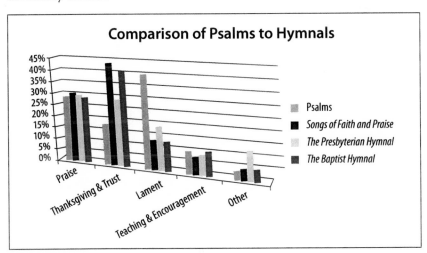

The loss of lament and its replacement by songs of thanksgiving and trust is alarming because the songs we sing week after week influence our theology as much as, or more than, the words of a sermon or Scripture itself. Our worship is not just something we do but something that transforms us. Michael Jinkins aptly says, "We cannot expect a people's understanding of God to reach much higher than their hymn books. The hymns we sing and the readings of Scripture we hear in worship form the texts that form us" (*In the House of the Lord*, 34). Regardless of what we may claim to believe, our hymnals reflect and articulate the theology that shapes us. Consequently, when we observe such massive shifts in what the church sings, we are, in fact, catching a glimpse of major theological changes that carry enormous practical significance for churches and individual believers. Worse, as Denise Hopkins puts it, "If 'we are what we sing' then we are in trouble in terms of expressing the reality of the life of faith" (*Journey through the Psalms*, 8).

The data and initial conclusions raise critical questions for our study. Why is it that in our churches confidence has replaced recognition of need? Is this actually true or merely what we want to believe about our lives? Why do our hymnals portray Christianity as a celebration of one victory after another while neglecting voices crying out from the margins of loss and defeat? Is this portrayal true to our world? Is it true to biblical theology? How do we account for the shift in what people of faith sing and pray? Is this change due to Western philosophy or American optimism of the individual? It appears that while the Psalms recognize humanity to be in a constant state of need and conflict, our churches celebrate the well-being experienced by few people today. While the world starves and lives in fear of abuse at the hands of the powerful, the church only thinks to sing another song of thanksgiving. Why are we singing so many happy songs? What does our practice say about us—and how is our practice forming us into (or deforming us away from) the image of Christ?

Investigation of what has happened is always easier than discerning why it has happened. If the loss of lament were a recent development, it would be easy to affix blame on the contemporary praise movement, "worshiptainment" as it is sometimes called. Perhaps this recent trend has pushed lament further to the margins, but lament was already on life support long before the contemporary praise movement. I don't believe it is fair to blame our worship leaders. They select and lead songs that are in our hymnals or popular among Christian music artists. Nor should blame fall on the editors or compilers of our hymnals. Their books collect, edit, and publish songs that churches want to sing. The process is cyclical: churches sing songs that are published and editors publish songs that churches sing. Both can act in ways to break the trend and help the church learn to lament, and we will consider some steps in this direction in coming chapters. Most significantly, we require a shift in theology that may be brought about only by learning a new language, a language capable of expressing the reality of our lives and our world—the language of lament.

Before we turn to language acquisition, however, we need to consider the practice of lament in the biblical records of the earliest Christian churches. One pervasive argument against lament is that the early church purposefully jettisoned lament along with other Old Testament practices unneeded or inappropriate for Christians. In other words, the church did not lose lament—it got rid of such language and replaced it with more faithful dialects of thanksgiving and confidence. In the next chapter, we will examine whether or not lament found a home in the life of Jesus or the early disciples in order to resolve the question of whether the language of lament is appropriate for Christians.

CHAPTER THREE

My God, My God, Why?

Prayer, we think, means presenting ourselves before God
so that he will be pleased with us.
We put on our Sunday best in our prayers. . . .

Prayers of lament fail to observe the niceties of due process.
They are jarring, even violent in their assault on decency and order.
They are the language of the nobody, the outsider, and the foreigner. . . . Blind
Bartimaeus will not lower his voice, speak civilly, and wait his turn.
—SCOTT A. ELLINGTON (*Risking Truth*, 182)

Jesus wept.
—JOHN 11:35

No one escapes the chaotic seas. Even if we are like the poet of Psalm 30 and say in our prosperity "I shall never be moved" and acknowledge that it is the Lord who "established me as a strong mountain" (vv. 6–7), without notice we may find ourselves in a storm (vv. 7b–10). And while we hope for a favorable outcome that turns "our mourning into dancing" and exchanges our sackcloth for joy (v. 11), too often the rain and wind continue without change. Yet, as we have seen, the language most used by our faith ancestors to express their experience in the storm has almost completely vanished from our faith communities. The most common form of prayer and song in the Psalms—lament—has become uncommon, even rare among us. And though I've heard it expressed in various ways, it is difficult to believe that our lack of lament is because the seas have calmed. Life has not gotten easier. I have to agree with Ecclesiastes that despite what may appear to be improvements, human experience has not and will not fundamentally change. "What has been is what will be, and what has been done is what will be done; there is nothing new under the sun" (Eccles. 1:9).

Or is there something new? Another explanation for the loss of lament is rooted in a perceived difference between the practice of faith in the Old and New Testaments. I frequently hear this viewpoint (despite strong evidence in the Bible to the contrary) expressed in a variety of ways: the Old Testament promoted an ethic inferior to that of the New Testament, the Old Testament was about works while the New Testament is about grace, or the Old Testament was only concerned with actions but the New Testament cares about attitudes. To be sure, there are differences between the covenants—due to changes in culture, not God's desires or expectations (but that is another book). Nonetheless, this negative view of the Old Testament creates a double jeopardy for lament as a Christian practice: 1) the nature and tone of lament, complaint and questioning, don't seem to be Christian, and 2) lament seems to be an Old Testament practice, replaced by greater confidence and praise in the New Testament. In other words, some view the absence of lament not as a loss but as a positive gain for Christians.

A number of Christian writers take a moderate form of this perspective about the psalms of lament when they discuss prayer but exclude the Psalms from consideration: they regard Christian prayer as a new thing. They caution us from turning to the Old Testament for instruction on prayer because Israel was a theocracy (both a spiritual and political entity), Israelite religion presumed the existence of the temple, and Israel did not understand the afterlife. As a result, the content and practice of prayer should differ for Christians. Our instruction on prayer should reflect the Lord's Prayer and Christian theology, not the Psalms and Israel's theology. More specifically in regard to lament, these writers emphasize that, since the followers of Jesus have a vision of resurrection that enables them to overcome every obstacle, Christian prayer should not lament.

C. S. Lewis takes a more aggressive and negative posture regarding the Old Testament laments. Lewis summarizes his feelings:

> The dominant impression I get from reading the Psalms is one
> of antiquity. I seem to be looking into a deep pit of time, but
> looking through a lens which brings the figures who inhabit
> that depth up close to my eye. In that momentary proximity
> they are almost shockingly alien; creatures of unrestrained
> emotion, wallowing in self-pity, sobbing, cursing, screaming
> in exultation, clashing uncouth weapons or dancing to the din
> of strange musical instruments. (*Christian Reflections*, 114)

With such an appraisal of lament, Lewis questions the spiritual benefit of such psalms and whether they have any value for Christian practice. He takes as an example Psalm 109, one of the most extreme of the laments, which he describes as an "unabashed hymn of hate as was ever written" (118):

> He [the psalmist] gives hatred free rein—encourages and
> spurs it on—in a sort of ghastly innocence. . . . The man him-
> self, of course, lived very long ago. His injuries may have been
> (humanly speaking) beyond endurance. He was doubtless
> a hot-blooded barbarian, more like a modern child than a
> modern man. And though we believe (and can even see from
> the last verse) that some knowledge of the real God had come
> to his race, yet he lived in the cold of the year, the early spring
> of Revelation, and those first gleams of knowledge were like
> snow drops, exposed to the frosts. For him, then, there may
> have been excuses. But we—what good can we find in reading
> such stuff?

Lewis later suggests that the "good" from our reading "such stuff" may be in realizing that our own ill treatment of others could tempt them to hate us and speak like this psalmist. But insofar as the psalm itself, Lewis bluntly says that God does not hear such prayers: "They are wicked. He condemns them" (120).

Regrettably, Lewis views the Old Testament practice of lament as sub-Christian. He points out that Christians have a greater hope and a deeper understanding of life (Heb. 1:1–4). On this side of the cross, we have knowledge of resurrection, a concept that was murky at best to Israel. As a result, Christ-followers should take a different view of trouble and pain. James urges us to consider trials all joy because they are productive to spiritual growth (James 1:2–4). Paul says, writing to a church facing opposition and persecution, "Rejoice in the Lord always; again I will say, Rejoice" (Phil. 4:4). And Peter adds that we know that our suffering, however great, will end with "eternal glory in Christ" (1 Pet. 5:10). So, it is argued, evidence from the Old Testament regarding lament is irrelevant. In Christ everything has changed for the better. Lament is contrary to the teaching of the New Testament and has no rightful place in the church or among its members.

To be fair, this line of argument does not suggest that the church should ignore the pain or hardship of its members—far from it. The New Testament not only recognizes suffering but teaches Christians to bear one another's burdens (Gal. 6:2), console one another (2 Cor. 1:3–4), and encourage the weary (Heb. 10:24–25). Those who are sick should call on the elders for prayer (James 5:14–15); those who sin should confess to others and pray for one another (James 5:16). In no way should the church acquiesce to the temptation to be a health club for the physically fit or a social club for the wealthy and thereby become a home for the neurotic because no one can speak the truth about their lives. That said, however, Lewis' argument does hold that none of these things should lead Christians to lament as Israel did in the Psalms.

For many people of deep faith, then, lament is a suspicious language because of its theological content and its initial appearance in the Old Testament. So it is at least possible that the loss of lament is no accident, but rather the intentional Christian exile of an unfaithful language. Israel lamented, but Christians do not and should not. To establish the validity of this claim, however, we need to look at the evidence within the New Testament itself. What can we learn about the practice of Jesus and the earliest churches? Does lament belong only to Israel in her "developmental stage of faith" or does this language step over testamental boundaries?

The Book of Psalms in the Time of Jesus

Researchers generally regard the book of Psalms as the hymnal of Second Temple Judaism, the stormy era in Judea from the rebuilding of the temple under the direction of Zerubbabel (Ezra 3–6) until the Roman destruction in 70 CE. Because of a lack of evidence, it is not clear how the book as a whole or its individual psalms functioned in worship. What is clear, however, is how highly Judaism valued and used the Psalms. Further, we know that it is from these roots that two well-known movements sprang that equally esteemed the Psalms, the Jewish sect at Qumran and Christianity.

Of the eight hundred different manuscripts recovered at Qumran (the Dead Sea Scrolls), approximately one-fourth are fragments of biblical texts (i.e., from the Old Testament). The Qumran sect had or produced more copies of some biblical books than others, with the book of Psalms leading the way. Fragmentary copies from thirty-six different scrolls of Psalms have been recovered, attesting to 115 individual psalms. By comparison, the next most common books are Deuteronomy (twenty-nine scrolls) and Isaiah (twenty-one). A scroll, even fragmentary, represents the meticulous efforts of scribes to hand copy a text and preserve the manuscript. Thus, the number of surviving manuscripts reflects where the community placed its emphasis and limited resources. For Qumran it was Psalms, Deuteronomy, and Isaiah because these books best served their interests and needs.

Since the Qumran community thrived geographically near the center of early Christianity (Jerusalem) and at approximately the same time (some suggest that John the Baptist came from Qumran), it should not be surprising that early Christian writings mirror the same regard for Psalms, Deuteronomy, and Isaiah. Writers of the New Testament books frequently cite Old Testament texts, refer to events recorded in the Old Testament, allude to passages, or use nuanced language to echo well-known texts. Precise counts of such instances vary from one researcher to another because of disagreements over ambiguous allusions and echoes; nonetheless, the top three texts to which New Testament writers refer remain stable: Psalms (seventy-nine citations, 333 allusions), Isaiah (sixty-six citations, 348 allusions), and Deuteronomy (fifty citations, 164 allusions; see *Novum Testamentum Graece*, 27th ed.). This data suggests that New Testament writers, especially Paul, knew the Book of Praises so well that it was second nature for them to incorporate bits and pieces of psalmic language into their letters and books.

Lament in the Life of Jesus

The simplest and shortest text in the Gospels says, "Jesus wept" (John 11:35). In the presence of two sisters (Martha and Mary) grieving for their brother (Lazarus) and in response to a stinging welcome from Mary ("Lord, if you had been here, my brother would not have died" [John 11:32]), Jesus weeps—for the sisters, for his friend Lazarus, and for himself. The text says nothing about lament (although Mary's statement to the Lord echoes the sentiments of several lament psalms), and my point here is not so much about lament but about the acceptance of human emotion and its expression. Jesus, who knows about the resurrection and the afterlife and who knows that he will raise Lazarus from the grave (John 11:11, 15), still weeps. Perfect faith casts out fear, but it does not exempt a person from feelings of deep sadness and their expression in tears. So an initial, simple observation and word of encouragement is in order: let's not try to be less human than the Son of God. Stoicism and its fake smiles in the face of life's pain and disappointment are not more godly or faithful than tears. After all, Jesus wept.

Jesus also lamented. Luke tells us that when Jesus came near Jerusalem during the triumphal entry he saw the city, wept, and lamented:

> If you, even you, had only recognized on this day the things that make for peace! But now they are hidden from your eyes. Indeed, the days will come upon you, when your enemies will set up ramparts around you and surround you, and hem you

in on every side. They will crush you to the ground, you and your children within you, and they will not leave within you one stone upon another, because you did not recognize the time of your visitation from God. (Luke 19:42–44)

We can also assume a good deal about Jesus' personal use of the Psalms from what we know about Jewish customs of the first century, though we should exercise reasonable restraint on our assumptions. For example, both Mark and Matthew mention that after the Passover meal "when [Jesus and the disciples] had sung the hymn, they went out to the Mount of Olives" (Matt. 26:30; Mark 14:26). Stable Jewish tradition regarding the Passover enables us to be fairly certain that the songs Jesus and his disciples sang came from the "Great Hallel" of Psalms 113–18. In Hebrew, *Hallel* means "to praise"—as in the plural imperative *Hallelujah*: "(Everyone) Praise the Lord!" Each of the psalms of the Great Hallel offers such praise, beginning with the first verse of Psalm 113.

> Praise the LORD!
>> Praise, O servants of the LORD;
>> praise the name of the LORD. (v. 1)

The first psalm of the Great Hallel exalts a God like no other, one who is "seated on high" (113:5) and yet who has regard for those on the margins of society: the poor, the needy, and the barren (113:7–9). Psalm 114 recalls the Lord's power exerted in the exodus and crossing into the land of promise (vv. 1–6), and the next of the Great Hallel psalms contrasts the powerless idols of the nations with "our God" who is in the heavens and who "does whatever he pleases" (115:3). So the psalmist urges Israel to trust her God (115:9–11), a God who has been mindful of Israel and who will bless her (115:12–13). Psalm 116 gives thanks to the Lord for rescue from death (vv. 3–11) and pledges to lift a drink offering (vv. 12–14) along with a thanksgiving sacrifice for God's blessing (vv. 17–19). Finally, the last psalm of the group (117) extends the call to praise the Lord beyond the boundaries of Israel:

Praise the LORD, all you nations!
>> Extol him, all you peoples!
For great is his steadfast love towards us,
>> and the faithfulness of the LORD endures forever.
Praise the LORD! (117:1–2)

Shortly after he sings the Great Hallel with his disciples, the Gospels record a different type of speech on the lips of Jesus. At Gethsemane, Jesus instructed his disciples to wait for him while he prayed. He then took Peter, James, and John with him deeper into the garden, and as they went he began "to be grieved and agitated" (NRSV), or, as Peterson captures the idea in *The Message*, "he plunged into an agonizing sorrow" (Matt. 26:37). He left the three, went a little farther, and then "threw himself on the ground and prayed, 'My Father, if it is possible, let this cup pass from me; yet not what I want but what you want'" (Matt. 26:39). The circumstances, Jesus' anguish, and the language are all reminiscent of the psalms of lament, in particular, the laments which appeal to God with great confidence that God hears and will respond. Jesus, then, demonstrates a capacity for a wide and rapid swing in how he sings or prays to God; he may address God with great songs of praise and then, only a short time later, speak heart-piercing words of lament: "My Father, if there is any way, get me out of this" (*The Message*).

The next instance of Jesus' use of the Psalms also draws from the language of lament, this time a specific psalm. Jesus' trial is completed, as are the flogging and scarlet-robed mockery, and the journey to Golgotha finished with the help of Simon (Matt. 27). Crucifixion, with all its shame, has begun. And it would seem that, when the Father could not stand to watch his Son suffer any longer, he turned off the lights (Matt. 27:45). Then Jesus screamed out the opening words of Psalm 22: "*Eli, Eli, lema sabachthani?*" That is, "My God, my God, why have you forsaken me?" (Matt. 27:46).

I am content to let many debates about the interpretation of this text pass by without resolution: For example, did God really abandon Jesus? Was God separating himself from the sin that Jesus bore or from Jesus himself? For our purposes, these questions are unimportant. I am content to observe that Jesus spoke these words; he was in agony and *felt* (at least and in any case) *that his Father had abandoned him.* So, calling to mind the words of a harsh lament, Jesus cited Psalm 22:1 to express his feelings to God. And though I am stating the obvious, his lament—his questioning of God's presence—was not the result of doubt or some lack of faith that came over him. Jesus knows the plan; he is aware of resurrection in three days and the ascension to follow. But none of this knowledge changes the pain, the human sense of desperation, and the feeling of abandonment. *My God, what are you doing? Where are you? Why have you left me all alone?* And then, using words from another lament, Jesus says, "'Father, into your hands I commend my spirit,'" and dies (Luke 23:46; Ps. 31:5).

Perhaps the writer of Hebrews knew even more about Jesus' prayer life, especially all of those times that Jesus slipped away from the crowds to pray. I have always imagined these nights alone with God to be friendly conversations, perhaps asking for direction or advice and certainly filled with thanksgiving and praise. But that is not how Hebrews describes Jesus' prayers:

> In the days of his flesh, Jesus offered up prayers and supplications, with loud cries and tears, to the one who was able to save him from death, and he was heard because of his reverent submission. (5:7)

In other words, the prayers at the garden and cross were not exceptions. The writer of Hebrews claims that a good portion of the prayer life of Jesus may best be characterized as lament—"prayers and supplications, with loud cries and tears"—much more like the beginning of Psalm 22 than the Great Hallel of Psalms 113–18.

I have omitted in this survey the many times in which Jesus, the disciples, or the Gospels use verses or phrases from the Psalms in conversation or teaching. I have also bypassed stories in which the Gospels extol the virtue of persistent prayer (Luke 18:1–8; Mark 7:28). Instead, we have focused our attention on Jesus' personal use of the Psalms in his own communion with God through song and prayer. And while I do not want to be offensive, I do want to make the conclusion of our survey clear. Jesus sang psalms of praise, but he also knew the language of lament and did not hesitate to engage God with the strongest of this language. When Jesus encountered grieving sisters, contemplated his own impending death, or hung on a cross, he did not try to comfort everyone by telling them to have more faith, that God has a plan, or not to worry because "all things work together for the good of those who love the Lord." He did not lead them in a song of praise—*he lamented*—not for lack of faith or doubt in the Father, but because of his faith and because of his relationship with a Father who understands life at sea. *LAMENT HAPPENS BECAUSE OF FAITH NOT IN SPITE OF IT*

Lament in the Early Church

Considerable evidence supports the early church's love for singing. On occasion, Paul's writings included brief encouragement for churches to sing (e.g., Eph. 5:18–20), but not because they were not already singing and praying. These texts give the sense that the churches were already engaged in these practices. Like early Judaism from which it sprang, the early church seized upon the Psalms as their hymnbook, to which they added new songs about Christ. In fact, researchers are fairly confident that the content of at least a few of these early Christian hymns has been preserved for us in the New Testament (e.g., the Christ hymn in Phil. 2:5–11).

Awareness of the church's early adoption of the Psalms contributes initial evidence toward the question of lament in Christian practice. It would seem logical that if 40 percent of the church's hymnal consisted of lament, the church accepted and used at least some of these psalms. But despite the intuitive strength of this evidence, it is not conclusive; just because the church accepted the book of Psalms does not necessarily mean they used *all* of the psalms. Perhaps, as counterclaims insist, other passages (James 1:2–4; Phil. 4:4; 1 Pet. 5:10, reviewed above) that urge Christians to rejoice despite difficult circumstances should lead us to a different outcome: praise instead of lament. For example, at first glance,

Paul's admonition to the Ephesians appears to omit lament as a proper Christian language:

> Do not get drunk with wine, for that is debauchery; but be filled with the Spirit, as you sing psalms and hymns and spiritual songs among yourselves, singing and making melody to the Lord in you hearts, giving thanks to God the Father at all times and for everything in the name of our Lord Jesus Christ. (Eph. 5:18–20)

Paul tells the early Christians to sing psalms, hymns, and spiritual songs—not lament. Even more, it seems that we can know with precision what they sang if we define these three terms. The problem with this approach, however, is that in Greek it is customary to combine three similar terms in sequence in order to convey the idea of all-inclusiveness. In other words, when Paul says to sing psalms, hymns, and spiritual songs, the idea is to sing these types of songs and all others like these. In which case, Paul implicitly includes the idea of lament even though it is not specified. This initial evidence, the Psalms (as the church's hymnal) and Paul's statement to the Ephesians, is admittedly soft evidence—an implied use of lament. Strong explicit evidence, however, emerges from the book of Acts.

Early in the book of Acts, Peter and John were arrested and detained overnight by Jewish leaders (Sadducees) for preaching the resurrection of Jesus. The next day at their hearing, the council was at a loss for what to do with these men who "had been with Jesus" and so decided to let them off with a warning "to speak no more to anyone in this name [Jesus]" (Acts 4:13, 17). Peter and John immediately protested the warning based on their responsibility to a higher authority; they must obey God rather than people (4:19–20), which elicited more threats against them before the authorities let them go.

Upon their release, they went to the church to report what had happened, including the warnings and threats made by the religious establishment (4:23). In response, they prayed, first addressing God: "Sovereign Lord, who made the heavens and the earth, the sea, and everything in them" (4:24). And then through a citation from Psalm 2, a royal psalm of lament, they introduced their situation:

> Why did the Gentiles rage,
>> and the peoples imagine vain things?
> The kings of the earth took their stand,
>> and the rulers have gathered together
>>> against the Lord and against his Messiah. (4:25–26)

The church described to God what happened when Jesus encountered these same religious leaders (4:27–28) and the threat that these leaders (enemies of the cross) now posed to the church. Then they made a specific request of the Lord: "Lord, look at their threats, and grant to your servants to speak your word with all boldness" (4:29). And God's response left no doubt that he heard and would do just as the church has asked (4:31).

In addition to the use of verses from a royal lament psalm in their prayer, the language of Acts 4:25–31 follows the standard conventions of a lament: an address to God, description of the opponent or enemy who threatens not only the psalmist but God, a request for God to act in specific ways, and reasons or motivations for why God should act (see Chapter Four). In other words, the prayer in Acts 4 is a lament that expresses strong confidence in the Lord to respond. Only a matter of weeks after the resurrection of Jesus and beginnings of the church, the church has found its voice in the language of lament.

The next two cases in Acts are more ambiguous but deserve some consideration. First, in Acts 7, the Sanhedrin (a council of Jewish leaders in Jerusalem) became enraged after hearing a great sermon, and, tossing due process out the window, they dragged the preacher, Stephen, out of the city and stoned him to death. It is a dangerous thing to preach an authentically great sermon. Stephen's final words draw from the last words of Jesus, just as Jesus drew his words from the Psalms. Stephen prayed, "Lord Jesus, receive my spirit" (Acts 7:59; see Luke 23:46; Ps. 31:5) and in a loud voice shouted "Lord, do not hold this sin against them" (Acts 7:60; see Luke 23:34).

In response to Stephen's death and despite the severe persecution that broke out that day against all Christ-followers, devout members of the Jerusalem church buried Stephen and "made loud lamentation over him" (Acts 8:2 NRSV). Other translations handle the key Greek terms (*kopeton megan*) in different ways: "and mourned deeply for him" (TNIV) or "mourning for him with loud cries" (TEV). The Greek term *kopeton* most likely denotes customary mourning rituals associated with death and burial; for example, weeping, wearing sackcloth, striking one's chest, and singing dirges—the language of lament or select lament psalms (e.g., Ps. 90).

In view of this data, three observations are in order about the lamentation made for Stephen. One, despite Stephen's murder, these disciples were not afraid to let everyone know of their connection to him and, thus, their own faith in Jesus. They made "loud" or "great" lamentation for him, not a quiet or secretive burial. Two, I suspect that Jewish Christians who make "great lamentation" are going to turn to the easiest resource at hand: the laments in the book of Psalms. And three, Saul was present at Stephen's death (Acts 8:1) and perhaps became aware of the "loud lamentation." Maybe (and only maybe) Saul noticed a difference in their lament because, later, he writes to the church at Thessalonica regarding their concern for those who have died "so that you may not grieve as others do who have no hope" (1 Thess. 4:13). The Christ-event does not stop the church from making "loud lamentation" for Stephen. But the confidence expressed in their lament was of such a nature that maybe, just maybe, it began to get Saul's attention.

In any event, the tables are turned on Saul/Paul in Acts 16. Here, Paul finds himself and Silas the targets of Jewish opposition. Upon a direct summons to go to Macedonia (Acts 16:6–10), Paul and Silas had traveled west, crossed the sea, and come to Philippi. Here, under the dictum "No good deed ever goes unpunished," the team of missionaries are flogged and thrown into prison for casting a spirit out of a slave girl—and costing her owners a fortune in future profits (Acts 16:16–24). Then, in prison, "about midnight Paul and Silas were praying and singing hymns to God, and the prisoners were listening to them" (Acts 16:25).

Like Jesus' times of solitude in the mountains, my presuppositions have dictated the way I have imagined this scene in the Philippian jail. I once thought of Paul and Silas alternately singing and then praying: two distinct acts of worship. The Greek, however, does not read "praying *and* singing" but rather "praying songs" or perhaps "singing prayers." The line between singing and praying is thin, if it exists at all in this and other texts. I have also assumed that Paul and Silas were singing songs of praise. And this may be true, at least in part. But the text does not explicitly make such a claim; it says only they were singing "hymns"—a broad, inclusive, and ambiguous term, not a narrow claim for praise songs. The ambiguity leads me to recheck my assumptions and consider other clues in the text as to what Paul and Silas were doing that night.

After the Lord responds to Paul and Silas by setting them free, the jailor is astounded and asks them, "Sirs, what must I do to be saved?" (Acts 16:27–30). The earthquake and non-escape of any prisoners could explain his reaction or the earthquake plus prior praise songs, but perhaps even more plausibly his response may have been the result of hearing lament songs plus the earthquake. As we will see, most laments describe to God what has happened to the psalmist (so the jailor would have heard their story), make requests to God, most often for vindication and release from opponents (e.g., release from jail and vindication from false accusations), and then express praise and confidence in God's power to act. So if Paul and Silas' song list included lament, the jailor's response makes better sense than if he had heard only praise songs in the night. Through their songs and God's answer in the earthquake, the jailor has learned that the God to whom Paul and Silas pray is the God to be reckoned with.

The point to which all the evidence is driving is that lament and praise existed together in the early church just as they did in the life of Jesus. The Jerusalem church prayed lament (Acts 4), devout followers lamented the death of Stephen (Acts 8), and Paul and Silas possibly had lament in their prison repertoire (Acts 16). Outside of Acts, Paul insists that mourning should be different for followers of Christ than it is for those who lack the hope he provides (1 Thess. 4), but he does not exclude grief or lament.

Paul tells the church in Rome that the whole creation groans with them as they await the redemption of their bodies (8:23), and as we wait the Spirit helps us when we are unable to find adequate words for prayer (8:26). He insists that Christians sing every kind of psalm, hymn, and spiritual song (Eph. 5). In fact, as we will see in Chapter Twelve, thanksgiving and lament have a close, even symbiotic relationship. Thanksgiving cannot exist without lament, or lament without thanksgiving. They belong together as two mutually dependent languages. And our last example of lament from the New Testament is a striking instance of this mutuality of lament and praise.

John's apocalypse captures a vision of the church at its fullest potential for praise. After a brief greeting to the seven churches, John immediately turns to doxology:

> To him who loves us and freed us from our sins by his blood,
> and made us to be a kingdom, priests serving his God and
> Father, to him be glory and dominion forever and ever. Amen.
> (Rev. 1:5–6)

John writes letters on behalf of the Lord to the churches (Rev. 2–3) and then attempts to convey a vision of heavenly worship that defies words. How does one describe the indescribable? God seated on a throne which emits flashes of lightning and peals of thunder, surrounded by twenty-four white-robed, golden-crowned elders and four creepy, otherworldly creatures who can do no more or less than sing God's praise:

> Holy, holy, holy,
> the Lord God the Almighty,
>   who was and is and is to come. (4:8)

At which, the twenty-four elders throw down their crowns and respond in song:

> You are worthy, our Lord and God,
>   to receive glory and honor and power,

> for you created all things,
>> and by your will they existed and were created. (4:11)

Praise never ends in John's vision but only expands in scope and intensity. In chapter 5, "myriads of myriads and thousands of thousands" of angels sing with full voice:

> Worthy is the Lamb that was slaughtered
>> to receive power and wealth and wisdom and might
>> and honor and glory and blessing! (vv. 11–12)

In chapter 7, John sees "a great multitude that no one could count, from every nation, from all tribes and peoples and languages" (v. 9), and they too sing praise: "salvation belongs to our God who is seated on the throne, and to the Lamb" (v. 10).

The martyrs make their first appearance in chapter 6, sandwiched between the myriads of angels in full voice of praise (ch. 5) and the multitudes of people crying out in worship (ch. 7). More faithful to God than I can ever hope to be, these saints gave up their lives for the sake of the good news and for the One who is enthroned. Under the altar, however, the martyrs cry out with another faith language:

> Sovereign Lord, holy and true,
>> how long will it be before you judge
>> and avenge our blood on the inhabitants of the earth? (6:10)

The martyrs, surrounded by praise, speak lament. In fact, they articulate an extreme form of lament that begs God to take action against an enemy (imprecation). Their appeal is identical to the "sub-Christian" language that C. S. Lewis said was understandable for childish Israelites, the hot-blooded barbarians living before the clear revelation of Christ. But here it is, on the lips of God's most faithful and devout servants. What's more, no one, not the elders, creatures, or God, react in shock or correct the martyrs for inappropriate words or feelings. Instead, they are given white robes (for the victorious) and encouraged to rest a bit longer (6:11).

Praise and lament live side by side not only in the Psalms, the lives of Israel's heroes, but also in the life of Jesus, the early church, and in John's revelation of the saints at worship in the presence of the enthroned God. New revelation may change the confidence with which a person laments and greater faith may change the content of lament, but neither displaces the need for or appropriateness of lament. If anything, greater faith only intensifies lament as our faith intersects the harsh realities of life. Lament lives alongside praise in the lives of God's people for the simple reason that not every event in life calls for a response of praise or thanksgiving. And if we are going to be honest with God, following the example of the faithful from Israel to the saints in heaven, then we need to learn how to speak this long neglected language—a language spoken by the trailblazer of our faith as he offered prayers with cries and tears to the Father.

CHAPTER FOUR

The Contours of Lament

It is this form {lament} that *enhances* experience and brings it to articulation
and also *limits* the experience of suffering so that it can be received
and coped with according to the perspectives, perceptions, and
resources of the community.
—WALTER BRUEGGEMANN (*The Psalms and the Life of Faith*, 86)

By engaging in the regular, programmatic expression of pain through the act
of lament, Israel insures that doctrinal structures are re-formed, rather than
obliterated, and that their relationship with Yahweh remains vibrant and
healthy, rather than becoming cripplingly destructive.
—SCOTT A. ELLINGTON (*Risking Truth*, 21)

B ailey Hobart Pemberton came into my life at the age of two; that's
fourteen in canine years. He was a soft-eyed, low-set, tricolor basset
hound with a personality to match: gentle, playful, and eager to love. When
Bailey arrived, however, he came with baggage. To be blunt, he needed
therapy. When Bailey had been just a young pup tripping over his ears, his
backyard was in the path of the F-5 tornado that rolled through Norman
and Moore, just south of Oklahoma City (May 5, 1999). The tornado veered
north, leaving a massive debris trail that stretched for miles and lasted a
lifetime for those in its path.

Bailey joined a younger fellow basset, Beauregard Horatio, in the task
of staking out and protecting the Pemberton family residence. Birds and
butterflies were public enemy number one; strangers were always welcome.

And of course, Bailey became our weather alert system. If he could sense a storm he would set off the siren and continue to bay at full volume until someone let him inside. Should a drop of rain land on his head the alarm would escalate to pacing and digging at the door—anything to call attention to the fact that he was outside and the apocalypse was coming. Meanwhile, Beauregard would sit calmly to the side watching his step-brother with his own befuddled expression.

A few months later, in the wake of a hot dry summer and strong wind, even by Oklahoma standards ("where the wind comes sweeping down the plain"), a wildfire jumped a row of houses, a city street, and landed in our crispy dry grass; I got out of the house in time to see the cedars on the south side of the house explode into giant fireballs. Neighbors appeared from every direction, cars stopped, and sirens blared as chaos broke loose. After a few minutes, it dawned on me that the backyard was also burning . . . with its picket fence, a stack of firewood, and the bassets. A neighbor and I ran back through the house one last time, and we found Bailey and Beauregard huddled together at the back door. We each grabbed a hound and ran.

The insurance company considered the house a total loss, and even more than ten years later the fire is still a difficult memory. We were blessed in more ways that I could ever recount—by churches, friends, students—by God. No one was injured in the fire, no other houses were damaged, and we recovered. But the daily rhythm of life was disrupted and replaced with tiresome tasks related to rebuilding. I had to cope with new and seemingly irrational fears—a whiff of smoke or a siren in the distance could set me off in the early days. Nothing really felt right for the next year—from the day of the fire until months after settling back in a rebuilt house, and even then it wasn't the same. I've often wondered if Job had the same feeling? New blessings are wonderful, but with the new gifts come a greater realization that they too could be taken away in a heartbeat.

A few hectic days after the fire, Bailey and Beauregard came "home" to the apartment we had leased for the interim. Bailey was diplomatic about the whole thing. He came into the apartment, looked around for a few minutes, then found my bedroom, jumped up on the bed, sniffed until he found my pillow, and then proceeded to pee.

With the aid of our veterinarian, we were able to translate Bailey's canine communication. Obviously, he felt a need to make a few things absolutely clear. One, he acknowledged and even respected my leadership in his family (thus his selection of *my* pillow). Two, he was not running away because life was out of sorts; we were still his family and he was here to stay. But, three, he needed me to know that his world was out of control and he didn't like it. He already had neurosis from dodging an F-5 tornado, and now his backyard had burned with all its hidden treasure of bones and toys. The night of the fire, he had been carried around like a fifty-pound bag of dog chow, tossed from one strange backyard to another by people he didn't even know. And he could not hold it inside any longer. In a manner that was both fully under control and fully expressive of his feelings, he sent the clearest memo I've ever received.

Liminal Space and Seasons of Life

Those who have thought deeply about human life describe times of upheaval and change with the terms liminal or liminality (Bailey described the time with his own unique language). Liminal space denotes the threshold between two states of being—when we are no longer this, but not yet that. In a liminal state, we are caught by circumstances in an in-between time or space of ambiguity, and as a result we feel displaced, confused, frustrated, or even angry. We are not certain who we are or what we are becoming, we only know that life is changing.

Long-standing societies develop rituals to help people cope with the ambiguity of our most significant liminal spaces. We conduct graduation exercises for students and their families who are dealing with the liminal time between school and career (or more school). We arrange funerals for families suspended in liminal space as they grieve what they have lost and anticipate adjusting to life without their loved one. We use inaugurations to dismiss a prior leader while installing a new one, most likely elected weeks or even months in the past (a "lame duck" period is an instance of liminal space). And weddings culminate a time of waiting for what is anticipated, but does not yet exist—this couple married.

Walter Brueggemann builds on the idea of liminality to describe the seasons of life: seasons of orientation, disorientation, and new orientation. He explains that sometimes "human life consists in satisfied seasons of well-being that evoke gratitude for the constancy of blessing" (*The Message of the Psalms*, 19). And so the believer sings songs of joy and praise for God's constancy and reliability. But, as we all learn, human life doesn't consist only of seasons of well-being, but also "anguished seasons of hurt, alienation, suffering, and death" (19). We struggle with how to live, how to adjust to a life that is far less than we desire. More, Brueggemann claims that the challenge is not only the season of disorientation but the move

> *out of a settled orientation into a season of disorientation.* This move is experienced partly as changed circumstance, but it is much more a personal awareness and acknowledgment of the changed circumstance. This may be abrupt or a slowly dawning acknowledgment. It constitutes a dismantling of the old, known world and a relinquishment of safe, reliable confidence in God's good creation. (20, emphasis in original)

Our challenge is not only how to live faithfully in a season of disorientation but also how to negotiate the liminal space as we move into a season of disorientation.

The concept of liminal space and seasons of disorientation are both helpful ways to describe and so talk about the difficult times we encounter. Of course, we respectfully acknowledge that however we may describe this time, for those living in deep ambiguity or pain, nothing can accurately depict their world. What we need as people of faith goes far beyond descriptions and analyses. We need the consolation of fellow believers (2 Cor. 1:3–7), those who will encourage and pray for us (Heb. 10:24–25), and the presence of a spiritual family who will walk alongside us and help carry the load (Gal. 6:2). But even more, we need God with us. We need an authentic faith language that will enable us to stay in relationship with God by speaking the truth of our lives to God and, at the same time, provide appropriate controls on our expressions so that we may pray as Jesus did, "with reverent submission" (Heb. 5:7). I believe that in the psalms of lament we find both: a vocabulary to express the realities of our brokenness and a grammar that helps us control the vocabulary. In brief, what we really need and what the psalms of lament provide is a way to live through times of disorientation with God as an intimate traveling companion.

The Contours of Lament

The language of lament is not an outburst of unrestrained speech that gives free reign to an emotional torrent of words. It is not venting for the sake of venting. Instead, lament is a structured, controlled language that by its methodical cadence helps restore a modicum of structure in times of disorientation. Lament psalms accomplish this restraint or control by providing a form of speech consisting of five common elements: an address to God, complaints, requests, motivation (why God should act), and confidence in God. Like the ritual actions of a wedding or even a funeral, these movements of lament enable us to negotiate the liminal space of pain with words that communicate to our God within a controlled setting. In a way, lament itself begins to restore some sense of order in the midst of chaos.

Here, to illustrate the contours of lament, we will explore how two short psalms deploy the elements of lament to bring their pain to God: Psalm 13 (in detail) and Psalm 54 (in less detail). Both texts are individual psalms of lament (i.e., spoken by an individual), although "I" may stand for a group. Psalm 13 emerges from broad and ambiguous trouble; Psalm 54 is somewhat more limited and specific in its complaint. Both psalms, however, demonstrate remarkable faith in the midst of conflict and express confidence not only in the Lord's willingness to hear difficult words but also in the Lord's faithfulness to act.

Psalm 13

Psalm 13 is the standard referent for a prototypical lament. Not only does the psalm include full expression of all five common elements, but the parts appear in order.

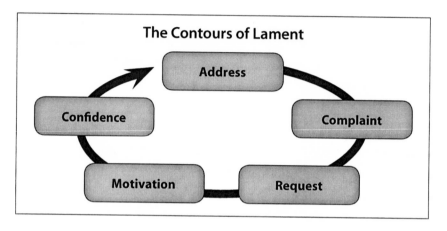

The Contours of Lament

Address

Confidence

Complaint

Motivation

Request

Part I: Address

> How long, O LORD? (v. 1)

The custom before prayer in one of my small groups was to ask who was "dialing" and who would "hang up." In other words, who would begin and end our prayers. The address in a lament psalm is a matter of "dialing" God's number, the one who is the recipient of our speech because he alone can make a difference. In Psalm 13, like other laments, the address is short, "How long, O LORD?," stated at the beginning of the psalm, and repeated later, "O LORD, my God!" (v. 3). Hymns of praise and songs of thanksgiving typically address God in elaborate words of descriptive praise: "O LORD, our Sovereign, how majestic is your name in all the earth" (8:1) or "The LORD is king; he is robed in majesty; the LORD is robed, he is girded with strength" (93:1). But those who lament have neither the serenity nor the luxury of time for such expansive words. Instead, the one who laments cries out with single words of address (in Hebrew): "O LORD" (*Yahweh*), "My God" (*Eli*), or perhaps an extravagant two words "O LORD, my God"

(*Yahweh Elohi*). The crisis or disorientation that summons lament permits little more than a visceral call to God and nothing less than an address to *my* God. Thus, lament is not mere complaint about life's troubles but speech directed to God with an expectation that God will respond.

Part II: Complaint

> Will you forget me forever?
> > How long will you hide your face from me?
> How long must I bear pain in my soul,
> > and have sorrow in my heart all day long?
> > How long shall my enemy be exalted over me? (Ps. 13:1b–2)

In the second movement of lament, the psalmist describes the problem(s) he or she is experiencing to God, often through the use of rhetorical questions: e.g., How long . . . ? Why do you . . . ? Where is . . . ? Have you not . . . ? In most cases, the question does not seek information but is a rhetorical form of objection to the situation. If a psalmist asks "how long?" it has already been too long. Much as when someone asks how much longer a sermon will last, the question is a thinly veiled complaint that the sermon is too long.

A complaint typically moves in three distinct directions, often combining all three in a single lament. First, the psalmist describes the trouble or difficulty that he or she personally faces. In Psalm 13, this personal trouble includes "pain in my soul" and "sorrow in my heart" (v. 2). The psalmist lodges both complaints through rhetorical questions ("how long?"). He is worn out from the affliction, and the only good answer to "how long?" is agreement that it has been too long and will now stop. As in many psalms, the precise nature of the psalmist's pain and sorrow is ambiguous; it could be physical, psychological, social, spiritual, or a combination of any of these. The reality of the personal suffering, however, is not ambiguous; the psalmist says I hurt all day long, every day—too long.

Second, the psalmist explains the trouble coming from others. Again a rhetorical question expresses the difficulty: "how long shall my enemy be exalted over me?" (v. 2c). These unidentified opponents are somehow getting an upper hand and are eager to proclaim victory over the psalmist and rejoice at his downfall (v. 4), a situation that the psalmist cannot imagine to be within God's desire. Later we will examine in some detail the issues pertaining to the "enemy" in lament psalms (see Chapters Eight and Nine). At this point, it is enough to say that others often are, in fact, a primary or contributing source of hardship in our seasons of disorientation. They may be the root cause of our demise, or they may be taking full advantage of our sudden weakness for their own benefit. But in any case, their presence cannot be ignored in an honest assessment of our trouble.

The third source of hardship that the psalmist often identifies is God. Later, we will study at length the complaints directed to and about God (see Chapters Ten and Eleven). In Psalm 13, as the writer sees it, God is the first and perhaps primary cause for all his trouble. Stated once again in the form of a rhetorical question, the psalmist asks how long God plans to forget about him. Or if God's intent is never again to look his direction and so bless him again, "how long will you hide your face from me?" (v. 1b; cf. Num. 6:24–26). Such words are shocking to most readers, and to some it is an unthinkable outrage to blame God! But it is also an inescapable accusation if we really believe in the sovereignty of God and if our lament is going to be honest, with no denial or cover-up of our feelings. Whether we have the nerve to say it, sometimes our disorientation is so intense that it seems the only possible cause must be God's deliberate or lax decision not to pay attention. When that is the situation, the psalmists speak out with bold and respectful words rooted in their own unwavering faith: Do you plan to forget me forever?

In most psalms, like Psalm 13, the complaint will identify difficulties coming from all three directions (myself, others, and God), because most significant problems in life are complex. And so, while the fundamental source of trouble may be my own sin, the psalmist may still flag others for personal fouls and charge God with acting in anger (Ps. 38). Or the complaint may be stated as simply as in Psalm 13: 1) I am in pain. 2) They want my demise. 3) God, where are you?

Part III: Request

> Consider and answer me, O LORD my God!
>> Give light to my eyes, or I will sleep the sleep of death.
> (Ps. 13:3)

Requests commonly follow or are interlaced among the complaints. In Psalm 13, the writer makes two appeals. First, in view of God's apparent forgetfulness and neglect (v. 1), he asks for God's attention and response (v. 3a). Second, he asks that God "Give light to my eyes" (v. 3b). Because the remainder of the line contrasts "light to my eyes" with sleeping the "sleep of death," the request does not appear to be for clearer physical vision or spiritual enlightenment but for revival of physical life or strength. First Samuel uses a similar phrase to describe Jonathan eating honey during a battle against the Philistines with the result that "his eyes brightened" (1 Sam. 14:27), in other words he regained his strength or vitality.

Just as complaints may be read literally (e.g., the enemy is a real person) or metaphorically (e.g., the enemy stands for anything opposed to me), so the requests vary in meaning. On the one hand, it could be that the appeal for "light" in 13:3b denotes a concern for the psalmist's physical life (as in 1 Samuel). If God does not intervene, the writer will "sleep the sleep of death"; that is, he will stop breathing and die. On the other hand, the contrast of life and death in the laments oftentimes reaches beyond a literal meaning to represent the difference between genuine life and a "living death." Life denotes well-being, joy, and peace. Death represents a person who goes through the motions of being alive but does not live with any sense of joy or fulfillment.

Part IV: Motivations

> Give light to my eyes, or I will sleep the sleep of death,
>> and my enemy will say, "I have prevailed";
>>> my foes will rejoice because I am shaken.
>> But I trusted in your steadfast love;
>>> my heart shall rejoice in your salvation. (Ps. 13:3b–5)

For many readers, the most shocking element of lament is not naming God as part of the problem but the freedom with which psalmists try to persuade God to act. Just as the laments do not hesitate to make specific requests, so they do not hesitate to use every rhetorical method—direct and indirect—to coerce, convince, and motivate God to do what they want. Stated bluntly, the psalmists are not afraid to engage in divine arm twisting if that's what it takes to get God to answer. Walter Brueggemann identifies seven common motivations, or reasons the psalmists frequently give for why God should intervene (*The Psalms and the Life of Faith*, 71):

1) God's reputation (13:4; 25:11; 57:5),
2) consistency with God's past actions (22:4–5; 143:5),
3) the speaker's guilt (25:11; 38:18),
4) the speaker's innocence (26:3–7; 35:7; 69:7),
5) a promise of praise (6:5; 22:22),
6) the helplessness of the speaker (25:16; 69:1), and
7) the speaker's trust in the Lord (17:8–9; 43:2).

Psalm 13, like most laments, develops its motivation along the same lines or topics of the complaint; God should act a) because of my situation (me), b) because of what they are doing (others), and c) because of you (God). a) The psalmist presents the depths of his misery to persuade God to act on his behalf. *I* am in a sorry state; *my pain* persists day after day with no relief in sight (v. 2); and, I am going to die—whether literally or metaphorically—unless you (God) intervene. The descriptive depth of the language works to touch God's heart. b) Others are responding to my predicament in an unthinkable and ungodly manner. Instead of helping me, they are celebrating (v. 2c) and anticipating an opportunity to declare victory over me, your servant (v. 4). (I cannot escape images of Muslims dancing in the streets after 9-11—and Christians cheering in the streets to celebrate the death of Osama bin Laden.) The description of the opponent also functions to stir God into action. How could the Lord see what they are doing and not intervene on my behalf? The Lord should respond out of a sense of justice and concern for how the powerful mistreat the weak. c) The psalmist tries to motivate divine action through direct and indirect statements about God. The opening rhetorical questions complain about God's attentiveness and hiding his face (v. 1) and in the process seek to touch God's heart, especially when the psalmist reminds God that he ("your servant") has "trusted in your steadfast love" (v. 5a). God's reputation is on the line in his response. The Lord has always claimed to be a "God merciful and gracious, slow to anger, and abounding in steadfast love and faithfulness" (Exod. 34:6). But if God does not act in the interest of those who trust his love, these words are meaningless and empty claims.

The psalmists do not worry about a charge of manipulating the divine because, I believe, they know that it is impossible. They know that God will always act in a way that is best for them (and others). But they also believe with all their hearts that their prayers make a difference in what God does (e.g., James 5:16). Perhaps these poets recall Moses' successful arguments with God (Exod. 32:11–14; Num. 14:13–20). So, given the opportunity to persuade God, they go to the task with every plausible idea or argument that might make a difference. In many cases, they have nothing to lose.

Part V: Confidence and Praise

> I will sing to the LORD,
>> because he has dealt bountifully with me. (Ps. 13:6)

After a multidirectional complaint, an appeal that sets out a new course of action, and motivations that systematically assert why God should pay closer attention and get involved, we are hardly prepared for the fifth and final movement of lament: an expression of confidence in God or even praise. It is such a remarkable shift in tone and outlook that it has sent interpreters tumbling in search of some explanation. One possibility is that between the psalmist's words of complaint and the statement of confidence (between vv. 5 and 6) we are to understand that a priest spoke an oracle of assurance (not recorded as part of the psalm). In fact, the previous psalm may contain an example of such an oracle. In Psalm 12, the poet addresses the Lord, states several complaints, requests, and reasons the Lord should act (vv. 1–4). Then, in verse five, the Lord speaks words of reassurance: "Because the poor are despoiled, because the needy groan, I will now rise up . . . I will place them in the safety for which they long." And, in response, the psalmist declares his confidence in the Lord (vv. 6–8). Another example of such an intervention is Hannah's prayer to which the priest Eli responds, "Go in peace; the God of Israel grant the petition you have made to him" (1 Sam. 1:17). So perhaps the explanation for the radical shift from complaint to praise was due to an oracle of salvation spoken by a priest or prophet included in Psalm 12 but not retained in other laments (cf. Pss. 91:15–16; 108:7).

Second, it is possible that the poet added the final verse of Psalm 13 at a later date—after the Lord had acted on his behalf. Like contemporary songs to which we add new verses, poets may have added verses to their prior lament psalms. We will consider this possibility more fully in Chapter Twelve. A third and I suspect more likely explanation for the dramatic swing from complaint to praise has nothing to do with priestly intervention or change in the psalmist's situation. No one has intervened or made promises on behalf of God. Instead, the psalmist concludes with what prompted the lament in the first place and undergirded its every word: a deep faith in the Lord. Regardless of how God may respond to my complaint—whether God does what I want, something else, or nothing at all—I want God to know that I always have and always will trust him (13:5). And, now that I have fully expressed my concerns, I relinquish the situation into God's hands and sing of my confidence in God. I know what God has done in the past and so I know that I can trust God with my future, even if I do not understand the present.

Two cautions regarding the shift from complaint to confidence are in order for our fast-paced, death-denying culture. First, Hopkins reminds us not to pole vault over complaint and petition in order to arrive more quickly at confidence and praise—to take a short-cut and so short-circuit the process of lament because of our discomfort with seasons of disorientation (*Journey through the Psalms*, 116). Lament is not a five-step process through which a person may move at a brisk pace; life is not so simple nor is the relinquishment of pain so easy. Second, while the crux of lament is hope over despair, it is not a matter of optimism in which we believe "everything will get better." But, as Clifton Black says, "the spine of lament is hope . . . the deep and irrepressible conviction, in the teeth of present evidence, that God has not severed the umbilical cord that has always bound us to the Lord" ("The Persistence of Wounds" in *Lament*, 54).

Psalm 54

The five distinct elements of lament are also present in Psalm 54, though they are intertwined in more complex ways than in Psalm 13. The poet addresses God with single words (in Hebrew) in verses one and two ("O God" [*Elohim*]), and verse six ("O LORD" [*adonay*]). As in Psalm 13, these unadorned vocatives convey urgency. The present need has no time or space for ornate greetings.

The complaint reveals the crisis that is creating such urgency for the psalmist. Insolent and ruthless people have risen against the poet and are seeking his life (v. 3). Unlike Psalm 13, the poet does not indict God for lax attention, nor does he describe the extent of his own suffering. Instead, the complaint focuses solely on the enemies and their efforts to victimize the psalmist. Here, as elsewhere in the Psalms, "enemies" may denote people or stand for anything that opposes God's followers. As a result, we may read the enemy of Psalm 54 as a person or persons making false accusations and chasing after the writer or as any possible opposition; for example, a diagnosis, lost dreams, or storms of any type.

The poet's requests are simple and correspond to the complaint. First, the psalmist implores God to save him—to take his side against his enemies and vindicate him over their life-threatening charges (v. 1). Second, he asks that God hear or pay attention to his words (v. 2). Verse five contains a third and final request: that God repay the enemies with the evil (or bad things) that they have done or planned to do to the psalmist. With this repayment, God will put an end to them and their threats (v. 5). The poet's vindictive tone requires further discussion (see Chapter Nine). At this point, we need to acknowledge that at least the psalmist surrenders his desire for vengeance into God's hands (see Rom. 12:19); God can decide what, if anything, needs to be done about his opponents.

In order to persuade God to act, the psalm depicts the enemies as evil people who refuse to follow God ("they do not set God before them" [v. 3]), unlike the psalmist who not only prays to God (vv. 1–2) but asserts that God is his helper (v. 4). In a sense, the poet puts God on the horns of a dilemma: either act on my behalf against them, or refuse to act and in effect support the insolent and arrogant people who threaten the life of your servant. Consequently, the psalmist asserts, "in your faithfulness put an end to them" (v. 5); in other words, God's prior pledge to be faithful (e.g., Exod. 34:6–7) requires God to act now on behalf of the psalmist.

Although our prior work with Psalm 13 prepares us for the final movement of lament, we may still be startled by the sudden shift from desperate cries for God's intervention (vv. 1–5) to assertions of confidence in God (vv. 6–7). Here, in Psalm 54, the poet is already planning for a future that includes a sacrifice of thanksgiving because God answered his prayer (v. 6). And he is confident that God will respond because God "has delivered me from *every trouble*" in the past (v. 7, emphasis mine). Memory of what God has done in my life enables confidence during future storms that God is reliable and faithful to his promises.

Conclusion

Lament typically works within the contours set out by Psalm 13 and 54: address, complaint, request, motivation, and confidence. A few psalms follow this formula in strict order with fairly distinct elements. Most psalmists, however, take these basic elements and create new art—rearranging, mixing, and pouring unique content into an elastic mold to speak the truth of their own lives in times of liminality and seasons of disorientation. Lament is more than the mere arranging and rearranging of cold, inflexible building blocks. Instead, like Psalm 13 and 54, the language of lament conveys a rich texture of tone and feeling. Psalm 54 expresses an urgent, even desperate, need. The poet is unable to cope with circumstances spiraling out of his control. Alone, he cannot get himself out of this storm of accusation and life-threatening opposition. He needs God—just a word from God to know that God hears and cares enough to act. And with this confidence, he relinquishes his circumstances and his desire for vindication into God's hands. Alternating threads of fear/trust and need/confidence are woven throughout the lament. In the same way, Psalm 13 weaves together doubt/faith, sorrow/joy, and death/life to convey not only descriptive information but also wide-ranging emotion. The poet is exhausted from pain with no energy to cope with another loss and too tired for more words. But he turns to God, placing hope in what only exists in the imagination and is only possible if God breaks through, and promising praise, confident in what God has yet to do.

Several years ago, I asked students in a semester-long course on Psalms, "What is the most significant thing you have learned about the Psalms so far?" Most students realized that the exam question only required some response to earn credit. One might say that the most significant thing they had learned was that there were 150 psalms in the book or that Psalm 117 was the shortest psalm. Maybe that is the most significant thing they have learned, who am I to disagree? And so I read through a number of predicable answers, until I came upon this response:

> Since my mother died my freshman year, and even more so after my father's death this year, it has often been a struggle for me to maintain a healthy prayer life. I did not question God or the relationship I have with him, but I wasn't honest. After the first week in this class, I began praying Psalm 13 and finding that if I was honest with God, sometimes angry with him, then I could truly talk and pray to God more earnestly. This class has taught me how to hurt *with* God, rather than without him. (emphasis from the student)

This is the benefit of learning to follow the contours of lament: lament provides a way for us to fully express what we are already thinking and feeling—a way to "hurt with God" when we are in the middle of a storm. And just as the faithful of Israel, Jesus, and the early church engaged in lament to give expression to their pain and hope—and so live with their God through disorientation—so this form for prayer awaits our use.

CHAPTER FIVE

Have Mercy on Me, O God, a Sinner

Have mercy on me, O God,
according to your steadfast love;
according to your abundant mercy
blot out my transgressions.
Wash me thoroughly from my iniquity,
and cleanse me from my sin.
—PSALM 51:1–3

Just as I am without one plea,
but that thy blood was shed for me,
and that thou bidd'st me come to thee,
O Lamb of God, I come. I come.
—CHARLOTTE ELLIOTT ("Just as I Am")

If lament is the practice of being honest with God, it stands to reason that I first must be honest about myself. And if I'm honest about that, I need to confess that telling the truth about myself is not easy. Most people want to appear better than we are—more together, more productive, and less flawed. It is hard for us to admit that we don't have our act together, and it is especially difficult to confess our sin with any clarity or concrete reference. Our hymnals testify against us. Most of our hymns that mention sin proclaim victory through Christ: *Victory in Jesus, What a Savior,* and *I Know That My Redeemer Lives.* Another large group of hymns about sin falls into the unique modern category of altar calls or invitation songs, inviting others to respond to the good news of Jesus and his offer of forgiveness: *Come to Jesus, Hark—The Gentle Voice, Jesus Is Tenderly Calling,* and *O Why Not Tonight.* Comparatively speaking, only a few songs take a subdued tone, express regret for sin, and request forgiveness: *Shall I Crucify My Savior?, On Bended Knee, My Eyes Are Dry,* and *I Bring My Sins to Thee.*

Perhaps surprisingly, on this point we compare favorably to the book of Psalms; the psalms also has few songs or prayers of lament in which sin is the primary problem—or is even mentioned. Tradition reaching back to the Middle Ages has identified seven "Penitential Psalms" to be recited at the times of life's greatest struggles: Psalms 6, 32, 38, 51, 102, 130, and 143. Of these seven psalms, however, one is a thanksgiving song for forgiveness (Ps. 32), two do not mention or even hint that sin is the problem (Pss. 6 and 102), and another briefly mentions that "no one living is righteous before you" (143:2b). Only three of the penitential psalms contain sustained lament for sin (38, 51, 130), and beyond these the book of Psalms has just two other psalms that identify sin as a primary cause of the psalmist's hardship (Pss. 25 and 39).

In this chapter, we will examine three of these five laments for sin (Pss. 130, 25, 51), first working through each text in some detail and then reflecting on the key themes shared by these psalms. To be sure, the psalmists consider sin to be a contributor to life's difficulties and a reason for lament, though perhaps not as great a singular cause as we might have thought. For them, life is more complicated than a one-sided explanation for trouble will allow; suffering is not always or often a direct result of sin. Forgiveness, on the other hand, is one sided—due to God's merciful character, not anything that we have done or might do.

Psalm 130

In July 2003, my first and so far last cruise sailed directly through hurricane Claudette. A day after the experience, the captain explained that when we left port Claudette was weakening on a westerly course; it was only when we were navigating oil rigs in the shallows of the Gulf of Mexico that she strengthened and turned north—there was nothing we could do but sail through her. He also mentioned that it is possible for a ship to go in six different directions—up/down, side/side, forward/backward—and during the storm we had done all six at the same time for several hours. Water poured down, came up, and smashed the sides of the ship. While trying not to be seasick, I gained new respect for Israel's use of the sea and storm as a symbol for the chaos that works against life.

Psalm 130 begins with a voice crying "out of the depths," shorthand for "the depths of the waters" (Ezek. 27:34), the last audible breath of a person being pulled under by deep floodwaters. He cries to the Lord from a sea of troubles that overwhelm, beat, choke, and drown. If only the Lord will hear and attend to my voice (130:1–2). With no time or words to spare, the poet confesses his only hope and by implication confesses what sunk him in such deep water:

> If you, O Lord, should mark iniquities,
>> Lord, who could stand?
> But there is forgiveness with you,
>> so that you may be revered. (vv. 3–4)

The root problem is sin; sin that by its nature wrecks human lives, warps relationships, and destroys everything in its path. For the psalmist, sin is not a lapse of judgment or unintentional error but a force that cracks open the dike, releasing the chaotic waters that destroy life. For him, sin matters not because it sends us to hell but because it makes life hell. But he also knows the good news that God does not "mark" (NRSV) or "keep a record" (NIV) of sin. God's disposition is not to keep a spreadsheet on sin and save it to multiple back-up systems in order to stay ready to accuse and convict. If God did there would be no hope; no one could ever stand, only drown in the sea. But the truth is that God's disposition is toward grace—to overlook, dismiss, and forgive (Exod. 34:6–7), and this truth is the poet's hope.

And it is this confidence in God that keeps the psalmist afloat— "waiting" and "hoping" (both key terms in vv. 5–8). The psalmist waits for the Lord like a bleary-eyed night sentry watches for the first light of dawn, the end of a dangerous night and the beginning of quiet rest in the safety of light (vv. 5–6). And speaking with tones of weary but determined hope, he repeats the same phrase again: "more than those who wait for the morning" (v. 6). For him, God's forgiveness is not about erasing marks off a cosmic slate, but relief from the squalls coming out of the center of the storm—from the sin itself. And when the water abates, he will know that God has indeed acted according to his true nature in forgiveness, an act that leads the poet to reverence (v. 4).

As we saw in Chapter Three, a shift from complaint/request to confidence/praise is common for lament. Here, the movement is dramatic as the psalmist turns his address to Israel and implores God's people to place their hope in the Lord (v. 7). The shift from the singular "I" to the plural "Israel" in verse 7 may indicate that we should read the entire psalm as the corporate voice of Israel ("I" = Israel). More likely, verses 1–6 are the voice of an individual reflecting on his own confession, while in verse 7 he turns in speech to his community, insistent that, as for him, the only way ahead for them is to confess and place their hope in the Lord's steadfast love and power to redeem them from the sin that threatens to overwhelm and drown out life (vv. 7–8).

Psalm 25

An acrostic is a literary or poetic device in which the first letter of each line uses each consecutive letter of the alphabet (technically, an "abecedarius"). Psalm 119, for example, is a massive acrostic in which the first eight verses each begin with the first letter of the Hebrew alphabet (*aleph*), then the next eight verses each begin with the second letter (vv. 9–16, *bet*), and so forth for the twenty-two letters of the alphabet, 176 verses. Because of their commitment to an alphabetic pattern, acrostics may seem less than coherent or somewhat jumpy as they move from line to line. The difficulty of achieving a smooth acrostic composition is understandable; try to write an acrostic psalm in English. The first few lines will be easy with *a b c d*, but imagine the difficulty when we reach *q r s t u v w x y z*.

Psalm 25 is an acrostic. Beginning with *aleph* (the first letter of the Hebrew alphabet), each verse begins with the next consecutive letter, concluding with *taw* (the final Hebrew letter) in verse 22. As a result of the acrostic form, the elements of lament do not appear in a tidy arrangement (as in Psalm 13) but are scattered throughout the psalm. For example, after a brief address to God ("O Lord," v. 1; repeated in vv. 6, 7, 11, 22), the psalm begins (vv. 1–2) and ends (vv. 19–21) with appeals regarding the psalmist's immediate problem: his enemies trying to shame him.

Honor and shame are core social values in most Mediterranean and Near Eastern cultures, without any close parallel in our Western society (one reason we have such difficulty understanding Eastern and Near Eastern nations today). For such cultures, to lose honor or be shamed is far more than suffering an embarrassment. In describing the first-century Mediterranean world, Vernon K. Robbins explains that "honor denotes a person's rightful place in society, one's social standing. . . . [it] is a claim to worth along with social acknowledgement of worth" (*Exploring the Texture of Texts*, 76). So to be "put to shame" (vv. 2, 20) means the loss of social position which negatively affects every familial relationship and business interaction. For an enemy to take honor (status) at the psalmist's expense is no small matter in a society with foundations built on the bedrock of honor and shame.

Because he trusts in God (v. 2) and takes refuge in the Lord (v. 20), the poet prays that his enemies not "exult over me" (v. 2) and that God will "not let me be put to shame" (vv. 2, 20). He asks that God not allow anyone who "waits" or who sets their hope on God to be put to shame (v. 3). Instead, shame should come to the "wantonly treacherous" (v. 3) and those who express violent hatred (v. 19), not those who live in "integrity and uprightness" and who, along with the psalmist, put their hope and trust in the Lord (v. 21). And so, the psalmist begins to build a persuasive case for God's intervention.

Despite the problem of the opposition, the middle verses of the acrostic attend to an even more serious concern: the writer's own sin. At first, he urges the Lord to remember or act in a way consistent with the Lord's own claims to be a merciful and gracious God (e.g., Exod. 34:6–7) and so forgive "the sins of my youth" (vv. 6–7). But it is his present sinfulness not the distant past that causes the gravest alarm. He asks God to pardon his guilt (v. 11) and "forgive all my sins" (v. 18). And, in the process of making these requests, he acknowledges that it is his own sin that is causing him so much trouble (vv. 16–18). It may be that the writer's enemies are capitalizing on his failures in an attempt to shame him and take away his honor in the community.

Interspersed throughout the complaints, appeals, and motivations are small units of wisdom or teaching related to the theme. For example, verses 8–10 identify God's goodness in the way he teaches sinners and instructs the humble in the right way. This is precisely the psalmist's hope for his own situation—that God will teach and lead him back to the correct path (vv. 4–5). In another short unit, verses 12–15 affirm that the Lord will teach those who "fear the LORD." Because of God's friendship, these people will be blessed with the joy of living in a permanent covenant relationship with God (vv. 13–14). Once again, this too is the psalmist's hope—that the Lord will "pluck my feet out of the net" (sin's net, the enemy's net, or both) and establish him on the right path (v. 15).

Psalm 51

The superscription, or heading, places Psalm 51 as a part of David's confession for his role in the Bathsheba-Uriah affair (2 Sam. 11), and this may be the origin of the psalm. David had the ability to write music (1 Sam. 17:16–23), and he certainly had reason to write a lament psalm. He was "the man" responsible for taking Bathsheba and murdering Uriah (2 Sam. 12:7–10), the man who took the neighbor's pet lamb for slaughter in Nathan's parable (2 Sam. 12:1–6). And once exposed, David admitted, "I have sinned against the LORD" (2 Sam. 12:13). Psalm 51 fits nicely into this background.

Careful study, however, raises questions about the reliability of the psalmic superscriptions. A total of one hundred psalms have some sort of heading in our standard Hebrew Bible (the *Biblia Hebraica Stuttgartensia*,

c. 1100 CE). Other manuscripts, however, differ in the number of superscriptions they include. For example, the Greek Old Testament (Septuagint)
includes 114 headings, fourteen more than the Hebrew text. Historically,
it appears that the headings were not part of the original psalms but were
later additions. As time passed, editors and copyists associated more and
more psalms with David (e.g., Pss. 4–6, 8) and particular moments in
David's life (e.g., Pss. 3, 7, 18) with the result of more headings appearing
in later manuscripts. What we don't know is whether these scribes were
following reliable traditions regarding these psalms, if they were divinely
inspired to know and so add the headings, if they meant to encourage
readers to think about David as they read the psalm, or if they were merely
providing their understanding or opinion—much as translators or editors
of modern Bibles add chapter and paragraph headings to the biblical text.
Consequently, despite the heading, though possible, we cannot be certain
that David wrote Psalm 51.

Psalm 51 seamlessly integrates the five elements of lament to express
remorse for sin and make an extended appeal for forgiveness. The address
is short ("O God") and repeated at several points in the psalm (vv. 10, 14, 15
["O Lord"], 17), and the poet condenses his complaint in verses 3–5: I am
constantly and painfully aware of my sin against God and so acknowledge
that any sentence God decides is just (on verse 5, see below). The writer's
request overwhelms the psalm. Nineteen of the forty-four lines appeal for
God's grace in one form or another (vv. 1a, 1d, 2, 6b–12, 14a, and 15a), and,
in his appeal, the psalmist provides a near complete Hebrew thesaurus for
the idea of forgiveness, including common and unusual images for forgiveness: have mercy (v. 1a), blot out (vv. 1d, 9b), wash me (vv. 2a, 7b), cleanse
me (v. 2b), teach me (v. 6b), purge me (v. 7a), let me hear joy (v. 8), hide your
face (v. 9a), create in me a clean heart (v. 10a), put in me a new and right
spirit (v. 10b), don't cast me away (v. 11a), don't take away your holy spirit
(v. 11b), restore the joy of your salvation (v. 12a) sustain in me a willing
spirit (v. 12b), deliver me (v. 14a), and open my lips to declare praise (v. 15a).
The psalmist asks for nothing more than God's mercy—and he asks for
mercy in every imaginable way to express his deep longing for God's grace.

Desperate to receive release from his sins, the psalmist asks God to forgive by appealing to God's character: "according to your steadfast love; according to your mercy" (v. 1bc) or, as *The Message* translates, "Generous in love . . . Huge in mercy." The poet confesses his sin (vv. 3–5) and cannot imagine taking God's mercy for granted; he is helpless without God's instruction (v. 6b), presence (v. 11), and sustaining spirit (v. 12). Apart from God's character, the psalmist can only appeal to the outcomes that forgiveness would produce. If God will only forgive me, then I will teach and lead others back to God (v. 13), I will declare how God has worked in my life (v. 14), and I will praise God (v. 15).

Despite the poet's desperation for forgiveness, the psalm possesses a tone of quiet confidence. The poet knows that God is willing to forgive because such is God's nature toward those with "a broken and contrite heart" (v. 17b). So although no dramatic shift from appeal to praise takes place in Psalm 51 (as in Ps. 13), the psalmist is no less sure of God's response or his own intention to praise the Lord.

Special Issues in Psalm 51

The poetic language of Psalm 51 has often confused readers and been misused in support of larger theological claims. For example, proponents of a theology of original sin often appeal to verse five for support: "Indeed, I was born guilty, a sinner when my mother conceived me." In fact, read in a literal fashion, the verse does assume guilt or sinfulness from the moment of conception. At least two arguments, however, stand against such a reading. First, we are reading poetry not prose or a legal brief. And Hebrew poetry, like its kin across languages, uses a full spectrum of literary devices, including metaphor and hyperbole, or exaggeration, in order to convey feeling (e.g., Pss. 98:7–9; 137:8–9). Thus, we need to evaluate extreme statements in the Psalms for the possibility of overstatement to make the writer's point. Second, a literal reading works against the psalm's message by making an excuse for the psalmist's behavior (it was because he was born guilty that he sinned)—he had no chance. But such an idea is against every other line of the psalm; elsewhere the psalmist takes full responsibility for his sin. So it seems best to read verse five as an instance of a hyperbolic metaphor that conveys how guilty the psalmist feels—so guilty that he cannot remember a time when he was not mired in sin.

A second difficulty raised by the poetic language of Psalm 51 concerns its conflicting statements about sacrifice. Verses 15–17 appear to take an antisacrificial attitude: God wants a "broken and contrite heart," not sacrifice. But the next two verses claim that, after the walls of Jerusalem are rebuilt, sacrifices will be offered again and God will take delight in them (vv. 18–19). So does God want sacrifice or not? Among the possible solutions to this tension is that one or more of these verses may be later additions to the original psalm. In the same way that we add new stanzas to existing songs, so a poet may have added verses 15–17 to what was already a complete lament (vv. 1–14), and then another poet much later (perhaps after the return from captivity) added verses 18–19 to provide new hope to the dismal situation in Jerusalem and correct any misunderstanding of what had been said about sacrifice in verses 15–17. Regardless of its compositional history, taken as a whole, the conclusion of the psalm sets out a coherent theology or understanding of sacrifice that is in harmony with what precedes (vv. 1–14) and what the Old Testament teaches elsewhere. God has never desired sacrifice without a person's heart (e.g. Isa. 1:10–17; Amos 5:21–24; Mic. 6:6–8). Michael Jinkins explains,

> God is at work in the hearts of sinners. . . . Underlying this affirmation is a critique of formal religious acts which have somehow lost their essential faith motivation. The criticism is not, in other words, merely a rejection of temple sacrifices, but a call to reformation of those sacrifices, so that they symbolize God's transformational activity in the hearts of the faithful. (*In the House of the Lord*, 92)

The first and genuine expense is our heart, ourselves—the gift that must precede any acceptable sacrifice. And it is this offering of brokenness in Psalm 51 that makes every other sacrifice "right sacrifice(s)" in which God takes delight (v. 19).

A third issue in Psalm 51 is also related to the nature of Hebrew poetry. Some readings of the phrase "your holy spirit" (v. 11) take these words to be a reference to the Holy Spirit of the trinity and so capitalize the phrase (e.g., NIV, NASV). Synonymous parallelism, a prevalent feature of Hebrew poetry, weighs heavily against such a translation or understanding. In synonymous parallelism, a poet restates the idea of the previous line with new or different terms in order to emphasize the prior thought or to add nuance in some way. For example, the opening lines of Psalm 148 are filled with synonymous parallelism: "Praise the Lord from the heavens; praise him in the heights!" (the heavens = the heights) "Praise him, all his angels; praise him, all his host!" (his angels = his host). In the same way, Psalm 51:11b ("and do not take your holy spirit from me") is in synonymous parallelism to the previous line ("Do not cast me away from your presence"). So in this text "your holy spirit" is another way of referring to God's presence, not necessarily a reference to the Holy Spirit. What the psalmist expresses is fear of lost intimacy in his relationship to God.

Lament for Sin

Psalms 130, 25, and 51 present a healthy theology of sin and self that takes sin seriously while at the same time acknowledging that God is greater than our sin. Each psalm reflects the heartache of guilt caused by sin (25:17; 51:3–5, 130:3), though it is impossible to discern with any precision what specific sin or sins lay behind each lament. Confession of specific offenses is bypassed in favor of a passionate confession that sin is my problem, disrupting and destroying every other aspect of my life. That said, however, we need to exercise caution with any conclusion that says suffering is the consequence of sin. It is true that the writer of Psalm 25 believes that as a result of his sin he is "lonely and afflicted" (v. 16); his sin has caused disruption and the loss of relationships. And perhaps the other "troubles of my heart," "my distress," and "my affliction and my trouble" are also the result of "all my sins" (vv. 17–18). Perhaps. But even then the precise nature of his sin is still vague. The same is true for Psalm 130. The psalmist faults his sin for landing him (and Israel) in "the depths." But the link is fuzzy and the exact sin concealed. And even for Psalm 51, if we disregard the superscription, the sin or sins that have led to this massive appeal for forgiveness are not explicitly stated. To be sure, each of these psalmists knew and confessed their sins through these psalms—and so have countless generations of believers who have taken up these psalms as their own. Because the writers bypassed precision in favor of poetic, elastic words—open rather than closed to new meaning—we, too, can acknowledge the hellish nature of our own sins through these laments. With their words, we can confront our own failures, naming and confessing what is destroying our own lives.

Another shared commitment in these laments is their reliance on God's character for forgiveness. The psalmists urge God to have mercy for the sake of his own reputation (25:11), for the result of reverence (130:4), or so that the one forgiven will teach others (51:13) and sing God's praise (51:15). But this cajolery is insignificant window dressing around their appeal to God's own character. Each psalm draws upon some knowledge of the ideas, if not the text itself, of God's revelation to Moses:

> The LORD, the LORD,
> a God merciful and gracious,
> slow to anger,
> and abounding in steadfast love and faithfulness,
> keeping steadfast love for the thousandth generation,
> forgiving iniquity and transgression and sin. (Exod. 34:6b–7a)

So Psalm 25 urges the Lord to remember his mercy and steadfast love "for they have been of old" (v. 6) and on this basis forgive "according to your steadfast love" (v. 7). And in a similar manner, Psalm 51 asks for grace "according to your steadfast love, according to your abundant mercy" (v. 1)—to forgive, not because of anything that I have done or will ever do, but because of who you have revealed yourself to be. Or, as Psalm 130 says, "there is forgiveness with you" (v. 4a). We need not hide in the garden from fear of our sin or our God (Gen. 3). God forgives. Mercy is God's first disposition and the only real basis of hope for those mired in sin.

Our twenty-first century Western world tends to take sin as a private matter between God and me—if we recognize sin at all. In these psalms, however, the lament is not complete until it makes some movement toward others, breaking through the restrictive walls of individualism and reaching out to the larger community. This move may be as simple as a pledge to teach others and lead sinners back to God (51:13) or a declaration of thanksgiving for God's intervention (51:15; see Chapter Twelve). But it also extends to an inclusion of the community in my confession and appeal for forgiveness. "Do good to Zion in your good pleasure; rebuild the walls of Jerusalem" (v. 18), so ends Psalm 51. Or, as Psalm 25 concludes, "Redeem Israel, O God, out of all its troubles" (v. 22). And Psalm 130 finishes with words both to and for Israel: "O Israel, hope in the LORD. . . . It is he who will redeem Israel from all its iniquities" (vv. 7–8). Like Isaiah, each of these psalmists recognizes that sin and guilt are not just personal matters, but are communal issues. "I am a man of unclean lips" and "I live among a people of unclean lips" (Isa. 6:5). And so the final move of lament for my sin is a turn toward the community, in speech to the community and in speech to God on behalf of the community. *Me* becomes *we; I* becomes *us.* The realization of sin in my life leads to recognition of sin in the life of the community, and so lament for my sin can never remain lament for only my sin but for a world at risk. Sin is more than an isolated individual activity; it is symptomatic of a diseased communal heart—systemic evil woven into the fabric of society.

These psalms chart a course back to God: admitting our failures and identifying the ways in which our sins unleash storms against our lives and impact the lives of others and locating our sins within a larger communal and societal whole. Indeed, all creation is in "bondage to decay," and our irresponsibility is to blame (Rom. 8:21). Most important, the course back to God is open because God makes it so. Mercy, grace, and unfailing love are God's first disposition, eager to welcome faltering steps in the right direction—even providing the language we need to speak the truth of our lives.

CHAPTER SIX

Why Are You Cast Down, O My Soul?

A study of lament may be a corrective for some religion in the church that wishes
to withdraw from life as it really is, to pretense and romance in the unreal
world of heavenly or holy things. The lament makes clear that faith and worship
deal with and are shaped by life as it comes to us.
—WALTER BRUEGGEMANN (*The Psalms and the Life of Faith*, 67)

If we were to pray cautiously, guardedly, elegantly, passionlessly, passively,
our prayer would be not only useless but harmful. Prayer of this sort sickens
the soul because it only contributes to a spirit of hopelessness and resignation
in face of evil. It makes us less than the subjects, less than the agents that God
has created and called us to be.
—KATHLEEN D. BILLMAN AND DANIEL L. MIGLIORE (*Rachel's Cry*, 118)

In previous chapters, we have discussed common objections to the
Christian practice of lament; for example, lament is a sub-Christian
language, lament belonged to Israel's developmental stage of faith, and,
this side of the cross, we have no need for lament. Two undisputable truths
form the basis of another common critique of lament.

Truth #1: No one is exempt from hardship. Just as the sun rises on the
evil and the good and rain falls on the just and the unjust (Matt. 5:45), so
too the storms of life come to both. One psalmist concluded, "[the wicked]
are like chaff that the wind drives away" (1:4), and another, "many are the

afflictions of the righteous" (34:19a). Towers collapse on the good and the bad (Luke 13:4). Disease does not discriminate, not even to favor those with healthy eating habits and exercise routines. A bad economy spreads its losses among the frugal and the wasteful. And no number of seminars or books will provide an iron-clad warranty for a happy marriage or well-adjusted children. Life is an equal opportunity employer; we all experience joy and pain.

Truth #2: People complain about Truth #1. Most people complain that life is not fair—and many people are spectacularly gifted at throwing tantrums about their lot in life from years of intense practice. And these people, of course, are an absolute delight to be around. They provide a running commentary on all that is unfair about their lives and the world. If not for their constant complaining, we would never know that their suffering is about to eclipse Job's record. They groan about their spouses and mutter about how the coaches selectively discriminate against their children. They make sure their colleagues realize that their workplace falls short of perfection; the bosses make decisions without adequate consultation (i.e., the bosses didn't ask their opinion) and do things that are too risky (i.e., not what they would have done). Above all, we should be grateful to complainers for reminding us of the problems in the church: ineffective church leadership, a lack of vision, too few people involved, and too many people who complain about their lives and the problems in the church.

The validity of Truth #1 (everyone experiences hardship) and Truth #2 (people complain about their troubles), raises another question about lament: What is the difference, if any, between commonplace groaning and lament as a language? Is there any substantial distinction between the two? Or is it, as some have suggested, that the laments are complaining put into religious jargon. Strip away the pretense of God-talk and all that remains is murmuring—just like Israel in the wilderness. And for Israel, such language was not "of faith" but due to an obstinate lack of trust in the Lord. What is supposed to distinguish Christians from nonbelievers is that Christians have a different attitude toward life. Christians have put to death our earthly nature and gotten rid of such shortcomings as "anger, wrath, malice, slander, and abusive language" (Col. 3:8). In place of the old self, we have clothed ourselves with "compassion, kindness, humility, meekness, and patience" (Col. 3:12). And so we "bear with one another and, if anyone has a complaint against another," we forgive just as the Lord has forgiven us (Col. 3:13). So some conclude that what distinguishes the Christian is indeed a new faith language, a language of thanksgiving, gratitude, and trust—not a language of lament (Col. 3:15–16).

This critique of lament provides a healthy skepticism that merits our consideration. It is true that Christians are a changed people, a people in the process of transformation into the image of Christ. It is also true that while everyone has problems, believers have a new and unique hope for the work of God in our lives, in the world, and in the world to come. Nonetheless, biblical lament is significantly different than Israel's murmuring or commonplace complaining; and the difference, ironically, is that lament comes from two robust and daring faith claims.

Faith Claim #1: The Lord Reigns

Few believers would dispute this assertion, despite the lack of direct evidence we might expect or hope for on occasion. But for the book of Psalms and its laments, the claim that the Lord is sovereign takes special significance. James Mays, among others, has argued that the declaration "the Lord reigns" is a prevailing or organizing metaphor for Psalms and its theology (*The Lord Reigns*, 12–22). And the book of Psalms does, in fact, appear to express a thematic movement toward the idea of God's reign through the arrangement of its individual psalms.

At the outset, the book of Psalms introduces a conflict between the king, ordained by God (2:6–7), and the nations—who should take warning and honor the Lord and his anointed on the throne of Israel, but do not (2:10–11). As the conflict develops in the book, not all is well for Israel's king: he suffers at the hands of many enemies and struggles with diverse problems (e.g., Pss. 3, 4, 6, 7, 17). The Lord upholds the king (Ps. 41) and the people pray that God will always bless him (Ps. 72). But the situation deteriorates. As Psalms reaches the end of Book 3, enemies have sacked

Jerusalem and the temple (Ps. 79), God has rejected the Davidic covenant and the current king (Ps. 89), and the nation appears to be dead, turned back to dust (Ps. 90).

It is at precisely this point in the book of Psalms that we hear the strongest affirmation that the Lord reigns. While the Davidic monarchy and nation have collapsed (Ps. 89), Psalm 93 begins the chant:

> The LORD is king, he is robed in majesty;
>> the LORD is robed; he is girded with strength.
> He has established the world; it shall never be moved. (v. 1)

The next six psalms pick up and expand the theme. Psalm 94 calls on the "judge of the earth" to rise up and deal with the proud and wicked (vv. 1–3), while Psalm 95 calls the people to give thanks to the Lord, "a great God, and a great King above all gods" (v. 3). Psalm 96 gives its own "great commission" to the reader:

> Say among the nations, "The LORD is King!"
>> The world is firmly established; it shall never be moved.
>> He will judge the peoples with equity. (v. 10)

Psalm 97 asserts the same theme, "The LORD is king! Let the earth rejoice, let the many coastlands be glad!" (v. 1), and the next psalm continues: "with trumpets and the sound of the horn make a joyful noise before the king, the LORD" (98:6). Finally, Psalm 99 concludes the proclamation of the Lord's reign in grand fashion:

> The LORD is king; let the peoples tremble!
>> He sits enthroned upon the cherubim; let the
> earth rejoice!
> . . . Mighty King, lover of justice,
>> you have established equity;
> you have executed justice
>> and righteousness in Jacob.
> Extol the LORD our God;

worship at his footstool.

Holy is he! (vv. 1, 4–5)

Despite the collapse of the Davidic monarchy in Judah, the Psalms boldly proclaim the reign of God. The true king of God's people has not been deposed or lost his kingdom. The Lord (still) reigns—alone and sovereign.

The poets of lament take this confession at face value: the Lord, a God of justice, equity, and righteousness—this God has uncompromised dominion over *all* of life, ordering the lives of his people. And it is this faith in a sovereign God that causes confusion. Why does an all-powerful king suddenly and inexplicably no longer bless, no longer order life, and no longer hold things together? If a person did not believe that God was sovereign, then there would be no cause for lament. But these writers *do believe* and have *high expectations* of the God whom they praise as king. So, the first faith claim that distinguishes lament from mere complaint is the deep faith from which lament emerges, a faith that the Lord reigns, and so a faith bewildered by the ambiguity and inadequacy of the Lord's reign.

Faith Claim #2: Bewildered Faith Evokes Speech to God

Faith connotes relationship, a harmony of expectations and trust. So when our understanding and expectations of God crash face first into the actualities of our lives, the resultant dissonance leads people of faith to lament. Faith cannot pretend, as Brueggemann contends, that life is well ordered when it is not. Nor can faith remain silent when life is experienced as pain rather than a gift. Just as the community must praise God when life is ordered and blessed, so must the church lament when life is no longer well ordered. For the trusting community, lament is an act of bold faith that "insists that the world must be experienced as it really is and not in some pretended way" (*The Message of the Psalms*, 52). So as everything is brought to speech, everything is submitted to the sovereignty of God. Brueggemann explains, to withhold parts of life from that conversation is in fact to withhold part of life from the sovereignty of God. Thus these psalms make the important connection: everything must be *brought to speech*, and everything brought to speech must be *addressed to God*, who is the final reference for all of life. (52, emphasis in original)

Lament is not mere complaint that life is not fair. Lament is of faith and for faith, born of the sovereignty of God and upholding the reign of God. The difference between complaint and lament is a faith that must speak the truth of our lives to the only One who can make a difference (the King), and, when we speak, we expect that God will respond.

The psalms we examine in this chapter (42–43 and 27) exemplify this struggle of faith for two writers in ancient Israel who found life to take sudden and prolonged turns across difficult terrain. And these poets, like their sisters and brothers of faith then and now, found this rugged place to be immensely complicated by their faith in the reign of God. So they speak boldly for the sake of their faith and passionately for the sake of their relationship with the Lord who reigns.

Psalm 42–43

Substantial evidence suggests that Psalms 42 and 43 originally constituted one psalm that at some point was inadvertently split into two chapters. In addition to manuscripts that read 42 and 43 as one psalm, other indications of unity include: 1) A recurring refrain:

> Why are you cast down, O my soul,
>> and why are you disquieted within me?
> Hope in God, for I shall again praise him,
>> my help and my God. (42:5, 11; 43:5)

This refrain occurs twice in Psalm 42 (dividing it into two stanzas; 42:5, 11) and concludes chapter 43 (marking 43:1–4 as the third and final stanza of the psalm). Like a chorus to a song, the refrain unites the three stanzas into one psalm. 2) The lack of a heading for Psalm 43. A survey of surrounding psalms reveals the presence of superscriptions (headings) extending back to Psalm 34 and forward to Psalm 70—except for Psalm 43. This lack or omission indicates that when scribes were adding the various headings to Psalms 34–70, Psalm 43 was still part of Psalm 42, not a distinct psalm. Otherwise, the scribes would most likely have added a superscription to 43 as they did for the surrounding psalms. 3) Together, Psalm 42–43 constitutes a complete lament. As we have seen, laments commonly include five elements (see Chapter Four: address, complaint, request, motivation, and confidence). Only by reading Psalm 42 and 43 together, however, do we find all five components. In Psalm 42, the psalmist calls to God (the address; v. 1) and expresses his troubles (the complaint; vv. 1–4, 7–10), but not until Psalm 43 does the psalmist complete his lament by asking God to vindicate and rescue him (the request; vv. 1, 3) with reasons why God should do these things (the motivation; vv. 2, 4). Only together are Psalms 42 and 43 a complete lament. 4) The thematic unity of Psalm 42–43. The unity of Psalm 42–43 is not only formal (with all five elements of lament) but also thematic. Psalm 42 introduces concerns about the psalmist's inner turmoil, his adversaries, and the distance he feels from God. In Psalm 43, the writer asks God to resolve each of these concerns—to vindicate

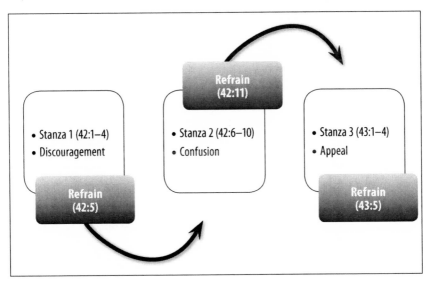

him against his enemies (v. 1), to restore him to God's presence (v. 3), and together these actions will resolve his inner turmoil (v. 4). Psalm 42–43 is, therefore, just that—one psalm with three stanzas.

Each stanza in Psalm 42–43 articulates distinctive feelings. In the first, the prevailing emotion is discouragement born as a result of separation from God (42:1–4). Like a deer cut off from and unable to locate water, for some unidentified reason, the psalmist is cut off from the presence of God—most likely physical separation from the Jerusalem temple. Clues within the psalm locate the poet in North Israel (e.g., 42:5). But the poet's problem is not just geography. The writer's physical circumstance has given cause for opponents to claim that God has abandoned him (42:3). And spurred by their harassment, the poet remembers better days, times when he enjoyed the presence of God, shouting joy and praise with others (42:4 NIV) or perhaps even leading the praise (42:4 NRSV). But not now—now he is homesick for God, existing on his tears rather than the streams of water that spring from the city of God (46:4). Cut off from God, taunted by enemies, and haunted by his memories, the psalmist is disheartened.

In the second stanza, discouragement becomes confusion. Without question, the psalmist believes in God's love ("By day the LORD commands his steadfast love," 42:8) and God's power (God is a "rock," 42:9). He also claims a personal relationship with God. He addresses himself to the "God of *my* life" (42:8) and speaks to "God *my* rock" (42:9). Whatever may be the cause of his separation from God's presence in the temple, the problem is not his sin. The psalmist says nothing about sin and gives no hint that sin is the underlying cause.

His confusion stems from his faith, not a lack of faith. The God in whom he believes and with whom he has a relationship has inexplicably let loose the chaotic waters that have swept over him and knocked him off his feet (42:7). And while he suffers "as with a deadly wound," people use his circumstances as evidence that God has abandoned him—or to question God's power to help or even God's concern for him (Where is *your* God?). God seems to have forgotten about him (42:9). His God confuses him; he believes—he just doesn't understand. If he didn't believe in the reign of

God, it would be easier to explain and perhaps even easier to live through the trouble. But he does believe and refuses to set aside his faith or be silent just because it would make life more bearable.

When what we believe to be true about our God clashes with the actualities of our lives so that nothing makes sense, our faith requires speech. Faith must appeal to God, the theme of the final stanza (43:1–4). The poet asks God for vindication and rescue from wicked and deceitful enemies, those who have been challenging God's faithfulness (43:1). He asks that God send his light and truth to bring him back home to the Jerusalem temple, the holy place where God symbolically lives with his people (43:3; cf. 1 Kings 8:22–53). Here the poet will rejoin a pilgrimage to worship God "my exceeding joy" (43:4). But above all, he asks that God, the stronghold of his life, no longer reject him. This request is posed as two questions: "Why have you cast me off? Why must I walk about mournfully because of the oppression of the enemy?" (43:2). The psalmist is not asking for an explanation of why God has acted as he has; reasons and explanations rarely matter in the middle of suffering. Rather, to ask "why" in these circumstances is to assert a fundamental objection: God should no longer treat him like an outcast. He should not have to live in perpetual mourning just because his opponents—and God's opponents—choose to make life difficult.

I have had the opportunity to read Psalm 42–43 with many groups over the past ten years, and each time I have raised the same final question: How should we read the recurring refrain? The text is straight-forward self-talk:

> Why are you cast down, O my soul,
> and why are you disquieted within me?
> Hope in God; for I shall again praise him,
> my help and my God. (42:5, 11; 43:5)

But the *tone* is not clear at all—and it is the tone of the refrain that makes all the difference in how we understand the psalm. Do we read the refrain with an optimistic voice of confidence? *Don't be so discouraged; everything is going to be fine—you know that you can count on God!* Or do we read with despair, a kind of hope against hope that somehow God will break through even though we can't bring ourselves to believe it? *I want to believe that things are going to be okay, but I can't. It's been too long and too hard. Maybe God will do something; he's my only chance—but it doesn't seem much of a chance.* Or is the psalmist angry, frustrated, or worried?

To make things easy, I reduce the options to two possible readings: Is the psalmist optimistic or in deep despair? The results are most always split with deep despair holding a slight lead. My training to look for a single meaning in a text leads me to think that the refrain cannot be both optimistic and despairing, unless, as some of my students have suggested, we read the refrain as a progression from despair (in the first instance of the refrain, 42:5) to hope (in the final refrain, 43:5). Or perhaps, the genius of this and other poets is that they allow us to read their psalms with different moods or tones based on our own situation. We bring ourselves to the text and fill it with our experience. The refrain itself is open and pliable with layers of possible meaning; it is the reader that makes the difference. The psalms read our lives just as we read the psalms. And within this interplay between text and reader, we are able to make the psalms our own, to fit them into our own situation and needs. The brilliance of the psalms is that this interaction works time after time. Psalm 42–43 is a resource for devastated readers who cannot bring themselves to give up on God and for readers confident that God will deliver them.

Psalm 27

While Psalms 42 and 43 are one psalm inadvertently split into two chapters, at first glance, it appears that in Psalm 27 two psalms have been combined in one chapter. The first six verses constitute a psalm of confidence (27:1–6) similar in tone to Psalm 23, and the last eight verses form a lament, complete with all five typical elements (27:7–14). So distinct are the two parts that Artur Weiser, among others, concludes that the dissimilarity in tone, mood, and poet's inward attitude "can hardly be accounted for in any other way than by assuming that we are now dealing [in vv. 7–14] with an independent psalm by another author" (*The Psalms*, 251). In Psalm 27, somehow we have "two originally independent poems" juxtaposed in one chapter.

Weiser may be correct about the situation, but the radical movement from confidence to lament may also be the product of a single voice trying to make his or her way on a faith journey that is more like a roller coaster than a predictable merry-go-round. If we give this perspective a chance, internal evidence emerges in favor of unity. First, key words lace the two halves together: "my salvation" (vv. 1 and 9), "heart" (vv. 3, 8, and 14), "hide" (vv. 5 and 9), "seek" (vv. 4 and 8), and "foes/enemies" (vv. 2 and 6). Second, both parts have the same persistent theme of a desire to live in the presence of God in spite of obstacles (vv. 4–5 and 7–9, 13; cf. Richard Clifford, *Psalms 1–72*, 146).

All this psalmist has ever wanted is to live in an intimate relationship with God, expressed through multiple metaphors in verses 1–6. His one desire has been to "live in the house of the LORD" and so to "behold the beauty of the LORD" (v. 4). Along with other references to the temple in verse four ("to inquire in his temple"), verse six ("I will offer in his tent sacrifices with shouts of joy"), and possibly verse five ("he will conceal me under the cover of his tent"), it would be easy to read the poet's hope literally as moving physically to a locale nearby or even in the temple. But such a reading misses the power of these metaphors to voice a desire greater than physical proximity. To "live in the house of the LORD" connotes enjoying God's hospitality (e.g., Ps. 23:5–6), just as "to behold" the Lord signifies fellowship with the Lord (e.g., Exod. 24:9–11). The hope is spiritual, not geographical. So, in close relationship to God, the psalmist refers to the Lord as "my light," "my salvation," and "my stronghold" or "refuge" (27:1). The Lord's presence and alliance is all that he needs in a time of trouble. God will "hide me" in his shelter (booth), "conceal me" within his tent, and even set me on a high rock/cliff that no one dares to assault (v. 5). And so with this one thing—intimacy with God—"I will be confident" no matter if people attack me like wild animals (v. 2) or whole armies surround me (v. 3). I will not be afraid; my one desire is all that matters.

Such faith comes from long experience with God. The poet knows that when enemies come again (and they will come) that the Lord will be with him; he knows because he and God have walked down this path together for a long time. He knows, but that doesn't change his sudden turn to lament (vv. 7–14). His questions are more intense because the poet's greatest desire has not changed; he still wants God's intimate presence. And so his confidence, under pressure, does not wilt but neither does it remain silent: Don't take away the only thing that matters—the one thing that I care about (v. 8). Don't hide your face, don't turn me away, don't toss me aside (v. 9), and don't give me up (v. 12). And even as these appeals come out of his mouth, his confidence remains: I know that if everyone else abandons me, the Lord will never leave me (v. 10). I know that I will experience the Lord's goodness (v. 13). I know that I must "wait" in hope for the Lord (v. 13).

As in Psalm 42–43, the lament of Psalm 27 does not come from weak faith but from strong faith. The psalmist's greatest desire is to live in close relationship with God, and he is confident that God not only shares his desire but will also act in such a way as to make relationship possible. The poet knows this—he has confidence in God. He has not suddenly lost faith between verses six and seven. He has, however, been brought down from the serenity of a high place and thrust back into the haze of conflict. But, even back here, he does not give up on God; rather, because of his experience with God, he calls on him to make his presence in the fray more visible.

Two recent commentaries on Psalms from James Mays and Richard Clifford provide excellent summaries and insight into the message of Psalm 27:

> The psalm in its present form is a text to teach and express trust for a way of life whose living will again and again be misrepresented, misunderstood, and put in question in the cultures in which it is undertaken. . . . The two parts of the psalm are one more way in which the Psalter teaches how

closely related are trust and need. The urgent prayers of the second part is the complement of the confident confession of the first part. Trust is active and real precisely when one is aware of one's vulnerability, of one's ultimate helplessness before the threats of life, "in the day of trouble," as the psalmist puts it. On the other hand, the voice of neediness speaking urgent pleas for help arises from trust, which transforms mere anxiety to prayer. (Mays, *Psalms*, 132)

Few psalms celebrate so eloquently the human hunger for God amid dangers and delays. It is a long journey from the opening "whom shall I fear?" to the final "wait for the Lord!" Between beginning and end there is desire, (anticipated) joyous thanks, anguish, and pleas not to be abandoned and to be guided home. These are the emotions of the great Christian saints, and they are also the emotions of ordinary people trying to remain faithful to God. Life does not move in a straight line from desire to fulfillment and neither does this psalm. It guides people through the turns and delays of life before God, teaching people to honor and nurture their desire for God. (Clifford, *Psalms 1–72*, 149)

Lament, Common Complaint, and Faith

Lament is not the same thing as common complaining about life's problems. In Psalms 42–43 and 27, the writers reflect on a long history of relationship with God and a strong desire for a continuing and deepening communion. Their problem, if it should be described as such, is that their faith has grown to expect something of the relationship. And when they are disappointed by unmet expectations, disappointed by God, they cannot remain silent. On one hand, when God works in their lives as he promised, these psalmists offer exuberant praise (27:6; 42:4; 43:3–4). On the other hand, these psalmists cannot escape the logical conclusion of praise. If we praise God for blessing our lives, we must lament when there is no blessing. If God is responsible for blessing, God is also accountable for the lack of blessing. Otherwise, faith is a one-sided Pollyanna approach to life. In my experience, it is at this point that the church typically falls silent or reverts back to another praise song. Not these psalmists—their faith will not allow it.

Genuine faith in a God who reigns is risky. Randy Harris explains, "When you have high expectations of God and he doesn't always operate the way you think he's going to, you're going to have some disappointments. And I'll grant you that's a dicey world." But the opposite is even more dangerous. Too many Christians never lament because they never really expect anything of God.

> Our expectations are so low that we are never disappointed. I don't want to do that. I want us to pray believing God answers. I want us to expect God to interact with us in the world. I want us to be brave enough to call upon him when he doesn't seem to be coming through. I want us to be bold enough to badger God when he seems reluctant. To cry out to God when he seems to have left the field. (*God Work*, 93)

To do this, to risk expectation and disappointment—to pray like the poets in Psalms 42–43 and 27—we need to dare to believe what we sing every Sunday: the Lord reigns.

CHAPTER SEVEN

There Is No Health in My Bones

Physical pain has the power to destroy language.
When the body is tormented with pain,
a person may lose the capacity to concentrate her attention and
coordinate her breathing and voice-producing
organs in ways necessary to speak clearly and coherently.
She may be able only to sign and groan.
—Kathleen D. Billman and Daniel Migliore (*Rachel's Cry*, 105)

Likewise the Spirit helps us in our weakness;
for we do not know how to pray as we ought,
but that very Spirit intercedes with sighs too deep for words.
And God, who searches the heart,
knows what is the mind of the Spirit, because the Spirit intercedes
for the saints according to the will of God.
—Romans 8:26–27

I've learned a lot about pain over the past five years. On one hand, acute pain lasts only as long as it takes the body to react or to heal. Acute pain is a good thing; it is the body's way of alerting the system and protecting itself. Step on a thorn and your whole body will instinctively react (a fight or flight response), shifting weight off the injured foot and reaching with your hands to find and remove the source of pain. In a similar way, many symptoms of illness are manifestations of our body's efforts to fight infection. When the acute pain or illness heals, we celebrate it as God's gift. On the other hand, chronic pain lasts longer (technically more than three months) and may be the result of multiple causes, most of which are not fully understood or treatable. My own chronic pain is most likely due to a combination of odd sounding terms such as RSD, CRPS, or CMT– the jury is still out. Today, all I know is that my pain is neither productive nor reliable; it is a fire alarm that blares despite the lack of smoke, fire, or any danger at all. And, like other people with these or similar conditions, I am learning how to live with these constant alarms that are unlikely to ever stop. I suppose my own physical struggles have led me to have special regard for body and health images in the laments.

In most cases, the psalmists refer to health problems metaphorically to represent other struggles; for example, a poet unable to answer false accusations is "like the mute, who cannot speak" (38:13). Nonetheless, compiled as one comprehensive list of symptoms, the various psalmists refer to ailments from head to toe and every point in-between. His hair has turned gray (71:18), his ears deaf (38:13, 14), and his face is covered with shame (44:15; 69:7). He is unable to speak (38:13–14; 77:4) except with moans (77:3) and groans (102:3), in part because his mouth is dried up (22:15) and his throat parched (69:3). God has fed the poet the "bread of tears" (80:5), and the psalmist has mixed tears with his drink (102:9). And, while his eyes have looked to the Lord for mercy (123:2; 141:8), they waste away (6:7; 31:9), grow dim (69:3; 88:9), and cannot see (40:12) because their light is gone (38:10). In a similar fashion, the psalmist's hands are stretched out (77:2; 88:9; 143:6) and lifted to God for help (141:2), while his body wastes away (102:4), withers (102:11), and becomes gaunt (109:24). His emaciated condition is evident from bones that waste away (31:10), cling to his skin (102:3), and protrude so far that they can be counted (22:17). More painful, his bones are shaking (6:2), out of joint (22:14), crushed (51:8), and burning (102:3; so too his loins, 38:7). He stumbles around on weak knees (109:24), with an aching back (129:3), shriveled feet (22:16), and unending pain (38:17; 69:29). Deadly wounds (42:10) that fester and stink from infection (38:5) contribute to his failing strength (31:10) and to his fainting and failing spirit (77:3; 142:3; 143:4, 8). After all this, it comes as no surprise that the poet(s) also has heart problems—a heart that throbs (38:10), melts like wax (22:14), burns (39:3), faints (61:2), and fails (40:12).

This catalogue of maladies is overwhelming even if most of the symptoms are metaphoric, which is precisely why the psalmists employ this category of images. These metaphors evoke our emotions. They make us cringe because of our own experience with illness and pain—or our fears of illness. Sooner or later, everyone confronts their mortality: a serious accident, a life-threatening illness, or a body that begins to wear out and become unreliable. While we may not fear death, we are afraid of losing our health and having to live with disability. So, with these metaphors, we can not only identify with the poet for his parched throat or weak knees, we *feel* the weakness and pain—and this feeling is what makes these metaphors work.

In this chapter, we will explore the language of physical health in the laments. We begin with a pair of psalms that utilize this language metaphorically; that is, health problems represent something other than physical well-being (Pss. 102 and 38). Next, we will examine another pair of psalms that use health language more literally to lament the brevity and difficulty of life (Pss. 90 and 71). Finally, we turn to the reluctant poet of Psalm 39 and what he tried not to say, but couldn't hold back.

Health as Metaphor: Psalms 102 and 38

Psalm 102 begins, like many other laments, with an extended appeal to the Lord to listen and answer quickly (vv. 1–2). The poet then develops his complaint through extensive use of body and health images: bones (vv. 3, 5), heart (v. 4), sleeplessness (v. 7), inability to eat (v. 4), and tears (v. 9). A vivid picture emerges of a lone individual in grief, wasting away in part because of enemies who taunt (v. 8), but most of all because God, in anger, has "lifted me up and tossed me aside" (v. 10). So the psalmist laments a life cut short (vv. 3, 11, 23–24) by a God who endures forever (vv. 25–28).

In poetry, however, first appearances are not always reliable. It may initially appear that the psalmist cries for himself—his own life cut short and tossed aside. But, as we continue to read, we discover that the poet has drawn us into a lament for Zion, the city of Jerusalem. As the psalmist paints a word picture with body and health images to express intense suffering, he has personified and brought Zion to life. It is the city that laments God's rejection, opponents' taunts, and a life cut short. In this way, verses 1–11 integrate seamlessly with verses 12–22; the psalm's object of concern is Zion.

In verses 12–22, the poet writes confidently that the Lord will have compassion on Zion (v. 13), will build up Zion (v. 16), and will look down from on high to listen and set free those doomed to die (vv. 19–20; perhaps exiled prisoners from Jerusalem). As a result, in an unthinkable reversal, nations will revere the Lord (v. 15) and gather together as one in Zion to declare the Lord's praise (vv. 21–22)—a universal vision of worldwide praise far beyond the imagination of even the most optimistic dreamer, but not for this poet. For this poet, what happens to Jerusalem matters not only for "the children of your servants"(v. 28) but for the kingdom of God. The Lord reigns. But the nations can only come to know the Lord and his reign as they see God's glory in and through Zion (v. 16), and see God's intervention on behalf of a city that was as good as dead (vv. 18–20).

For the sake of the psalmist, I hope that the maladies in Psalm 38 are also metaphorical. Otherwise, the writer has multiple serious physical issues: infected wounds (v. 5), burning loins (v. 7), loss of sight (v. 10), a throbbing heart (v. 10), diminished strength (v. 10), and constant pain (v. 17). Though it is not beyond imagination that one person could suffer all these problems, I expect that at least some of this language is metaphoric. But even so, the psalmist's physical complaints are only one facet of a much greater whole.

The poet also describes social, psychological, and theological problems. Social: abandoned by friends (v. 11) and chased by enemies who return evil for his good (vv. 12, 19–20). Psychological: spent and crushed by the weight of his problems (v. 8), "utterly bowed down" all day long in mourning (v. 6), as well as groaning (v. 8), longing, and sighing (v. 9). Theological: while he confesses his sin (v. 18) and acknowledges that he has brought many of his troubles on himself because of his sin (vv. 3–4), he also believes that God is overreacting in anger (vv. 1, 3). And this is his most pressing need: that God stop hurting him. Enough is enough. God has already shot him with arrows and smashed him with his hand (v. 2). Now God needs to calm down, to return to his true self (v. 1; see Chapters Ten and Eleven regarding God). And remarkably, although the psalmist identifies God as the problem at the beginning of the psalm (vv. 1–3), at the end, God is the only possible solution (vv. 21–22).

Life Is But a Dream: Psalms 90 and 71

In their own ways, the poets of Psalms 90 and 71 reflect on the brevity of life and its hardships. Psalm 90 approaches these subjects from a universal perspective, a common human problem. Psalm 71 makes its appeal to God from a more personal point of view, a person growing near the end of life. Both poets, however, share the same unqualified trust in the Lord. Psalm 90 begins with the declaration,

> LORD, you have been our dwelling place
>> in all generations.
> Before the mountains were brought forth,
>> or ever you had formed the earth and the world,
>> from everlasting to everlasting you are God. (vv. 1–2)

Psalm 71 asserts no less of a lifelong relationship to God in its opening lines ("In you, O LORD, I take refuge," v. 1a) and then states,

> For you, O LORD, are my hope,
>> my trust, O LORD, from my youth.
> Upon you I have leaned from my birth;
>> it was you who took me from my mother's womb.
> My praise is continually of you. (vv. 5–6)

Whatever else may follow, both psalmists make certain up front that God knows of their reverence and their lives of faith; as we will see, the words of confidence and praise must come first to ensure that God does not misunderstand what follows. Like a friend beginning a difficult conversation with words of love and affirmation, now he or she can say what must be said.

God causes death, abbreviating the human lifespan to no more than a dream or grass that flourishes and dies in a single day (90:3, 5–6). At least that's the best the poet of Psalm 90 can calculate (on the superscription "A Psalm of Moses," see the discussion in Chapter Five). God is eternal, so for God even a thousand years is nothing, like yesterday (so fast that it is already gone) or like a few hours standing watch in the night (v. 4). In contrast, humans are short lived at best because God orders us to turn back to dust (v. 3). But why? The psalmist asks why death must come so soon. Even more, he asks why our brief stay has to be characterized by pain, grief, and sorrow (vv. 10, 15) so that when we do reach the finish, it's a like a sigh at the end of a hard day's work (v. 9).

God is angry with us (v. 7). And it seems to the psalmist that God's anger has reached a deadly extreme. God has worked himself into a fury by deciding to focus on our sins; instead of forgiving, he has "set our iniquities" before him, "our secret sins in the light of your countenance" (v. 8). The predictable result is an anger that consumes and overwhelms human life (v. 7), cutting life short and turning it into "only toil and trouble" (v. 10). In the view of this psalmist, the so-called "angry God" of the Old Testament is precisely the human predicament for which there is no human solution. Perhaps we could live more wisely in view of the situation (v. 12), but the poet knows that humans are sinful beings who cannot stop or change our sinful nature (Gen. 8:21). If God decides to concentrate on our sins rather than giving attention to compassion, we are fated to short lives of pain and sorrow.

Only God can "turn" (NRSV), "relent" (NIV), or change (Hebrew *sub*, 90:13), and the psalmist begs him to do so—to "turn" from wrath to compassion (v. 13), from anger to steadfast love (v. 14). Like Abraham and Moses, he bargains with the Lord: give us as many good days and years as you have already given us bad days (v. 15). The ledger is way out of balance. Turn and favor us instead of overwhelming us with wrath; simply put, "prosper for us the work of our hands—O prosper the work of our hands!" (v. 17). Life is too short and difficult enough on its own to live it under God's wrath! Little wonder why the poet began with such strong affirmations of trust and reliance on God. He had to ensure that God knew where he was coming from before he spoke these challenging words. He had to make certain that God knew he was coming from a perspective of faith.

Even more so than the poet of Psalm 90, the poet of Psalm 71 articulates a lifetime of experience with God. For as long as he can remember, he has leaned on and learned from God (71:5, 6, 17). He and God have been through many difficult times together (v. 20). And while God has proven to be a reliable and sturdy refuge, the poet has proven to be a dependable example of gratitude and praise ("like a portent to many" [71:7], also vv. 8, 16, 22–23), telling others about what God has done in his life (vv. 15, 24). Now, however, he has a growing concern: he is getting old.

My students and I have an ongoing disagreement about the age of this psalmist. I think he is old, meaning older than me. He is disturbed about his age; now that he is no longer able to do all that he has done for God in the past, he is worried that God will leave him (vv. 9, 18). His enemies, sensing his waning physical strength, are sure to try to take advantage of him and claim that "God has forsaken" him, and he has no one else to help him (v. 11). As the poet reflects on a long life spent with God, he asks, "even to old age and gray hairs, O God, do not forsake me" (v. 18). He has so much more that he wants to do for God. It seems to me that the psalmist's insight into aging comes from his own experience; he is old.

My students, however, claim the poet was about *my age* (strike one). Then, realizing what they have just said, these young people try to rescue their grade by explaining that they did not mean that the psalmist and I are old, but middle aged and worrying about the *near* future (strike two). Benevolent teacher that I am, I interrupt and stop them from saying any more and grant that they could be correct. In either case, the cause of the lament is essentially the same: life has difficult times and seasons, especially the season of growing old—not because this psalmist or we have done anything in particular to cause our suffering. Pain, illness, growing old, and death are simply part of life as we know it. Life is just that way—for the faithful and unbeliever alike.

We are "fearfully and wonderfully made" (139:14) by a God who has crowned us "with glory and honor," given us co-regency or dominion over creation (8:5–6), and is intimately concerned about his human creation (33:13–19). But our world is hardly what God originally created or intended (see Gen. 2–3). We live a brief life in which no one escapes a share of pain, illness, and suffering. The only questions are what, when, and how? What will we face? When will it come? And, most important, how will we as a people of faith respond? What Psalm 90 and 71 teach us is that we may continue in relationship with God, speaking to God with honest words about our needs and expecting God to act.

Psalm 39

A student favorite on "Praise Friday" at the university where I teach is the gospel song, "Said I Wasn't Gonna Tell Nobody." The first verse sets a vibrant tone for the whole:

> I said I wasn't gonna tell nobody but I
>> couldn't keep it to myself,
>> couldn't keep it to myself,
>> couldn't keep it to myself.
> I said I wasn't gonna tell nobody but I
>> couldn't keep it to myself,
>> what the LORD has done for me.

Students love the rhythm and positive message of the song, even to the point of clapping with the beat and a bit of shuffling in the aisles. The poet of Psalm 39 had similar feelings—at least the reluctance to bring to speech what he felt, though he had a very different understanding of what "the LORD has done for me" that he was trying to keep silent.

In the opening verses of the poem, the psalmist describes his futile efforts to muzzle his own mouth (v. 1), to be "silent and still" and hold his "peace" (v. 2). While inside, his distress was burning, becoming hotter and hotter until finally, like a fire exploding, "I spoke with my tongue" (v. 3). He just could not keep it to himself no matter how hard he tried. A little later in the psalm, he returns to the theme of silence and explains rather bluntly that the reason he tried to be silent was because it was "you [God] who have done it" (v. 9b). Unlike the gospel song that rejoices in an inability to hold back praise for God's wonderful work, this psalmist says he tried his best not to say anything because what he had to say would implicate God. Obviously, he speaks anyway (vv. 4–13), but only because he has no choice—as a person of faith, he must speak the truth, the whole truth, and nothing but the truth, so help him God—even if the truth brings God into question.

God has made human life short, just a few "handbreadths" (the width of four fingers at their base, 3¾ inches for my hand), a mere breath (*hebel*, the same Hebrew term in Ecclesiastes for "vanity" [Eccles. 1:2; 12:8]), or only a shadow; in relation to God, my lifetime is nothing (39:5–6). And yet people live at a frenetic pace to acquire stuff, to save up the "necessities" of life—without any apparent realization that their lives are so short that they are only storing up goods for someone else to take away—someone they don't even know (v. 6). These people need what the psalmist asks for himself: to know "my end," "the measure of my days," to know "how fleeting" life really is. Perhaps if they knew the brevity of life they would slow down and not chase things so much.

Up to verse 6, it is not clear why the psalmist thought he needed to be silent. Most everyone already knows, more or less, about the brevity of life. Even in verses 7–9, as the poet acknowledges his sinfulness, he also confesses that his only hope is in God—hardly anything shocking or that needs to be kept quiet. But with a few strokes of his quill, the poet unleashes the underlying problem and throws an entirely different light over all that has been said. *God has done it; God is responsible* (v. 9b). It is God who is beating the psalmist senseless; completely and totally exhausting him:

> Remove your stroke from me;
> I am worn down by the blows of your hand. (39:10 NRSV)

> Remove your scourge from me;
> I am overcome by the blow of your hand. (NIV)

> But please stop striking me!
> I am exhausted by the blows from your hand. (NTL)

Once silence has been broken, the psalmist cannot stop the words. He knows that God punishes humans for sin (v. 11ab), but in the process God destroys everything they hold dear (like a moth that consumes everything, (v. 11c). And God does this even though the psalmist knows and God knows that human life is "a mere breath" (v. 11d). The poet understands the need for punishment but not for what God is doing now, what God is doing to his life. It is too much; it is going too far against a life that goes only a few inches and vanishes.

The poet never specifies what he believes God is doing. Most inter- preters guess that the trouble involves some illness or physical suffering based on the terms in verses 10–11. To be sure, for the ancient Israelite, God was sovereign and responsible for all life—and therefore responsible for all suffering. Israel did not remove God from responsibility for illness or pain by drawing fine lines, such as God "allows" trouble but is not its ultimate cause or source. To them, such a claim would be a denial of God's sovereignty, and this psalmist cannot make that move (we will discuss these ideas further in Chapters Ten and Eleven).

Instead, Psalm 39 must take the trouble to God and press God for a solution, though the proposed remedy is not what we would expect. The poet asks God to consider him as a "passing guest" or an "alien, like all my forebears" (v. 12b). In view of the brevity of life (vv. 4–5), the idea that humans are just sojourners passing through time and space is apt. But this is no innocent image or request. For God to accept the poet's status as a passing guest or alien has ethical implications. God has taught Israel that sojourners are to be treated fairly, hosted or accepted, and never to be harmed (Exod. 22:23; 23:9, 12; Deut. 24:17). So, for the poet, if humans are God's passing guest or alien, the implication is that God must stop mistreating him, stop beating him and taking away "what is dear to them." Not even Israel is allowed to treat aliens like that.

If God is not willing to accept and treat the poet as a resident alien, then the poet reaches for a final alternative: then please, *just leave me alone* so that I may smile again—after all, soon I will be gone anyway (v. 13). Asking for just a little joy, a little relief for a short life doesn't seem like too much to ask: "Give me a break, cut me some slack before it's too late and I'm out of here" (v. 13, *The Message*). Just divert your glance for a little while and I'll be gone.

If you have not read the laments before, you may need to catch your breath about now. But trust me, we have only touched the surface of what other psalmists will need to say to God. And we will deal with these psalms and the questions they raise for us later in the book. Here I propose only a brief reminder and one more detail. The Reminder: the psalmist did not want to say these things to or about God. But, after a long time of enduring pain, he finally got to the point that he had to speak what was boiling over in his heart. Before he speaks, while he speaks, and after—the psalmist has not lost his faith. It is from faith that he speaks; his only hope is God (v. 7). He has nowhere else to turn.

The Detail: one reason the psalmist kept silent was out of concern for other people who don't follow God (v. 1). As long as they were around, he would never say anything like this aloud to God. Others would not understand. They would think that he had lost faith in God. They would turn his words against him and would not be helped by his prayer. So the poet waited until the right time and then spoke his heart—perhaps alone, but I suspect in the presence of other believers who would understand. This is an important principle for lament: lament is not an unrestrained rant, but controlled speech that has its proper time and place in the faith community.

Illness and Pain: Psalm 41

While some psalms use the language of health and physical suffering metaphorically (e.g., Pss. 102 and 38), others address these problems in and of themselves. At times, psalmists marvel at God's human creation ("I praise you, for I am fearfully and wonderfully made" [139:14]) and reflect on God's intimate and faithful concern for humanity ("what are human beings that you are mindful of them, mortals that you care for them?" [8:4; cf. 139:7–18]), but not in Psalm 41. Here we find a poet who struggles with a body that no longer works so wonderfully and a God who no longer seems so attentive. Instead, like the poets of Psalms 90 and 71, his life is marked by prolonged pain, disease, and the social stigma and psychological struggles that parade along with chronic illness.

Interpreters disagree on the genre of Psalm 41: lament or thanksgiving? Those who identify the poetry as lament point to verses 4–10, which contain all the components of a lament. Those who classify the psalm as thanksgiving agree that verses 4–10 are lament but point out that in its present setting this lament is set inside a thanksgiving song. As we will see in Chapter Twelve, a crucial part of thanksgiving is the inclusion of a report of what God has done that merits thanksgiving. In some poems, an easy way to provide this report is to quote the prior lament to which God has responded and for which the psalmist now gives thanks (e.g., Ps. 30:8–12). Such citation is what we find in Psalm 41. And despite the fact that I, too, identify the psalm as a song of thanksgiving, I include it in this discussion because of the original lament's concern for failing health.

The song of thanksgiving begins in the form of a blessing or "beatitude" (similar to Pss. 1 and 32): "happy are those who consider the poor" (41:1). Here, the term "poor" is not restrictive in meaning (i.e., only those without money) but open: the "poor" designate any who are "weak" (NIV), "helpless" (NASV), or ill. In other words, the psalmist gives thanks by speaking a blessing over all who take an active concern for those who are sick and, more specifically, a blessing for those who looked after him when he was ill. For these caretakers, he prays that the Lord will deliver them "in the day" of their trouble when they fall ill (41:1), keeping them alive (v. 2), sustaining them "on their sickbed" (v. 3a), and healing them (v. 3b). In addition, he asks that when they are weak, the Lord will not hand them over to enemies who would take advantage of them (v. 2). Through this blessing the poet prays for those who came to his aid—that the Lord will go to their aid when they become ill; a blessing especially suitable for health-care workers today.

We know from two statements at the conclusion of the psalm that the psalmist has recovered from his brush with death. First, the enemy has not triumphed but has been defeated by the poet's healing (v. 11). His recovery has shown that his enemies were wrong in their claims about him; by getting well, he defeated them. Second, the poet asserts that the Lord has upheld him because of his integrity (v. 12), a direct answer to his earlier prayer that God "raise me up" (v. 10). (The doxology in verse 13 is not part of Psalm 41 but denotes the end of Book 1 of the Psalms. See Chapter Two.)

As we have observed, the lament in verses 4–11 now serves to give thanks to all those who heard and responded to its appeal: God and people. But originally this lament must have sounded like the last words of a dying man. He was seriously ill, in his reckoning as the result of some unspecified sin (v. 4). On one hand, that disease and hardship come as the result of sin was a common theological idea in the ancient world (e.g., Job and his friends), which Jesus warned must be applied with discretion; just because a person is sick does not mean they have sinned (Luke 13:1–5). On the other hand, the poet may be aware of some sin that carries an obvious and specific physical consequence (e.g., drunkenness, Prov. 23:29–35). But, in any case, his first request connects a need for God's forgiveness with his need for healing (41:4, 10; cf. Mark 2:1–12).

His second request has to do with what other people ("my enemies") are doing during his illness. These people hope that the poet will die and cease to exist in any form—reputation, children, memory ("and my name perish"). They are two-faced. When they come to visit him, they say all the acceptable things; for example, we hope you get well soon. But they are bogus. Their visits are nothing more than reconnaissance missions to get more grist for the rumor mill (v. 6). Like Job's friends, these enemies assume that anyone with such a terrible illness must have committed some terrible sin. So they visit to gather clues, imagine the worst, and then go out and tell everyone what they have seen. Despite their words to the psalmist (v. 6), they do not believe for a moment that he will recover (v. 8). Their smear campaign devastates, and he is too weak and sick to respond. But what hurts even worse is that his trusted friend has also betrayed him (v. 9).

Helpless to defend himself, the psalmist asked God to intervene, to "be gracious to me, and raise me up, that I may repay them" (v. 10). The final request, "that I may repay them," is unusual in laments. As we will see in Chapters Eight and Nine, normally, the psalmist will ask *God* to repay his enemies. But even here, the idea may still be that God's action of raising him up (i.e., healing him) will be the repayment that the poet wants to give the enemies. When God heals him, that will prove the enemies were wrong, and they will be shamed.

Psalm 41 introduces issues that set the direction for the next few chapters in our study. We will further examine the problem of the enemies and the psalmist's request for vengeance in Chapters Eight and Nine. Then, we will turn our attention to accusations psalmists make against God in Chapters Ten and Eleven. Finally, we will explore the connection between lament and thanksgiving in Chapter Twelve. In Psalm 41, lament has led to thanksgiving, just as thanksgiving has sprung from the remnants of lament. In fact, the two are so closely related that thanksgiving, as practiced in the Psalms, is not possible without prior lament—a connection that not only raises further concern about our loss of lament but also about the content of our thanksgiving.

CHAPTER EIGHT

How Long, O God, Is the Foe to Scoff?

Thus I suggest that most of the Psalms can only be appropriately
prayed by people who are living at the edge of their lives, sensitive to
the raw hurts, the primitive passions, and the naïve elations that are
at the bottom of our life. . . . It asks us to depart from the closely
managed world of public survival, to move into the open, frightening,
healing world of speech with the Holy One.
—WALTER BRUEGGEMANN (*Praying the Psalms*, 8)

Our vocation as Church is not to provide the world with a spiritual
novocaine to make the injustice and cruelty a little easier for us to
accept. . . . These psalms speak the theological language of outrage
because sometimes outrage is the only possible redemptive response.
—MICHAEL JINKINS (*In the House of the Lord*, 97)

Sixty of the 150 psalms mention other people who are the past or
present cause or secondary contributor to the psalmist's trouble. The
poets describe these opponents in vivid terms, even if the psalm looks back
to give thanks (e.g., Ps. 30) or looks forward in confidence (e.g., Pss. 23, 27).
The enemies are young hungry lions lurking for prey to kill and drag away
(7:2; 10:9; 17:12; 22:13, 21; 35:17; 57:4); they are a pack of howling dogs
(22:16, 20; 59:6, 14), strong bulls (22:12), wild oxen with deadly horns (22:21),
and poisonous snakes eager to strike (58:4–5; 140:3). In human terms, the
opponents are murderous bandits waiting in ambush for innocent travelers

(10:8; 59:3; 64:3–4), hunters setting trap-nets and digging catch-pits to snare the unsuspecting (10:9; 35:7–8; 38:12; 57:6; 140:5; 141:9; 142:3), trackers chasing down people to the point of collapse (7:1; 17:11; 143:3), and demolition men battering their victim like a wall about to fall (62:3). Even allowing for hyperbole, these descriptions leave the impression of vicious opponents who intentionally contribute to the poet's troubles. And their presence is cause for serious alarm. They did not cut off the poet during rush-hour traffic. They are not people with whom we disagree on politics or religion. Rather, their identity is wrapped up with trouble making and taking advantage of those in need for their own personal gain—actions that are deliberate, grievous, and intentionally destructive.

Only eight of the sixty lament psalms lack reference to an enemy. Most notably, two of these exceptions are penitential psalms in which the poet identifies sin to be the problem, wholly of his or her own doing (Pss. 51, 130; see Chapter Five). Another set of psalms wrestles with God regarding the brevity and difficulty of life without mention of opponents (Pss. 39, 90; see Chapter Seven). Three others deal with God's overwhelming wrath (Ps. 88, with brief mention of companions who have deserted the psalmist), God's absence (Ps. 77), and God's failure to keep promises (Ps. 85; see Chapters Ten and Eleven). The remaining exception asks for the restoration of Zion without any explicit or implied complaint about enemies (Ps. 126). Consequently, these exceptions prove the general rule for lament. At our times of greatest need, people often appear who are eager to take advantage of us in our weakness or to aggravate the situation to cause more pain. Sometimes these others do not merely contribute to our suffering, they are the primary cause—deliberately and with malice. These opponents are those who are "out to get" whoever stands between them and what they want.

In this chapter we will examine several important topics related to the enemy in lament psalms. First, we will explore the ambiguous identity of the opponents and possible reasons for such anonymity. Second, we will consider the ethical teaching of the New and Old Testaments regarding our enemies and how this teaching relates to the laments. Third, we will observe how the poets draw a close connection between themselves and God—over against their common enemies. Fourth, we will begin to analyze what the laments say or pray to God regarding the enemies (a project that will continue into Chapter Nine).

Who is My ~~Neighbor~~ Enemy?

Although the enemy is ever present in the lament psalms, in most cases even our best investigative tools cannot unmask their identity. On three occasions, clues within psalms identify Babylon as the opponent or, more precisely, the army of Babylon that has invaded Jerusalem and ruthlessly destroyed the temple (Ps. 74, 79, 137). At other times, we find a psalmist devastated by a friend who has unexpectedly turned against him. When he is most needed, a trusted companion is nowhere to be found (38:11; 88:18). The pain of personal betrayal is evident in Psalm 55:

> It is not enemies who taunt me—
>> I could bear that;
> it is not adversaries who deal insolently with me—
>> I could hide from them.
> But it is you, my equal,
>> my companion, my familiar friend,
> with whom I kept pleasant company;
>> we walked in the house of God with the throng.
> (vv. 12–14; cf. 41:9)

A number of psalms also describe the enemy in terms reminiscent of a legal opponent in a criminal trial or civil lawsuit. For example, in Psalm 35, the psalmist is on the defense against false charges while the enemy testifies against him, "Aha, Aha, our eyes have seen it" (v. 21), and concludes, "Aha, we have our heart's desire . . . we have swallowed you up" (v. 25; cf. 70:3). In a similar fashion, the opponents in Psalm 64 have concocted what they believe to be a foolproof scheme to take down the psalmist, thinking to themselves,

> Who can see us?
>
>> Who can search out our crimes?
>
> We have thought out a cunningly conceived plot. (vv. 5–6)

Both of these psalms may have originated from court cases in which the psalmist faced false and serious charges. As for the psalmist, he can only appeal to God for vindication and assert his innocence:

> Vindicate me, O LORD,
>
>> for I have walked in my integrity
>>
>> and I have trusted in the LORD without wavering.
>
> Prove me, O LORD, and try me;
>
>> test my heart and mind . . .
>
> I wash my hands in innocence,
>
>> and go around your altar, O LORD. (26:1–2, 6)

Or from Psalm 17,

> Hear a just cause, O LORD; attend to my cry;
>
>> give ear to my prayer from lips free of deceit.
>
> From you let my vindication come;
>
>> let your eyes see the right.
>
> If you try my heart, if you visit me by night,
>
>> if you test me, you will find no wickedness in me;
>
> my mouth does not transgress. (vv. 1–3)

Threatened with serious legal charges supported by false witnesses and bribery (26:10), these poets call on God for legal aid. Without the Lord's help, the lions will tear into them (17:12; 35:17), they will fall to the ambush (64:2–4), and, though innocent, they will be convicted and taken away (64:5). While the legal language may be metaphorical, the situation with the enemy in these cases is grave—even to the point of threatening the psalmist's life.

Beyond this relatively small number of psalms that identify the opponent, the enemy remains anonymous in most laments. And I suspect the anonymity is purposeful on the part of the psalmist. What is important in these psalms is what the enemy does. The enemy is anyone or even anything that stands against life, the community, or against God and God's way in the world. Most often, the psalmists construct the enemy as an ambiguous or open character so that readers may pick up the text and make it their own. In this way, the enemy does not remain confined to a historical identity in the past. Instead, we may read *our* opponents onto the text and the opponents of justice and righteousness throughout the world, a metamorphosis in reading that makes these psalms relevant for our own prayers.

The Enemies and New Testament Ethics

The presence of enemies in the Psalms and the poets' honest prayers to God about their enemies inevitably leads to an avalanche of ethical objections. Some Christians dismiss these laments because these prayers come to us from a people who had lower ethical expectations for how a person should treat outsiders. As Christians, however, we live by a higher standard to love our enemies, pray for them, and return good for their wrong against us. As Paul said, "If your enemies are hungry, feed them; and if they are thirsty, give them something to drink" (Rom. 12:20). We are to love our neighbor—a term Jesus defined as any person we meet who needs our help (Luke 10). Not only should we not pray for the collapse of our enemies, we should not rejoice when we see their downfall. We should be compassionate. A Christian should not ever speak negatively about others, much less speak a curse against them or strike out physically. As God's people, we are to be like our God in all our actions, distinct from the world around us.

The problem with this line of argumentation is that the perceived difference in ethics between the Old and New Testaments does not stand up to critical examination. Neither God nor God's expectations for how we treat our enemies changes between the testaments. The book of Proverbs first records the adage cited by Paul in his letter to the Romans: "If your enemies are hungry, feed them; if they are thirsty, give them something to drink" (Prov. 25:21–22; Rom. 12:20). And it is Leviticus that originally states, "You shall not take vengeance or bear a grudge against any of your people, but you shall love your neighbor as yourself. I am the LORD " (Lev. 19:18). Then, to insure against any misunderstanding or reduction of the command to love only "my people," the same chapter concludes, "The alien who resides with you shall be to you as the citizen among you; you shall love the alien as yourself, for you were aliens in the land of Egypt; I am the LORD your God" (Lev. 19:34). The Old Testament, just as the New, sets a high ethical standard of love for all people—neighbors, strangers, and enemies. Personal vendettas and retaliation are unacceptable, even in our hearts. In Job's proclamation of innocence, he denies any impropriety in action and attitude toward his enemies. He denies inwardly rejoicing "at the ruin of those who hated me" or sinning by "asking for their lives with a curse" (Job 31:29–30). Job understands that righteousness is a matter of right attitudes toward his enemies, not just external actions.

To be sure, the New Testament affirms the same ethical standards with a greater example of love for an enemy. At his crucifixion, Jesus prays, "Father, forgive them; for they do not know what they are doing" (Luke 23:34). And, in the same manner, Jesus teaches his disciples to "love your enemies and pray for those who persecute you" (Matt. 5:44), a correction of misaligned teaching from parts of Judaism of his time, not a correction of the original ethic of the Hebrew Scriptures. So Paul and other writers urge their readers also to adopt the ethic of Christ: "Do not repay anyone evil for evil, but take thought for what is noble in the sight of all. . . . Beloved, never avenge yourselves, but leave room for the wrath of God" (Rom. 12:17–19; cf. 1 Sam. 24:17 and Lev. 19:18). The ethic is clear and as unchanging as the God who called Israel to be holy, distinct from the surrounding nations (Lev. 18:1–5; 19:1–2; 20:7–8, 26).

Just as in the Old Testament, however, other texts in the New Testament complicate our understanding of the ethic of love and nonre-taliation. In Acts 13, frustrated by Elymas' opposition and efforts to keep Sergius Paulus away from the faith, Paul "looked intently at him and said, 'You son of the devil, you enemy of all righteousness, full of all deceit and villainy, will you not stop making crooked the straight paths of the Lord?

And now listen—the hand of the Lord is against you, and you will be blind for a while, unable to see the sun'" (Acts 13:9–11). Paul then strikes Elymas blind! And this is not the only time Paul curses an opponent; at the end of 1 Corinthians, after the final exhortations and greetings, Paul picks up the pen with his own hand and writes, "Let anyone be accursed who has no love for the Lord" (1 Cor. 16:22).

Similar requests for God's intervention against opponents are voiced in John's vision of the heavenly worship. John has seen four strange creatures flying around the throne proclaiming the holiness of God (Rev. 4:8), twenty-four elders casting their crowns before the throne and singing the worthiness of the Lord to receive glory, honor, and power (4:11), and "myriads of myriads and thousands and thousands" of angels surrounding the throne "singing with full voice, 'Worthy is the Lamb that was slaughtered to receive power and wealth and wisdom and might and honor and glory and blessing!'" (5:12). Then, below the altar, John sees the martyrs, "the souls of those who had been slaughtered for the Word of God and for the testimony they had given" (6:9). And these faithful ones impatiently cry out, "Sovereign Lord, holy and true, how long will it be before you *judge and avenge* our blood on the inhabitants of the earth?" (6:10, emphasis mine). In view of the New Testament ethic of love and nonretaliation, we might wonder if these martyrs have lost their bearings. Perhaps even more confusing, a little later John describes the fate of those who worship the beast in violent and graphic terms: "they will also drink the wine of God's wrath, poured unmixed into the cup of his anger, and they will be tormented with fire and sulfur in the presence of the holy angels and in the presence of the Lamb" (14:10). Then, when the harvest is fully ripe, an angel swings his sickle over the earth, gathers the vintage, and throws it "into the great wine press of the wrath of God. And the wine press was trodden outside the city, and blood flowed from the wine press, as high as a horse's bridle, for a distance of about two hundred miles" (14:19–20). The wrath of God in the Old Testament is nothing compared to the wrath of God in Revelation.

Three conclusions are necessary at this point. First, the ethic of love and nonretaliation is the same in the Old and New Testaments. Second,

God does not change between the Old and New Testament. God does not have a multiple personality disorder. Or, as a colleague once told me, God did not need to repent and be baptized to become a Christian. "Jesus Christ is the same yesterday and today and forever" (Heb. 13:8). God's character is unchanged, and so God's ethic for loving opponents remains unchanged. Consequently, third, we cannot dismiss the laments regarding enemies because they express an old ethic below that of Christianity or because they only have to do with a God of wrath, not a God of love. The principles of love for the enemy and nonretaliation are rooted in the character of God and as unchanging as God. With these options set aside, we must push further into the Psalms to understand what we are to do with this language of lament about enemies.

The Enemies and God

Attention to the words of the enemy embedded in the psalms raises awareness of the seriousness of each poet's situation and the close identification of the psalmists with God. In other words, the psalmists understand the enemies' threats and attacks not only to be against the psalmist but also *against God*. For example, in Psalm 10, the poet complains that the enemy persecutes the poor and thinks, "God will not seek it out . . . there is no God" (v. 4) or "God has forgotten, he has hidden his face, he will never see it" (v. 10). So they believe that, despite their actions, "we shall not be moved; throughout all generations we shall not meet adversity" (v. 6) and "you [God] will not call us to account" (v. 13). Here, dealing with the enemy is a matter of justice, and God's attentiveness to the poor. How God responds to the mistreatment of the oppressed will contribute to or malign God's reputation.

In a similar way, the opponents in Psalm 22 mock the psalmist *and God* when they call out, "Commit your cause to the LORD; let him deliver— let him rescue the one in whom he delights" (v. 8). These opponents do not believe for a moment that the psalmist's God will show up, even less that he will deliver the psalmist. Their language calls God out as they belittle the poet for foolhardy faith in an unseen God. In a more succinct form, other foes simply ask, "Where is your God?" (42:3, 10; 79:5). The enemies ridicule the poet for his lifelong affirmation of a powerful God who cares for and rescues his people. If the Lord is so great, where is your God now? Why does he delay? Why is your God absent when you most need him? The question "Where is your God?" drives home the close association between the poet and the Lord in these psalms. What happens to the poet is directly related to the presence or absence of God—and to the reputation and character of God. The enemy's rhetoric and brutal attack are not just about the poet, but the poet's God.

What I am trying to establish here—and what many overlook in their reading of these laments—is that these psalms do not complain to God about petty issues; for example, *look what they did to me.* The complaints are not about people who slighted me, insulted me, or hurt me in some small way so that I now regard them as my enemy and ask God to even the score. Enemies and opponents in the Psalms belong to a wholly different category. The poets identify the enemies as a serious threat by drawing a close association between God and those at risk. God's reputation is at stake. Consequently, several psalms assert the hope that, as a result of God's intervention against the opponent, people will say, "Great is the LORD, who delights in the welfare of his servant" (35:27) or, "Surely there is a reward for the righteous; surely there is a God who judges on earth" (58:11). But, for this to happen, God must act against *his enemies.*

Responses and Prayers Regarding the Enemy

Despite the general similarities among laments that make some mention of an opponent—the common stock of metaphors, the anonymity of the foe, and the writers' close association with God—these laments are a diverse group when it comes to what they ask the Lord to do. In fact, the divergence among these prayers ranges from one extreme to the other, from silence (no request) to violent imprecation (curse), with laments falling all along the continuum. Our analysis then, for the sake of clarity, will plot five points on this spectrum of how the psalmists respond to their enemies and what they ask God to do. A graph, of course, is an artificial construct. The psalms are more complex than any reduction to a single idea, and so, many laments will scrape against the edges of the coordinates assigned here or overlap among the categories. Nonetheless, analysis of the points on this trajectory between extremes should prove helpful to our understanding, appreciation, and recovery of this language of lament. In what remains of this chapter, we will explore the first three of these positions, leaving the fourth and fifth groups to our next chapter.

1. *Silence.* On one extreme, a few psalms that mention opponents or oppression ask nothing of God either directly or indirectly in regard to the enemies. For example, Psalm 62 describes a group of people intent to bring down "a person of prominence" (the poet/king) through lies and double-talk (vv. 3–4). Their assault never stops; they are like men battering an unstable wall or tottering fence—and the wall is about to collapse. Yet the poet does not ask God to do anything about them. Instead, the psalm begins with self-talk about what the psalmist plans to do:

> For God alone my soul waits in silence;
>> from him comes my salvation.
> He alone is my rock and my salvation,
>> my fortress; I shall never be shaken. (vv. 1–2)

Then, after the description of the enemies, the poet repeats his opening thoughts and adds:

> On God rests my deliverance and honor;
>> my mighty rock, my refuge is God. (v. 7)

The remainder of the psalm addresses others, urging them to trust the Lord at all times and put no confidence in social status or wealth (vv. 8–10). Finally, the poet confidently asserts that power and steadfast love belong to the Lord, "for you repay to all according to their work" (vv. 11–12).

Although the psalmist's response to his adversaries is silence (no request regarding the enemies), the psalm clearly marks out its own response: trust God. The self-talk challenges the poet to trust God for help and reminds that God is his sturdy rock, mighty fortress, and safe refuge. The poet sees no need to ask God to deal with them—he only feels the need to wait patiently for God's intervention. And what the psalmist tells himself, he also tells others. In view of what people may do or try to do to us, striking out to discredit us, lying about us to cause our ruin—trust in God. Social status is temporary at best and wealth is not trustworthy. God, however, will repay everyone according to their work.

In Psalm 62 and others like it (e.g., Ps. 13), the response to enemies is to move our focus from the enemy to our God and to remind ourselves of the love, strength, and trustworthiness of our God. Technically, the response is silence, no request. But this silence is not passive; it entails a difficult stance in regard to opposition: faith.

2. *Please save us.* Like the first group, the second transfers our focal point. Where the first group turns the focus inward to our need to trust God in the face of opposition, the second focuses attention on what I need God to do for me. Oftentimes, these needs are expressed in short appeals:

> Vindicate me, O God, and defend my cause
> > against an ungodly people;
> from those who are deceitful and unjust deliver me! (43:1)

> But you, O LORD, do not be far away!
> > O my help, come quickly to my aid!
> Deliver my soul from the sword,
> > my life from the power of the dog!
> > Save me from the mouth of the lion! (22:19–21a)

> Wondrously show your steadfast love,
> > O savior of those who seek refuge
> > from their adversaries at your right hand.
> Guard me as the apple of your eye;
> > hide me in the shadow of your wings,
> from the wicked who despoil me,
> > my deadly enemies who surround me. (17:7–9)

Similar appeals occur in 74:18–23, 86:14–17, and 102:12–22. In these psalms, the poets do not ask God to do anything to their enemies. Instead, it is enough to ask God to rescue me.

The unspoken reality of these texts is the consequence my request will have on the enemy. In order for God to rescue me from the enemy, something must be done about the enemy. Neither Pharaoh nor Babylon will let God's people just walk away. To save Esther, Mordecai, and the Jews, someone has to stop Haman. And John knows that Rome will continue to persecute Christians until the moment the Lamb destroys the beast. Certainly, God can do as he pleases, but history demonstrates that God rarely works outside the human dimensions of politics and power. Victory requires someone to lose. Implicitly, to ask God to save me is a request for God to act against the opposition—even if we do not explicitly ask God to do something to them.

These psalmists are not naïve or unaware of the ramifications of their requests. I do wonder, however, if we have thought through our own prayers for "a speedy end to this war," "the safety of our men and women in the armed forces," or for "an end to the conflict in the Middle East." We routinely offer these requests, even if we would never ask God to act directly against our enemies or overthrow them violently. I wonder whether we take our prayers seriously and whether we understand the complex sociopolitical consequences implied by our prayers? While I grant that there is space between praying for our rescue from oppression and praying directly against our oppressors, that space is thin. To pray for our success, our prosperity, our victory, or our premiere status requires someone else to come up short. The poets in this second group of psalms chose to appeal to God for their need of rescue, but I suspect they did so with full realization that redemption always comes at a cost.

3. *What God will do to them.* In his letter to a church facing various trials, James urges reliance on God (James 1:2–4) before turning his words to what will happen to the rich oppressors: their wealth will rot, their clothes be moth eaten, and the cries of the laborers they defrauded will reach the Lord. They have fattened their hearts for a day of slaughter

(5:1–6). James' words are harsh and to the point—warning offenders and giving encouragement to those suffering as a result of unfair business practices.

The third group of psalms on our trajectory is similar to James' words. In these psalms, the poets describe what God will do to the foe or oppressors. For example:

> But God will shoot his arrow at them;
>> they will be wounded suddenly.
> Because of their tongue he will bring them to ruin;
>> all who see them will shake with horror.
> Then everyone will fear;
>> they will tell what God has brought about,
>> and ponder what he has done. (Ps. 64:7–9)

> But God will break you down forever;
>> he will snatch and tear you from your tent;
>> he will uproot you from the land of the living. *Selah*
> The righteous will see, and fear,
>> and will laugh at the evildoer, saying,
> "See the one who would not take
>> refuge in God,
> but trusted in abundant riches,
>> and sought refuge in wealth." (52:5–7)

Similar statements occur in 6:10, 9:17–18, 14:5 (53:5), 28:5, 54:5, 57:3, and 63:9–10. As in groups 1 and 2, these psalmists do not ask God to do anything to the enemy. Instead, they confidently assert what God will do to them: God will break them, uproot them, shoot them, and bring them to ruin. Such rhetoric in a prayer or song, such as Psalm 52 or James 5, warns any listener who might be tempted to trust in his or her wealth and encourages those who are suffering: God will attend to their situation. Perhaps indirectly, these writers ask God to do what they so confidently proclaim on God's behalf. Even so, like the psalms in group 2, the poets refrain from any explicit request for God to strike their enemy.

. A Tentative Pause

Examination of the fourth and fifth groups of lament that respond to opponents requires the complete space of the next chapter. Here we pause momentarily to reflect on what we have seen to this point. The presence of dangerous enemies aligned against believers and their God is not restricted to the era of the Old Testament. The problem of adversaries extends into the New Testament and deeply into the fabric of our own lives—and with this uncomfortable reality comes the need for a way or ways to speak to God about opponents in a manner that is honest with my feelings and faithful to God's way in the world. Since the Old Testament ethic regarding the treatment of enemies is identical to the New Testament ethic, the Psalms are a relevant and accessible starting point for this dialogue.

I expect most Christians would embrace the first three clusters of psalms on our map as ethically appropriate for how we should respond to our enemies: 1) silence that focuses on our own trust in God, 2) prayer for God's work of deliverance in my life (with at least some realization of what this may do to my enemy), and 3) confident reminders to ourselves and others of God's ultimate plans in regard to evil. The next two groups of psalms face a steeper uphill battle for acceptance.

I must admit to feeling a bit out of place in the psalmists' passionate conversation about enemies. Odds are good that if you had the financial ability to purchase this book, have the ability to read, and have the luxury of leisure time to read, you probably have few enemies like those described by the psalmists. At least I feel like I am in a different world—perhaps I am. And the reason disturbs me: songs and prayers like these tend to emerge from classes of socially oppressed people. As a number of writers have pointed out, the strongest strain of such songs in our United States history developed among African American slaves in the South—the "sorrow songs." While slave owners demanded happy songs (see Ps. 137), the slaves sang songs of anguish, pain, and hope. Those who are at ease have little use for songs that threaten the status quo.

So these psalms disturb me, not because of ethical objections to their content, but because we have so little regard or use for them in our refined services of worship. What we read, sing, and pray in our assemblies reflects not only who we are but the people with whom we have identified. Michael Jinkins calls it "the socio-economics of liturgy: issues of class, race, and financial status relate directly to what hymns are chosen and what psalms and other Scripture form the practical lectionary of a church's ordinary worship" (*In the House of the Lord*, 37). He explains,

> It is not merely coincidental that those churches which fail to use psalms of lament altogether and those which under-utilize these resources are most deeply invested in the status quo, while the members of those churches which make frequent use of the psalms of lament are usually not shakers and movers in society. (36)

It is possible that the reason the psalms about enemies disturb us and find no place in our churches is because we have chosen to live protected lives in insulated communities, whether our community is a middle- to upper-class neighborhood or a church with a fortress mentality. Our lack of solidarity with those in need is what causes us to wonder why these prayers are in the Bible and question who would ever need them. Our failure to engage these psalms calls our spiritual and physical isolation to account.

These psalms also disturb me because, like it or not, most of the world identifies the United States as the enemy. In their eyes we are the oppressors—the wealthy, powerful leaders of a world society in which they do not share privilege. The truth of such a charge, of course, depends on what we do with the words of these psalms of lament that plead with God for justice and righteousness to be experienced here and now. Do we really want God to deliver those suffering from oppression even if complex sociopolitical consequences cause us to experience less of the good life? Or would we prefer to sing another song that celebrates what we take to be God's blessings on our lives? Jinkins aptly challenges us:

But praise and thanksgiving divorced from lamentation, divorced from heart-felt observation of societal injustices and the cries of the oppressed, divorced from a critical assessment of our role in human society, become expressions of vanity. (*In the House of the Lord*, 38–39)

If nothing else, the laments about enemies challenge us to ask ourselves, whose side are we on? Could it be that we face no threats because, through our complacency, we have sided with or even become the enemy? These psalms disturb me.

CHAPTER NINE

Like a Snail Dissolves into Slime

Mine eyes have seen the glory of the coming of the Lord;
He is trampling out the vintage where the grapes of wrath are stored;
He hath loosed the fateful lightning of His terrible swift sword;
His truth is marching on.
Glory, glory, hallelujah!
—JULIA WARD HOWE ("Battle Hymn of the Republic")

How easy it is for us to condemn ancient Israel's cry for revenge
and support our own, hiding behind our more impersonal methods of warfare!
—DENISE DOMBKOWSKI HOPKINS (*Journey through the Psalms*, 93)

On April 6, 1994, an airplane carrying Burundian president Cyprien Ntaryamira and Rwandan president Juvénal Habyarimana was shot down by a rocket near the International Airport of Kigali, the capital of Rwanda. The crash sparked an unimaginable melee. Within hours, Rwandan Armed Forces set up roadblocks and began going from house to house killing Tutsis, an ethnic minority group accused of assassinating the president and plotting rebellion against the majority Hutus. United Nations peacekeeping forces in the country sheltered some citizens but most stood by without acting—forbidden to help because of their mandate to "monitor" not intervene.

The next day, ten Belgian soldiers with the United Nations were tortured and murdered, prompting the United Nations to order its forces to retreat to the airport (April 11) and then to withdraw almost all of its 2,500 troops from the country (April 21). Foreign internationals from France, Belgium, and the United States were airlifted to safety. Meanwhile, no one helped the Tutsis or the moderate Hutus who were also being caught up in the slaughter. Neighbors were forced to murder neighbors. Incentives of money, food, and land were given to those who would kill Tutsis. Their bodies were thrown into rivers, swamps, mass graves, and left in churches where they had sought refuge. On April 11, five days after the killing began, the International Red Cross estimated that tens of thousands of Rwandans had been murdered, by April 21, hundreds of thousands, by May 15, five hundred thousand, and by mid-July, when the Tutsi forces captured the capital and the genocide came to an end, eight hundred thousand had died—nearly 10 percent of the nation's population in one hundred days. The pace of the brutality surpassed Hitler's holocaust.

Today the world knows this tragedy by the phrase "One Hundred Days of Slaughter." But at the time, when Rwanda was disintegrating, the international community issued statements, postured, and debated the use of the term "genocide" for what was happening. Some voted to send troops and equipment to Rwanda—but then delayed over arguments about who would finance the effort.

Of course, a conflict of this magnitude has deep roots, in this case extending to colonial times when the Belgians considered the Tutsis to be superior to the Hutus and so extended privileges and opportunities to the Tutsis that were denied to the Hutus. And tensions remain, especially in the Democratic Republic of Congo (DRC, formerly Zaire) where, after Kigali fell to the Tutsis, an estimated two million Hutus fled and now live. Several times since 1994, the Rwandan army has crossed the border to attack Hutus in DRC, citing alarm over the large Hutu forces.

A Tutsi family living in Rwanda in April 1994 would have read the laments regarding enemies far differently than I do from the comfort of my study. In 1994, I lived in West Texas, where I preached for a church, took my son to little league games, and dropped off my daughter at preschool once a week. I was not on the run for my life, hiding among dead bodies in the swamp or watching my family be butchered. And this dissimilarity of experience makes all the difference as we come to the last two groups of psalms regarding enemies. Our lives and our relationship to the oppressed determine how we read these texts and what we do with them.

Psalms along the Trajectory of Extremes

In the previous chapter, we began to explore similarities among laments that mention others who are in some way responsible for the poet's suffering. On occasion, these psalms identify the enemy as an invading army, a legal adversary, or a former friend. But, most often, the psalmists cloak their opponents in a veil of anonymity, a move that makes their prayers available to others, including us. In our prayers, the enemy may be anyone or anything that stands against us or against those with whom we identify. We have also seen that the poets firmly assert that their lives and their interests are inexorably aligned with God and God's way in the world. Consequently, what was already a critical situation for the writer is made out to be a serious matter for God. My enemies, the psalmists claim, are God's enemies—giving God further warrant to intervene on my behalf (an issue we will return to later in this chapter).

The psalmists respond to their enemies in diverse ways—which we have begun to plot along a trajectory from one extreme to another.

1. *Silence.* Once a poet has mentioned or described an opponent, he or she may not ask God to do anything. Rather, the poet may turn his focus inward in self-talk and then outward to others in encouragement to trust God. Here, at least, what is most important is my reaction, not what happens to the enemy. Trust in God—that God knows how to handle the situation, and wait on God to act at the appropriate time.

2. *Please save us.* Like the first response, psalms in this group transfer the focal point from "them" (the enemy) to "us" (the poet and others in need) and ask God to rescue *us* from *them*—without telling God how to effect the rescue or what we think God should do to the enemy. To be sure,

these psalmists realize that their deliverance will have consequences for their opponents, but they bypass consideration of these effects in favor of a straightforward appeal to God to help us.

3. *What God will do to them.* In a rhetorical effort to warn would-be opponents, encourage those who are oppressed, and perhaps make an indirect appeal to God, a number of psalms describe what God will do to their enemies. Among other claims, the poets assert that God will judge them, strike them with terror, and put them to shame. But these texts do not ask God to act against the enemy, at least not directly. Here it is enough to proclaim and celebrate what the righteous know God will do to the wicked.

Two Final Categories: The Imprecatory Psalms

Along the trajectory between extremes, we now arrive at instances in which the psalmists explicitly ask God to do something against the enemy. Most literature on the book of Psalms describes these texts as "imprecatory psalms" (from the verb "imprecate"—to invoke a curse). Because of the large number of these psalms and the variety among them, I divide these texts into the two final groups on our spectrum.

4. *Please judge them.* Most imprecatory psalms make brief and simple requests regarding what God should do to the opponents. Four ideas are especially prevalent:

- that God would shame or dishonor the enemy; for example, "Let my accusers be put to shame and consumed; let those who seek to hurt me be covered with scorn and disgrace" (71:13; 13; cf. 25:3, 19, 20; 31:17; 40:13–15; 70:2–3);
- that God would judge them; for example, "Rise up, O LORD, in your anger; lift yourself up against the fury of my enemies; awake, O my God; you have appointed a judgment. Let the assembly of the peoples be gathered around you, and over it take your seat on high" (7:6–7; cf. 5:10; 17:13–14);
- that God would repay them what they deserve or what they had planned against the poet; for example, "Repay them

according to their works, and according to the evil of their
deeds; repay them according to the work of their hands;
render them their due reward" (28:4; cf. 5:10; 56:7; 141:10);

- that God would cut off or destroy the enemy—this request
  may be limited to the offending body part of the foe; for
  example, "May the LORD cut off all flattering lips, the
  tongue that makes great boasts, those who say, 'With our
  tongues we will prevail; our lips are our own—who is our
  master?'" (12:3–4; cf. 31:18), or be more comprehensive and
  vivid, "Let burning coals fall on them! Let them be flung
  into pits, no more to rise! Do not let the slanderer be established in the land; let evil speedily hunt down the violent!"
  (140:10–11; cf. 55:9, 15; 80:16; 143:12).

Each of these psalms makes a direct and concise request for God to act
against the enemy. Yet while their appeals are brief (only 1–2 verses) and
not developed in detail, these compact requests pack a powerful punch.
As we saw in Chapter Five, shame and dishonor were important societal
values in ancient Israel; loss of honor negatively affected a person's relationships, business, family, and religion—all of one's life. So a person who
requests that an enemy be shamed is asking God to act in a severe and
harmful manner. The psalmists' appeal for God's judgment is also harsh,
though less so when the poet adds to his prayer a request that God judge
him too (7:6–9). Nonetheless, their hope is that God give the enemy what
he or she deserves (28:4–5) and that this repayment will cause irreparable
damage. The final subcategory of these brief wishes clearly conveys in only
a few words its violent and deadly wish—that God cut off, destroy, and
bring death to the enemy.

5. *Slay them!* The final and most extreme group of laments on the trajectory of responses is the fully developed imprecation. By my count, only
eight psalms fall into this category: 35, 58, 59, 69, 79, 83, 109, and 137. But
eight is more than enough—because here we reach an extreme language.
Two examples will suffice:

O God, break the teeth in their mouths;
> tear out the fangs of the young lions, O LORD!
Let them vanish like water that runs away;
> like grass let them be trodden down and wither.
Let them be like the snail that dissolves into slime;
> like the untimely birth that never sees the sun.
Sooner than your pots can feel the heat of thorns,
> whether green or ablaze, may he sweep them away!
The righteous will rejoice when they see vengeance done;
> they will bathe their feet in the blood of the wicked.
People will say, "Surely there is a reward for righteousness;
> surely there is a God who judges on earth." (58:6–11)

Let them be put to shame and dishonor
> who seek after my life.
Let them be turned back and confounded
> who devise evil against me.
Let them be like chaff before the wind,
> with the angel of the LORD driving them on.
Let their way be dark and slippery,
> with the angel of the LORD pursuing them.
For without cause they hid their net for me;
> without cause they dug a pit for my life.
Let ruin come on them unawares.
And let the net that they hid ensnare them;
> let them fall in it—to their ruin. (35:4–8)

These imprecations do not come to us from eras of peace or even in cases where a national leader (e.g., the king) was wicked, even very wicked. Nor do the imprecations arise from petty personal or individual vendettas. These fully developed imprecations arise from the worst imaginable situations: where one is unjustly accused and on trial for his or her life (Pss. 35, 109), where the legal system and its judges are corrupt and beyond remediation (Ps. 58), in times of national crisis (Pss. 59, 69, 83) and national devastation (Pss. 79, 137).

Nonetheless, the violence seems over the top, rabid, and ultrafanatical. In these psalms, the poets are not content to merely describe the enemy or ask God's help for themselves. Nor are they satisfied with pronouncing what God will do to the opponents or demand that God judge them. Instead, these writers spell out what they want God to do to their enemy with precise and grotesque images: broken teeth, dissolved snails, withered grass, chaff in the wind, even miscarriage—and may they come to their fate quickly and unaware until the moment they fall into the trap net. Even if we allow for some hyperbole (or a lot) and admit that the writers may have never intended for anyone to take their words literally, their anger and appeals for retribution are nonetheless unnerving.

Dangers at the Extremes

At first sight, these imprecatory psalms look like a centuries-old mummy brought out into the clear light of day—decayed and still reeking of death. It is tempting to pronounce them dead and move at fast pace to bury them back in the pages of the Old Testament before they stink up the rest of Scripture. Why bother with further autopsy? They seem so devoid of any sign of spiritual life that it is difficult to understand how anyone in our Judeo-Christian heritage could have thought they contained life in the first place. This response is the first of two extremes: we edit out the imprecatory psalms with scissors and paste (or a few clicks of the mouse) according to our tastes, or we simply pretend these psalms do not exist by never reading them.

A pick-and-choose approach to the Psalms, however, is a dicey option that creates more problems than it solves. First, once we beginning excising texts, at what level do we decide a psalm or prayer is unacceptable: when it details what we think God should do to our enemy (eight psalms: 35, 58, 59, 69, 79, 83, 109, 137), when it asks God to judge or repay our enemy without spelling out the details (eleven psalms: 5, 7, 12, 17, 28, 31, 55, 56, 70, 71, 140), when it pronounces what God will do to them (eight psalms: 6, 52, 54,

57, 62, 63, 64, 141), or when it asks God to rescue me—realizing or not the consequences my rescue has for my enemy (seven psalms: 12, 17, 22, 43, 74, 86, 102)? Where do we draw the line? If we go this direction, our refined sensibilities may lead us to a place where we are unable to pray about much of anything because of inescapable and complex real-world consequences.

Second, once we begin deleting texts, what is to stop us from banishing texts from the New Testament? If we are to be theologically consistent, the same criteria we use to judge and dismiss imprecatory psalms from the Old Testament stands in judgment of James, John, and Paul. Like the psalms that declare what God will do to their wicked enemies, James tells the wealthy to "weep and wail for the miseries that are coming to you" (5:1) and describes the rust from accumulated gold and silver that "will eat your flesh like fire" (5:3). John also describes terrible judgment that is coming on the enemies of the Lamb (Rev. 14:10, 19:19–20), while the martyrs call out for vengeance (6:10). And Paul states bluntly, "Let anyone be accursed who has no love for the Lord" (1 Cor. 16:22). So, as tempting as it may appear, excising the language of imprecation in the Psalms does not solve the problem.

On the opposite end of the spectrum, a willy-nilly use of the imprecatory psalms has the potential to devastate God's way in this world. To take a recent example, in June 2009, Wiley Drake spoke openly about his prayers of imprecation regarding President Barack Obama in an interview on the Alan Colmes Show (Fox News Radio). Asked directly if he was praying for the death of the president, Drake said, "Yes." When Colmes asked again, "You would like for the president of the United States to die?" Drake replied, "If he does not turn to God and does not turn his life around, I am asking God to enforce imprecatory prayers that are throughout the Scripture that would cause him death, that's correct." His comments created a small sensation. Not only a Christian, Drake was a Southern Baptist pastor, political activist, and one-time second vice president in the Southern Baptist Convention. During the interview, Drake tried to explain his position: "I think it is appropriate to pray the word of God. I'm not saying anything. What I am doing is repeating what God is saying" (http://video.foxnews.com/v/3931975/prayer-of-death/).

While some may support Drake's use of the imprecatory psalms, I'm alarmed at the potential damage to the reputation of Christ and Christians. At the same time, the lure of his position is subtle and deceptively persuasive. It is tempting to conclude that our position is God's position with such confidence that we can stand in for God. Consequently, Paul's instruction to be subject to governing authorities (Rom 13:1–2) or any other biblical admonition does not apply to us. When we identify our cause as God's cause and ourselves as God's representatives, we feel entitled to pronounce God's curses on others (whether I speak them aloud or not). After all, we are right and everyone else is wrong. We've become like gods—or like God.

I want to be aligned with God's purposes, but it is risky to believe that an attack on my ideology is an attack on God, and therefore justification for the use of imprecatory psalms. In our last chapter, we took note of a similar move among the laments regarding enemies. The psalmists often claim that the enemies' threats and attacks are not just directed against them but also against God, and they used this claim to motivate God to act on behalf of God's own interests. The early church used the same strategy in its first recorded prayer as it asks God to view Jewish threats against Peter and John as threats against God and to enable "*your* servants to speak your word with all boldness" (Acts 4:29, emphasis mine). Of course we should want to represent God and act on behalf of God's interests. What we need, however, is humility equivalent to our confidence. We are not God and, even if we can't believe it, we may be wrong about what God wants. So before we deploy explosive words (these are not neutral prayers), we need to exercise caution and humility. Does this issue really matter that much to God? For who am I really praying—God's interests or my own? Who stands to gain as the result of my prayer?

If Nothing Else: Principles from Imprecatory Psalms

I am aware of potential pitfalls in the direction I am pointing; in fact, these missteps are more like stumbling off the side of Mt. Everest than twisting an ankle in a pothole. But since common objections against lament (see previous chapters) or outright dismissal of imprecatory psalms fail to exorcize these texts from the Bible, it seems possible that these psalms exist in the text because we need them. These disturbing, breath-taking imprecations enact basic principles of relationship with God, prayer, and even how to relate to our enemies. In other words, the problem is not the imprecatory psalms but us—not the text but the reader.

1. *If nothing else*, the imprecatory psalms teach us how to pray the ethic Paul taught the church in Rome. In his letter to the Romans, Paul cites Proverbs 25: "If your enemies are hungry, feed them; if they are thirsty, give them something to drink; for by doing this you will heap burning coals on their heads" (Rom. 12:20; Prov. 25:21–22). The meaning of the second half of this proverb is widely debated—are the coals helpful or harmful? The ethic, however, is clear: help your enemies. And this ethic is Paul's emphasis in the text:

> Do not repay anyone evil for evil, but take thought for what is noble in the sight of all. If it is possible, so far as it depends on you, live peaceably with all. Beloved, never avenge your-selves, but leave room for the wrath of God; for it is written, "Vengeance is mine, I will repay, says the Lord." No, "if your enemies are hungry, feed them; if they are thirsty, give them something to drink; for by doing this you will heap burning coals on their heads." Do not be overcome by evil, but over-come evil with good. (Rom. 12:17–21)

Paul's concern, on the one hand, is that the Christians in Rome not take matters into their own hands to repay or avenge a wrong. On the other hand, Paul urges them to leave the righting of wrongs to God, to "leave room for the wrath of God." So in essence his counsel is: refuse to avenge yourself—give the matter to God.

The martyrs' lament of Revelation 6 follows Paul's instruction to the Romans. Instead of taking vengeance into their own hands, they turn these desires over to God: "how long will it be before *you* judge and avenge our blood?" (v. 10, emphasis mine). And the imprecations from the book of

Psalms follow the same practice. In other words, the psalmists are doing exactly what Paul instructs us to do: instead of acting on our desire for revenge, give it to God. My hope for vengeance may be appropriate (e.g., to break the fangs of poisonous snakes [the wicked] before they strike and kill others [Ps. 58:3–6]), or inappropriate (e.g., it is difficult to imagine any situation in which dashing infants against rock would be the right thing to do [Ps. 137:9]), but what I want is largely irrelevant. In the final analysis, it is what I do with these feelings and wishes that is important—and these psalms exemplify leaving "room for the wrath of God" by giving my desire for revenge to God, then God may do what God deems best. It is out of my hands.

2. *If nothing else*, the imprecations also teach us the level of honesty God seeks in our prayers. When honesty is a high value in conversation with God, what I say or ask for may be good or terrible. Moses prayed that God would change his mind and let him enter the land—and God said no (Deut. 3:23–26). Paul prayed that God would remove his "thorn in the flesh"—and God said no (2 Cor. 12:7–10). Jesus prayed that God would remove "this cup from me"—and God said no (Matt. 26:39). Prayer is not a matter of agreeing with God. Prayer is confessing the truth about ourselves and our desires and letting God sort out what is appropriate or inappropriate, right or wrong, best or not good—and letting God act, not me. Such honest prayer runs counter to our intuitive pride. "Prayer, we think, means presenting ourselves before God so that he will be pleased with us. We put on our Sunday best in our prayers." Consequently, as Peterson continues, "It is easy to be honest before God with our hallelujahs; it is somewhat more difficult to be honest in our hurts; it is nearly impossible to be honest before God in the dark emotions of our hate" (*Answering God*, 100).

The imprecatory psalms teach us that God values honesty over pious posturing—and our efforts to censor these prayers indict our superficial engagement with God and the world. Our judgment against these psalms passes judgment on us. It might be that a particular lament regarding an enemy comes from a time and occasion in which God could agree that action needs to be taken. Or it might be that a lament finds God's veto. In either case, the psalmist practices the spiritual discipline of honesty with God and the ethic of nonretaliation against enemies.

3. *If nothing else,* the imprecatory psalms prompt us to take our eyes off ourselves and see the world. My prayers are too egocentric; they are all about me—my friends, my community, and my nation. Consequently, when all I pray about is what affects me, the imprecatory psalms make no sense. I don't have enemies like those attacking the psalmist. I don't suffer humiliation and threats against my life. These psalms disturb my moral sensitivities because I only think and pray about me.

What should disturb me is One Hundred Days of Slaughter, the Holocaust, adolescent girls taken out of Nepal and held as sex slaves in India, and little boys captured and forced to work fishing boats in Ghana. What is a parent supposed to say to God when their children have been kidnapped, they are powerless to do anything, and no one in power will help? Much more important for us, what are we saying to God on behalf of these parents and children? While we are drowning in a sea of egocentric prayers, a desperate world goes mute. If we do not speak up, who will speak to God on behalf of the oppressed? Our world desperately needs people of faith to speak strong language on behalf of those with no power, no strength, and no voice.

I shudder at the use of the imprecatory psalms in self-serving ways, but I also shudder to think we are so insulated from the world that we fail to ask or see who needs this language today.

In a discussion of Psalm 109, one of the extensive imprecations, Walter Brueggemann leads us to this question:

> One may conclude "This psalm does not concern me, because I have never been that angry." Such a response may be spoken as though it were a virtue, but I suggest it reflects someone who is only half living. It is a good idea, when encountering a psalm like this, to ask, "Whose psalm is this?" If I am not able to pray that way today, then I can ask, who needs to pray that way today? Who is justified in praying that way today? It

could be the voice of a woman who is victimized by rape, who surely knows that kind of rage and indignation and does not need "due process" to know the proper outcome. It could be the voice of a black in South Africa (or here?) who has yet again been brutalized or humiliated by the system. Or it could be a Palestinian peasant weary of war, resentful of displacement. (*The Message of the Psalms*, 87)

Paul told the Roman Christians to "weep with those who weep" (12:15), and to the Galatians he said, "Bear one another's burdens, and in this way you will fulfill the law of Christ" (6:2). Our failure to pray the imprecatory psalms is nothing less than a failure to bear the burdens of and pray for those who have wept so many tears they can no longer speak for themselves. Michael Jinkins asserts that our responsibility extends even further:

The Church from whose pulpits Jim Crow was preached as gospel has a responsibility to pray these psalms of God's fiery grace as it stands in the presence of African Americans lynched in the American South; the Church that benefited financially from oppressive juntas have a responsibility to cry out for God's justice in the presence of the peasants murdered by death squads in Central America; the Church which stood in silence suffers the need to call for God's righteousness in the presence of women raped and entire male populations exterminated in the "ethnic cleansing" crusades in the former Yugoslavia. (*In the House of the Lord*, 98)

When we are disturbed about what disturbs God, our prayers will change— as will what we do outside the safe confines of the sanctuary. Our prayers to God will compel us to take up God's work in the places where the only proper response is outrage.

At the end, we realize that our concerns about imprecatory psalms are misplaced. These psalms may not be about me or for me after all. I am not abused, terrorized, or left without a way to attend to my family's basic needs. But I am not the center of the universe. These psalms exist for people who are brutalized and suffering a life of injustice—so that we have the words to pray for them, on their behalf. Without these words, my prayers are too selfish. Love for neighbor challenges us to ask who needs us to pray imprecations for them because their voice has been taken away. Whose burden can I pick up and so fulfill the love of Christ?

CHAPTER TEN

Will You Hide Yourself Forever?

The collection of the Psalter is not for those whose life is one of
uninterrupted continuity and equilibrium. Such people should stay safely
in the book of Proverbs, which reflects on the continuities of life. But few
of us live that kind of life. Most of us who think our lives are that way
have been numbed, desensitized, and suppressed so that we are cut off
from what is in fact going on in our lives.
—WALTER BRUEGGEMANN (*Praying the Psalms*, 14)

Recovering the language of lament means finding the possibility
of this combination ⟨protest and trust⟩. The prayers of lament are
prayers of persuasion, full of reasons to try to persuade God to help,
so they do not assume God's deliverance; they are also prayers of
trust, so they do assume God's deliverance.
—PATRICK D. MILLER ("Heaven's Prisoners:
The Lament as Christian Prayer," 19–20)

As we have seen over the last few chapters, the psalmists teach
us how to approach God with our concerns about life and other
people, releasing to God our emotions, pain, and even our desire for vengeance. When life takes sudden and even prolonged turns into darkness,
these poets lead us in calling out to God, knowing that the God to whom
we call is himself the answer to our needs:

> Hear my cry, O God;
>> listen to my prayer.
> From the end of the earth I call to you,
>> when my heart is faint.
> Lead me to the rock
>> that is higher than I;
> for you are my refuge,
>> a strong tower against the enemy. (61:1–3)

And, with this language, they also provide an example of life lived with God when the valley is deep and lonely.

> For God alone my soul waits in silence;
>> for my hope is from him.
> He alone is my rock and my salvation,
>> my fortress; I shall not be shaken.
> On God rests my deliverance and honor;
>> my mighty rock, my refuge is in God. (62:5–7)

Confidence in spite of attack, trust when the foundations shake, a quiet, nonanxious spirit—not because we shut our eyes to our circumstances or retreat from reality, but because of a relationship with God. The Psalms teach us that in all these times what matters most is *God's presence*. If God is with us, we can rest under his protection.

> He will hide me in his shelter in the day of trouble;
>> he will conceal me under the cover of his tent;
>> he will set me high on a rock. (27:5)

> Even though I walk through the darkest valley,
>> I fear no evil;
> for you are with me;
>> your rod and your staff—
>> they comfort me. (23:4)

> God is our refuge and strength,
>> a very present help in trouble.

> Therefore we will not fear, though the earth should change,
>> though the mountains shake in the heart of the sea;
> though its waters roar and foam,
>> though the mountains tremble with its tumult. (46:1–3)

With God near *in relationship*, I can call out with confidence knowing that God hears and will respond. And, *in relationship*, God invites me to speak my heart with honesty and without fear. More than the words and patterns of lament, beyond any how-to guide for prayer, the psalmists lead us to an intimate *relationship* with God.

Relationship and Relationships

Though not codified or absolute, within every culture exists a set of rules for proper social conduct—appropriate and inappropriate behavior for different types of relationships. Most learn at a young age how to size up a situation and act according to the rules, though it may take a little time. For the first few years of her life, my daughter believed everyone in the grocery store should say hello to her; she would continue waving and calling to every stranger until they complied. To the relief of our mothers, we eventually learn that it is not appropriate to tell someone at the mall that his (or her) purple hair looks funny. Though it seems okay to tell our grandpa that he has big ears. Over time we come to understand that few friendships in life are capable of genuine transparency—only here with love and tact may we speak about what is needed and at the same time be willing to receive whatever the other person needs to say to us. Such friendships are rare. Most relationships operate at a far lower level, and appropriately so. We listen with internal gauges set to filter what we hear and answer carefully, not wanting to offend, dancing around what we really think to guard their feelings. In casual relationships we rarely confront or criticize—and we do not take criticism well.

So what about God? The Psalms exemplify honest speech to God about our failures, when we need to confess sin and turn to God for forgiveness. God also invites us to bring life's struggles and difficulties to him—openly and honestly. And when my problem has to do with others, God welcomes truthful speech about what they have done to me, my feelings toward them, and what I want God to do to them. God can handle it. God wants, so the psalmists claim by their practice, an intimate relationship with us that welcomes us to say what we think and feel, trusting God to sort it all out.

But what if God is the problem? Or if not *the* problem, God could resolve my trouble with minimal divine effort, if only he would get involved, but God doesn't help. Does God's desire for an honest relationship extend to speech about everyone and everything—except God? Is my relationship to God just one more among many others in which I may talk about anything except the person to whom I am speaking? What kind of relationship do I have with God? Can I talk to God about God's failures?

I realize that to suggest such questions raises a navy fleet of warning flags. The Lord is sovereign king over all creation, worthy of respect. Who can walk into a royal court and criticize the king? If we have an obligation to honor our parents, how much more respect is due our divine Father? We do not stand in judgment of God; God examines us. But with these concerns duly noted, we need to recognize another danger that we tend to overlook, a danger as ominous to our relationship as a lack of respect. My fears and experience of dysfunctional relationships may define and limit my relationship with God. Instead of God's invitation and hopes for relationship establishing what is appropriate, we decide based on what we want and are comfortable with. Our selective use of biblical metaphors for God exposes us. Our preference for the images of God as king, father, and judge marks a line in the sand for this relationship, a line further etched into concrete by a neglect of other biblical metaphors for God (e.g., friend, mother, husband). When we think of God only in terms of a sovereign king and judge, we become yes-men with endless affirmations for what God chooses to do; we limit appropriate speech—especially compared to how I might speak to my spouse or friend. Unless we are careful, our reduced set of metaphors for God leads us to an unstated set of assumptions for what is appropriate instead of the witness of Scripture leading us to what God wants in this relationship. The question we should be asking is *what does God dare us say*, not what *we* dare to do?

The psalmists do not pause to offer a descriptive answer to what we should or should not say to God. But, if there is a line in the sand marking how far a person may be honest with God, they leap across with abandon. If the problem is their sin, these poets say it. If the trouble lies with others, they bring it to God. And if the issue regards God, they refuse to be silent just because it is God. Rather, when the problem is God they not only *must* speak—they dare not exercise such caution that their speech becomes a ridicule of truthful conversation. As God's covenant partners, they ask difficult questions and make harsh accusations. They do not lack fear of God; it is because of their reverence and their relationship with God that they dare not engage in half-truths, dance around hidden thoughts, or suppress their feelings. They know that God will not stand for two-faced flattery. For these psalmists, either God is an intimate friend to whom we speak our true thoughts and feelings, or God, in fact, is no friend at all. The psalmists reject the false reverence of silence and dare to live in the relationship to which God called them—accusing, challenging, and questioning God about God.

Questions for God

Questions are not created equal. Rhetorical questions forecast their own answer, leading questions take us along a predetermined path, and trick questions catch an unsuspecting response. There are open-ended questions, lingering questions, personal questions, and dumb questions (what color is yes?). And there are loaded questions—the psalmists' preferred tool for engaging God. Loaded questions mask innuendo with an initial appearance of innocence. However, beyond what appears to be a simple or innocent inquiry about God's behavior, the innuendo packed in the psalmists' questions create barbs—rhetorical devices that prick and hook God's heart so that God must respond. As an entry point into our own need for difficult conversations with God, this chapter focuses on these questions. For the sake of simplicity, I arrange the psalmists' questions into seven recurring and overlapping requests, questions that engage God in the practice of intimate relationship—and questions that may help us re-engage God.

1. *Why are you standing so far away?* The poets often express confidence that God is present and aware of their needs, but bewilderment that God does nothing:

> Why do you stand so far off? (10:1)

> Why are you so far from helping me, from the words of my groaning? (22:1)

These and other questions use anthropomorphic language (putting God in human terms)—an inescapable move for theology (speech to or about God). We have no other way to understand or talk about God except with human language. So, the Psalms describe God as a shepherd, warrior, king, and judge—all limited but positive human images for the divine. In their questions, however, the psalmists depict God as an undependable and flawed human. The question "Why do you stand far off?" wonders whether God has become so nearsighted that he can't see what is happening. "Why are you so far from helping me?" suggests that God has wandered off in disregard of the poet or perhaps has lost his ability to help. And both questions raise the issue of whether God cares enough to stay close and help or whether God prefers to watch, sitting out this battle while the psalmist goes at it alone.

In a similar way, another psalmist questions why God has the power to intervene but doesn't.

> Why do you hold back your hand;
> Why do you keep you hand in your bosom? (74:11)

God's hand is a symbol of God's power. When he summoned Moses to go to Egypt, the Lord told him, "So I will stretch out my hand and strike Egypt with all my wonders that I will perform in it; after that he will let you go" (Exod. 3:20). But so far as the psalmist can see, God is like Napoleon posing for his portrait. God refuses to take his hands out of his pockets and do something to help. God is witnessing a crime, but chooses not to get involved.

2. *How long will you let this go on?* The most frequent interrogative for God in the psalms is *how long* (usually combined with other questions). Here, the psalmists assume that God is nearby, aware, and capable—but inexplicably not intervening.

> How long, O LORD? Will you forget me forever?
> How long will you hide your face from me?
> How long must I bear pain in my soul,
>> and have sorrow in my heart all day long?
> How long shall my enemy be exalted over me? (13:1–2)

> How long, O LORD, will you look on? (35:17)

> My soul also is struck with terror,
>> while you, O LORD—how long? (6:3)

> Turn, O LORD! How Long?
> Have compassion on your servants! (90:13)

In some contexts *how long* may be an inquiry of time—how much longer will this last? Most often, however, *how long* is an unconditional objection.

At one of the first places I preached, every Sunday, the same elderly couple sat in the third pew from the front. They were a gracious encouragement to me. The husband, however, had one particular habit that mortified his wife. When he thought the Bible class or sermon might be running long he would stand up, turn around, and squint at the clock on the back wall of the auditorium. He just stood there with his wife tugging at his arm; sometimes he would sit down and other times he would turn back for a second look at the clock. It was his way of asking "How long?"—and effectively putting an end to the sermon. In the same way, the psalmists who ask God "how long" about their pain are not asking whether they must endure another five minutes or five years. They are standing in the assembly asserting that it has already been too long, especially when there is a God who can end their suffering but does not.

3. *Why do you act more human than divine?* This question, as I have worded it, never occurs in the psalms. Nonetheless, many poets ask questions that propose this particular excuse for why a God so near in relationship fails to respond to our trouble.

> Rouse yourself! Why do you sleep, O LORD?
>> Awake, do not cast us off forever! (44:23)

> Wake up! Bestir yourself for my defense,
>> for my cause, my God and my LORD! (35:23)

> Rouse yourself, come to my help and see!
>> You, LORD God of hosts, are God of Israel.
> Awake to punish all the nations;
>> spare none of those who treacherously plot evil. (59:4e–5)

Their questions are not as innocent or naïve as they might first appear. What kind of God falls asleep when our lives are on the line? Maybe God is more human and less divine than we thought: God is tired, perhaps still worn out from the work of creation. Elijah, in his famous battle with the prophets of Baal on Mt. Carmel, mocked Baal's failure to respond by making similar excuses for him: "Cry aloud! Surely he is a god; either he is meditating, or he has wandered away, or he is on a journey, or *perhaps he is asleep and must be awakened*" (1 Kings 18:27, emphasis mine). The psalmists' question, "Why do you sleep?," is a vivid reminder of the battle of the gods on Mt. Carmel and a sharp jab at the Lord's claims to be the only true God. If the Lord is sleeping when his people need him, he is no more reliable than Baal.

Questions about God's memory or forgetfulness are equally powerful shots at God's failure to act. As divine, God does not forget because of absentmindedness or a faulty memory. Quite the opposite, Scripture asserts that God is reliable precisely because God does not forget. Isaiah 49 claims that God could no more forget his people than a nursing mother could forget her child (49:15). So the prophet urges Israel to remember the

God who will never forget her (44:21). When God forgets, it is not a lapse of memory but a deliberate decision to leave a person or people (Lam. 5:20). But if so, how do we explain God's forgetfulness?

> Will you forget our affliction and oppression? (44:24)

> Has God forgotten to be gracious? (77:9)

> Will you forget me forever? (13:1; 42:9)

The psalmists know that the divine nature does not forget. So to ask God "Why have you forgotten?" is to assert that God has deliberately decided to abandon his people (for which there is no excuse) or that God is more human than divine—with the onset of Alzheimer's that causes God to forget and no longer be reliable.

4. *Why are you hiding?* People hide for many reasons. In games such as peekaboo or hide and seek, we hide for the joy of being found. After all, it's not much fun to hide so well that the seeker never finds us, gives up, and leaves us hidden while they move on to other games. Sometimes we hide so that we can have a moment of peace away from the demands of the day. At other times we may hide from fear of bullies, abusive spouses, and situations raging beyond our control. But why would God hide?

> Why do you hide yourself in times of trouble? (10:1; 44:24)

> How long, O LORD? Will you hide yourself forever? (89:46)

> How long will you hide your face from me? (13:1)

> Why do you hide your face from me? (88:14)

Again, the psalmists' questions are not concerned with getting an explanation, but challenging God to look in the mirror. From their perspective, God's failure to intervene suggests that God is hiding from the situation. The question for God is *why?* Is God afraid of the opposition or does he just not want his personal time to be disturbed? Is God playing a game with us—at our expense? The poets know that these are untenable explanations.

The Lord is not a human who fears an enemy or who lacks compassion for those in need. God is not like us; he hides from nothing—unless God is more human and less divine than we thought. And this is the point these questions press God to consider: Who am I? A human who hides from trouble or a divine sovereign who does not hide?

The questions "How long will you hide your face from me?" and "Why do you hide your face from me?" push God's self-reflection even further. Prior to the Israelites leaving Mt. Sinai, the Lord gave explicit instructions for how the priests should bless the people:

> The LORD bless you and keep you;
> the LORD make his face to shine upon you, and be gracious
>   to you;
> the LORD lift his countenance upon you, and give you peace.
> (Num. 6:24–25)

The Lord's blessing is inextricably bound up with his "face" or "countenance" turning and looking upon his people. When God's face gazes on Israel, they are blessed; to look is to love and care for them. Consequently, to "hide your face" denotes to withdraw love. In daring fashion, the poets use God's own words to reprimand his failure to act. What the psalmists want to know is when did the Lord decide to become a God characterized by hiding his face from his people instead of shining his face on them? They challenge the Lord to consider how long he plans to act in contradiction of his own self-revelation?

5. *Why have you rejected me?* If the preceding questions used metaphors to skirt the issue, potent with implied claims, the next set of questions cuts to the center of the matter.

> Why have you cast me off? (43:2)

> O God, why do you cast us off forever? (74:1)

> O LORD, why do you cast me off? (88:14a)

> Have you not rejected us, O God? (108:11a)

My God, my God, why have you forsaken me? (22:1)

These questions are also rooted in Israel's experience with the Lord. Moses claimed that "he [the Lord] will be with you; he will not fail you or forsake you. Do not fear or be dismayed" (Deut. 31:1; Josh. 1:5). Other psalms assert the same fail-proof assurance that God will never abandon or toss aside his covenant people: "for the LORD will not forsake his people; he will not abandon his heritage" (94:14), "for the LORD loves justice; he will not forsake his faithful ones" (37:28). Against this covenant background, the poets' questions are biting rebukes: You [Lord] have walked out on your vows. You have left your people when they needed you most. You are unfaithful.

6. *Why are you so angry?* After the disastrous golden calf affair at Sinai, Moses begged God not to destroy the people but to go with them despite their stubbornness. In order to know that God was in fact with them, Moses asked to see God (Exod. 33:12–16). The Lord refused because of the danger; no human could handle a full view of God. But the Lord did agree to reveal part of himself to Moses (33:17–23). Hidden behind a rock, Moses heard the Lord speak:

> The LORD, the LORD,
> a God merciful and gracious,
> slow to anger,
> and abounding in steadfast love and faithfulness,
> keeping steadfast love for the thousandth generation,
> forgiving iniquity and transgression and sin,
> yet by no means clearing the guilty,
> but visiting the iniquity of the parents
> upon the children
> and the children's children
> to the third and fourth generation. (Exod. 34:6–7)

By God's own words, he is "slow to anger" and limits the consequences of iniquity to the third and fourth generation (perhaps an indication of the three to four generations living together in a typical family compound). God is merciful and gracious, abounding in love, not an angry or capricious god. The psalmists, however, challenge whether God is living up to his claims.

> Why does your anger smoke against the sheep of your pasture? (74:1)
>
> Has he [God] in anger shut up his compassion? (77:9)
>
> Will you be angry forever?
> Will you prolong your anger to all generations? (85:5)
>
> How long, O LORD? Will you be angry forever?
> Will your jealous wrath burn like fire? (79:5)
>
> How long will you be angry with your people's prayers? (80:4)
>
> How long will your wrath burn like fire? (89:46)

Divine anger is a controlled, reasonable choice, not an overpowering emotion that causes God to do irrational things. At least divine anger is supposed to be different. But these poets question whether God has lost control of his emotions: Your anger has taken over with nonsensical results—burning the pasture of *your own* sheep, locking away compassion. You are acting like a temperamental human, not the God of covenant. As before, the question "How long?" asserts an objection that, regardless of when or why God's anger began, it has gone on too long. Against his promises, God has decided to "be angry forever" and prolong his anger "to all generations" (85:5). You blow up on a whim and, instead of faithful love, you allow your anger to burn without control. The poets take God at his word and turn those words back on God, daring God to be true to himself.

7. *Why do you tolerate them?* This final category of questions has to do with the enemies, a topic we have already discussed at length in Chapters Eight and Nine. Here, however, the questions draw attention not so much to the activity of the enemy but the inactivity of God.

Why should the nations say, "Where is their God?" (79:10)

How long, O God, is the foe to scoff?
> Is the enemy to revile your name forever? (74:10)

Why do the wicked renounce God, and say in their hearts,
> "You will not call us to account"? (10:13)

Why must I walk about mournfully,
> because the enemy oppresses me? (42:9; 43:2)

How long shall my enemy be exalted over me? (13:2)

In the past, God has been anxious about his reputation in the world. More than once, Moses effectively argued that God should not destroy his people reasoning, what will the Egyptians say? (Exod. 32:12), or what will the nations say? (Num. 14:15). God invested his reputation in his relationship to his people; Egypt and the nations knew that Israel belonged to the Lord, so what happened to Israel reflected God's character to the world.

But in these psalms, God's concern for his reputation is a thing of the past. God seems unconcerned with what the enemy says and does to God's people, and God's lethargy is a mystery. With so much on the line—the wellbeing of God's people, God's reputation in the world, and God's hope for the world— why God allows enemies to run over his people and defame him makes no sense. Either God changed his plan and failed to tell us, or God needs a swift kick in the pants for his own good. The psalmists challenge God to decide who or what he cares about and to be faithful to his people and himself.

More Questions

Other questions slip through the cracks of these seven categories (e.g., 89:49; 77:8). Nonetheless, this brief analysis is enough to demonstrate that the psalmists' questions of God are far from innocent inquiries. These questions call to mind Israel's most memorable experiences with God and God's most fundamental claims about his own character. And based on the Lord's own words, the poets censure their God—a move that in my fifty years of church

I have never heard in any prayer or song. And I can only imagine the reaction that would come if we prayed publicly like this next Sunday morning. I suspect it would be the last time we were invited to pray in public.

At this point it is enough to state the obvious: somewhere along the path we have been separated from our spiritual mentors and only now do we enter a clearing where we can look up and see the psalmists on the other rim of the Grand Canyon. A geological chasm has come between us. We hear them from their side of the canyon—singing the psalms of praise that first drew us to them, chanting familiar songs of thanksgiving and asking questions of God that cause us to shudder. Some on our side will be happy to stay put, questioning the validity of such language and the faith of those who speak in such tongues. But what we need to realize is that language and relationship are inseparable. To content ourselves with a safe language that never raises difficult questions is to settle for a friendly acquaintance with God instead of the covenant relationship modeled by the Psalms.

The psalmists' questions of God raise important questions for us. What level of intimacy do we want with God? Do we really want covenant partnership, or a less risky affiliation? Will we withdraw, content with metaphors of God as king and judge, or do we dare to engage God as friend and spouse? Are we willing to risk ourselves in such love and reliance on God that it is possible to be disappointed by God? Will we take God at his word so that when God is unfaithful we call God out? Do we play it safe or trust God enough to say difficult words? Do we believe that God really wants an intimate relationship or do we not?

We pause here to consider our own questions before continuing in the next chapter with an exploration of three psalms that engage God with especially harsh accusations. To be sure, getting to the other side of the canyon and rejoining the psalmists will not be easy, but it is possible. The question is whether we want a covenant relationship with God that requires the risk and vulnerability of honest conversation.

CHAPTER ELEVEN

Where Is Your Steadfast Love of Old?

How is faith to endure, O God, when you allow all this scraping and tearing on us? You have allowed rivers of blood to flow, mountains of suffering to pile up, sobs to become humanity's song–all without lifting a finger that we could see. You have allowed bonds of love beyond number to be painfully snapped. If you have not abandoned us, explain yourself . . . instead of hearing an answer we catch sight of God himself scraped and torn. Through our tears we see the tears of God.

NICHOLAS WOLTERSTORFF (*Lament for a Son*, 80)

Where complaint against God is disallowed, there can be no lament in the strict sense of the word. The lament is excluded from prayer. Instead of complaint against God there perforce arises the doctrine of the righteousness of God.

CLAUS WESTERMANN (*Praise and Lament in the Psalms*, 203)

In the film *The Apostle* (1997), Euless "Sonny" Dewey (Robert Duvall) is praying late at night in his bedroom. Sonny is a charismatic Pentecostal preacher in rural East Texas and a deeply flawed man. He is a domineering husband with a violent temper—which has landed him in serious trouble with the law for attacking his estranged wife's boyfriend with a baseball bat (whether he will live is still uncertain). Yet, despite Sonny's obvious failures, Duvall portrays him as a man who is genuinely and passionately committed to serving his God. He may be morally corrupt, but Sonny is no televangelist charlatan.

So he prays—pacing the floor, looking up, and staring down. He is loud and intense: "I'm mad at you [God]; I can't take it! Give me a sign or something. Blow this pain out of me. Give it to me tonight, Lord God Jehovah. If you won't give me back my wife, give me peace.... I don't know who's been foolin' with me, you or the devil. I don't know...." Sonny continues about his wife and the other man, but soon turns back to God: "I'm confused. I'm mad. I love you Lord; I love you. But I'm mad at you. I am mad at you!" He confesses that he is a sinner and "once in a while—a womanizer." But he immediately adds, "I'm your servant... I'm your servant. What should I do? Tell me. I've always called you Jesus; you've always called me Sonny. What should I do Jesus?"

While Sonny continues to pray, downstairs the phone rings in his mother's room. It takes several rings to wake Mrs. Dewey (June Carter Cash) before she manages to get the phone to her ear. "Mrs. Dewey? It sounds like you got a wild man over there carrying on and whatever. I'm just—just who, who is that over there? Is that your son or just who is that?"

Mrs. Dewey hears Sonny upstairs, "Oh, that is my son. He's—I'll tell you, ever since he was a little bitty boy sometimes he talks to the Lord and sometimes he yells at the Lord. And tonight he just happens to be yelling at him." The caller is exasperated and insists Mrs. Dewey calm her son or at least get him to turn down the volume. Instead Mrs. Dewey hangs up the receiver, lays back in bed, hears Sonny still shouting at God, and chuckles to herself as she goes back to sleep.

On his first day in the Nazi concentration camp at Birkenau, Elie Wiesel watched a lorry deliver a load of dead children into a ditch gasping with gigantic flames. His father began to whisper the Jewish prayer for the dead, not only for the children but for him and his son. "May His Name be blessed and glorified...." But the younger Wiesel balked, repulsed: "For the first time, I felt revolt rise up in me. Why should I bless his name? The Eternal, Lord of the Universe, the All-Powerful and Terrible, was silent. What had I to thank him for?" (*Night*, 31). He reflects on that night:

> Never shall I forget that night, the first night in camp, which
> has turned my life into one long night, seven times cursed and
> seven times sealed. Never shall I forget that smoke. Never shall
> I forget the little faces of the children. . . . Never shall I forget
> those flames which consumed my faith forever. . . . Never shall
> I forget those moments which murdered my God and my soul
> and turned my dreams to dust. (32)

Yet, with his faith shaking from tremors beneath the foundations of the
earth, Wiesel could no more escape his faith than he could escape the
camps. As he moved from one place to another, with new guards search-
ing for upgrades for their own clothes, Wiesel would find himself giving
thanks to God for the mud that coated his new shoes so that the Kapos
did not notice.

As the weeks unfolded, he listened at night to others talk about God's
mysterious ways, the sins of the Jewish people, and their future deliverance. But his faith felt out of place. He was like Job listening to his three
friends trying to explain his suffering and defending God's ways. None of
their explanations rang true. "How I sympathized with Job! I did not deny
God's existence, but I doubted His absolute justice" (*Night*, 42). This theme
is common in Wiesel's writings. In a later book, *The Trial of God* (1979),
he expresses the questions and accusations of God rising from the clash of
his faith against the harsh experiences of his life. And it is these abrasive,
unflinching indictments of God that are the means by which he maintains
his faith. As Robert Brown explains, Jewish tradition invites us "not to bury
our concerns but to hold them up, to confront God with them, sometimes
in anger." We question God, challenge God, and demand an accounting
from God. "And this, rather than diminishing God is truly to take God
seriously" (*The Trial of God*, xvi).

Perhaps. But I know many believers for whom all this inflammatory
language about God is too much to absorb. Whatever happened to awe
and reverence, the fear of God and humility? Wiesel's experience, Jewish
tradition, and a fictional movie of a man yelling at God provide sparse

ground to support Christian practice. Except that, in this case, their words build on the foundation of Scripture—psalms that take us into the deepest recesses of the human heart in times of greatest despair. In this chapter, we continue our journey into these deep and dark places by examining three psalms that take God so seriously that their poets find it necessary to confront God and demand an accounting. After close reading of these psalms, keeping in mind our study of the psalmists' questions for God (Chapter Ten), we will step back and reflect on all this talk to and about God, whether we should follow these writers, and, if so, what principles might guide faithful reclamation of this difficult language.

Psalm 44

The poet of Psalm 44 begins with a rehearsal of praise for God's mighty actions during the era of the conquest (44:1–3). God and God alone was the cause of success. With "your own hand" God drove out the nations and planted his people in the land:

> For not by their own sword did they win the land,
>> Nor did their arm give them victory;
> But your right hand, and your arm. (44:3)

Speaking on behalf of God's people, this affirmation of God's work in the past leads to the psalmist's confession of trust in the present: "you are my King and my God" (v. 4), and it is only "through you" that we defeat our foes and assailants (v. 5). As a result, we do not trust in our own strength or weapons (v. 6) but only in God (v. 7): "in God we have boasted continually, and we will give thanks to your name forever" (v. 8).

These opening verses establish the poet's conviction that the Lord reigns—in the past (vv. 1–3) and the present (vv. 4–8). And because God is sovereign, God's people trust the Lord to reign over those in whom he delights—them (v. 3). We know that we cannot overcome anyone; only our King can save with his mighty arm. So we rely on our King to protect us. With these affirmations, like an agent conducting a sting operation, the poet has completed the set-up and the trap is ready to spring shut, catching its prey: God, the King.

A torrent of serious and specific charges against the King floods the middle verses of the psalm (vv. 9–16). At the center of the indictment, the poet says that the King in whom we placed our confidence has betrayed us and not gone with our armies into battle—with catastrophic consequences (vv. 9–10). A variety of metaphors flesh out the situation. We were like sheep going to slaughter, doomed, helpless (v. 11). We were treated like worthless store goods, sold dirt cheap or thrown away (v. 12). We have become the object of taunting (v. 13) and the butt of everyone's jokes (v. 14). We are disgraced and shamed by the words and presence of the enemy (vv. 15–16).

The stinging defeat in battle and shameful submission to foreigners expressed in the metaphors of verses 11–16 depict an unbearable setting. And yet these difficulties are not the primary dispute. God, our King, is the problem. In Hebrew, each of verses 10–14 address God with a second person ("you") verb:

> *You made us* turn back from the foe,
>> and our enemies have gotten spoil.
> *You have made us* like sheep for slaughter,
>> and have scattered us among the nations.
> *You have sold your people* for a trifle,
>> demanding no high price for them.
> *You have made us* the taunt of our neighbors,
>> the derision and scorn of those around us.
> *You have made us* a byword among the nations,
>> a laughing stock among the peoples. (emphasis mine)

The problem is not simply that Israel has become like sheep doomed for slaughter, worthless, shamed, and the punch line of every joke. It is that God has done it. Against his promises and record of faithfulness, God did not go out with their armies to give victory.

The poet's logic is impeccable. If God's people honor him as King and give him credit for victories, then God must take the blame for defeat. His "right hand, and arm" could have reversed fortunes on the field, but God kept his arms folded and his hands in his pockets. At no time does the poet question God's ability or God's ongoing reign as King. Nor does the psalmist doubt what has been claimed about God in the past. Instead, the poet arraigns God for criminal indifference in the present. As King, God has received the praise and service of his subjects, so he has covenant obligations to his people—but he has abandoned his responsibilities.

Our psalm has taken on the tone, if not the form, of a legal proceeding with God standing as the accused. Consequently, in verse 17 the poet further asserts that God's people are not to blame. This disaster is not our fault; we have not "forgotten" God or broken the covenant. We have not turned back from following God (v. 18), or turned aside after other gods (vv. 20–21). We have not been unfaithful—but God is treating us like we were. You (God) have broken us and "covered us with deep darkness" (v. 19b). Finally, the poet charges the Lord as an accessory to murder: "Because of you we are being killed all day long, and accounted as sheep for the slaughter" (v. 22).

After such a jarring accusation, we might expect one of two things to happen: 1) the psalmist to walk out on this unfaithful King, or 2) for the King to strike the poet for blasphemous words. But neither happens. Instead, the psalmist again calls on the Lord to intervene. The poet does not back down from his charges, but neither does he back down from his confidence in God. He urges God to act by asking three of the questions that we examined in our last chapter. Why do you sleep, O Lord? (v. 23) Why do you hide your face? (v. 24a) Why do you forget our affliction and oppression? (v. 24b). The psalmist calls God out to alert wakefulness, to being present with his people, and to memory of his promises—to be the true King of his people. Despite his disappointment with God, the poet turns to the Lord and leads the reader to make the same move: to take a long view of faith and relationship with God that stands against the present disillusionment. Because of his resilient faith, the poet maintains that regardless of the criminal charges he has brought, he still believes that the Lord will be faithful, a point emphasized by the final words of Psalm 44: "Redeem us for the sake of your steadfast love."

Psalm 88

A common feature of lament psalms, like Psalm 44, is to conclude with a note of praise or a statement of confidence in the Lord. Regardless of what a poet may have said to or about God, harsh accusations and stern words give way to a final acclamation of God's reliability. Occasionally, a lament may begin with affirmations of trust or pepper the entire psalm to give it a flavor of confidence in God. Consequently, no matter how harsh a lament might be, it returns to the ground from which it sprang—a robust faith that sees the light of God's faithfulness at the end of a long night. These writers, despite their complaints, are optimists in God's steadfast love. Except for Psalm 88.

Psalm 88 begins "at night" when "I cry out in your presence" (v. 1), concludes "in darkness" (v. 18), and, between these end points, the psalmist stumbles through the haze utterly and completely alone. Friends, companions, neighbors—everyone or anyone who might have stepped up to be with the poet have deserted him while he faces the battle of his life (vv. 4b, 8, 18). Images of death and dying overwhelm the psalm and the psalmist. His "life draws near to Sheol" (v. 3), other people regard him as good as dead and in the grave—Sheol, a shadowy realm of the dead beyond God's presence (vv. 4–5). In verses 10–12, the poet asks a string of rhetorical questions, each of which anticipates the response no: no one in the underworld expects to experience God's love (v. 11a), faithfulness (v. 11b), or saving help (v. 12)—just as no one expects the "shades" (the dead) to praise God (v. 10). Those who die "are cut off from your hand" (v. 5b), and, separated from God, they have no reason to praise him.

Worst of all is the recognition that God is to blame for this ongoing darkness. The shepherd's psalm may claim reassurance that the Lord will lead when I come to the "darkest valley" (23:4) and that I need not fear because God is with me, "your rod and your staff—they comfort me" (23:3–4). But in Psalm 88, it is God who has put me in the depths of this pit (v. 6), and it is God who has caused all my friends to leave me (vv. 8, 18). God is inexplicably and uncontrollably angry (v. 7), and in his anger he has carried out one military assault after another against the poet (v. 8). God has unleashed the chaotic waters to sweep over and drown him (vv. 16–17). Worse, God's attacks are nothing new, just a continuation of a lifelong pattern.

> Wretched and close to death from my youth up,
>> I suffer your terrors; I am desperate. (v. 15)

Imprisoned, he cannot escape God's anger (v. 8), nor can he understand why God is doing this to him. The psalmist searches for answers that never come.

> O LORD, why do you cast me off?
>> Why do you hide your face from me? (v. 14)

God has left him in the pit—dark, desperate, and alone.

It is little wonder that the psalm lacks any word of praise or expression of confidence in God; it is God who is killing me. And yet, as my students have pointed out to me and argued in many papers, perhaps there is more God-confidence in this psalm than I recognize. Despite what the psalmist says about God, he still reaches out to God:

> O LORD, God of my salvation,
>> when at night, I cry out in your presence,
> let my prayer come before you;
>> incline your ear to my cry. (vv. 1–2)

> Every day I call on you, O LORD;
> I spread my hands to you. (v. 9)

> But I, O LORD, cry out to you;
>> in the morning my prayer comes before you. (v. 13)

We often judge faithfulness on the basis of praise—the more enthusiastic the better. But, for the psalmists, it is not so much what we say to God that makes us faithful—the superlatives of praise—but that we keep coming back, reaching out to God when there is little evidence to suggest that God is remotely interested. Maybe we can only sigh a muffled cry in the dark. But directed to God, a tear-soaked allegation of betrayal may be the most courageous faith ever voiced. Like Job, we do not give up on God, even when there is every reason to walk away and no good reason to stay. We may go it alone. Few may ever appreciate the tenacity of such faith, perhaps only Job and the author of Psalm 88.

Psalm 89

Similar to Psalm 44 and in contrast to Psalm 88, Psalm 89 begins with the stated intention of declaring the Lord's steadfast love and faithfulness (89:1–2), and follows this intent with an overwhelming recital of God's love and fidelity (vv. 3–37). In the divine council of gods, an ancient Near Eastern way to depict the divine realm, no one exhibits faithfulness like the Lord (vv. 5–9). On earth, creation demonstrates the Lord's power as well as his steadfast love and faithfulness (vv. 10–14). As a result, the people who belong to the Lord rejoice because they know that their strength and shield is reliable (vv. 15–18). For the poet, however, the Lord's faithfulness is best seen in his covenant with David: "I will establish your descendants forever, and build your throne for all generations" (v. 4).

In verses 19–37, the psalmist unpacks the covenant promise to David with emphasis on the ideas of forever/always and steadfast love/faithfulness. When the Lord anointed David as king, he promised that he would always

- provide strength to David's dynasty (v. 21),
- defeat David's enemies (vv. 22–23),
- maintain faithfulness and steadfast love with David (v. 24),
- make David the greatest of kings (vv. 26–27), and
- keep covenant and establish David's dynasty forever (v. 28).

Even if David's children abandon the Lord's law, the Lord will punish them, but he will never revoke his covenant with David (vv. 30–35).

David's dynasty will continue forever, enduring like the sun and moon (vv. 36–37). The Lord's promise of faithful covenant evokes massive praise from the psalmist.

The danger of such massive praise, however, is that we might take what we say seriously. Praise is a double-edged sword: taking God at his word, praise boasts in God's steadfast love and faithfulness—and taking God at his word, praise evokes protest when God is not steadfast or faithful. Because the psalmist trusts that God is reliable and keeps his promises, his present situation (perhaps the Babylonian destruction of Jerusalem) demands that he level accusations of betrayal and infidelity against God. Faith demands that his accusations equal the intensity of his praise:

- You (God) have rejected David's dynasty and broken your own covenant (vv. 38–39, cf. vv. 19–21, 28).
- You have devastated his city and given your strength to his enemies (vv. 40–42, cf. vv. 22–23).
- You did not support him in battle (v. 43, cf. v. 21).
- You took the ruling scepter out of his hand and threw his crown to the ground (vv. 43–44).
- You cut short his days and covered him with shame (v. 45, cf. vv. 29, 33).

The poet concludes his charges with two sets of questions and two reminders. 1) How long will you hide and let your anger burn out of control? Remember that we live only a short time and can't wait forever for you to calm. 2) What happened to your steadfast love and faithfulness that you swore to maintain? Remember how your enemies are taunting your anointed king, and act. (Verse 52 is a concluding doxology for Book 3 of Psalms, not part of Psalm 89.)

Psalm 89 demonstrates the inextricable link between praise and lament. If what we say about God in praise is true (vv. 1–37) then, when God's work collapses, we must continue to speak the truth, even if it means indicting God on charges on faithlessness and violation of covenant (vv. 38–51). Otherwise, our praise is no more than hollow claims about God that we really do not believe, or we don't believe strongly enough to challenge God when God doesn't act in harmony with our praise. But if we take God's claims and our praise at face value, that we are God's covenant partners—chosen by God for authentic relationship—then we have more to do than stand about singing the same praise songs week after week. We are responsible for the authenticity of our side of the relationship. We have a choice as to whether we close our eyes to pain and chaos, suppress our thoughts and exchange our feelings for another happy song, or accept responsibility for prayer that includes difficult words. And we know from every other relationship in our lives that, as long as we avoid the tough conversations, our relationship with God will remain superficial at best—just an endless series of platitudes and pats on the back. But if we take God's covenant call on our lives seriously, instead of walking alone in the darkness we can walk with God in an intimate and authentic relationship.

Principles for Authentic Dialogue

As we observed at the end of the last chapter and see even more clearly now, a rift the size of the Grand Canyon stands between our practice of prayer and song and the practice of the psalmists. Accepting the witness of Scripture as normative for our lives, we need to find a path back to biblical faith languages: praise that asserts the truth about God's work and lament that dares to believe what we claim in praise. In our final chapter, we will consider specific ways in which we may traverse the divide. Here, we need to establish guiding principles for our trek, essential attitudes from which practices may emerge.

First, lament begins in submission to the reign of God. For the psalms, the point of asking God questions was rarely to get an answer or explanation for what God is doing. The psalmists were spiritually wise enough to know that "my [God's] ways are not your ways." And not only are God's purposes more complex than we can comprehend, we do not need to know. What we need is to articulate our thoughts and feelings, to put the doubts and questions that we are already thinking into speech—*to submit our speech, our questions to God our sovereign*—and trust that God and our relationship can handle our speech. My relationship to God demands submission of my mind by putting my thoughts and questions into words. To hold back my questions is, in a way, holding back part of my life from God's sovereignty.

Second, although it may appear counterintuitive, an ability to ask difficult questions of God comes not only from submission but also humility. To inquire, even to ask loaded questions, is to acknowledge that I do not understand everything in my life. I do not have it all together, nor do I have everything under control. To lament is to humble myself before my sovereign. It is pride that prevents me from telling God and others the truth. Masked by false piety, pride may look like authentic faith: we appear to be successful, we talk about our blessings, we minister to others in crisis, and we even talk a lot about God. But our pride prevents us from telling anyone the truth about ourselves—that I am not okay, that I am confused, that I am angry, that I feel as if God has abandoned me. Arrogance, not humility, keeps us from speaking the truth of our lives.

Third, with submission and humility, the psalmists challenge us to decide how serious we plan to be about our relationship with God. And here, the greatest danger is not our questions but our silence. Silence in the place of difficult questions may come because we fear inappropriate, irreverent speech toward God. But silence may also be due to giving up on a relationship or because we have no real expectations of God. Oftentimes, we never ask God difficult questions because we are never disappointed or confused by God—and we are never disappointed because we never really expected God to do anything in the first place. No expectations, no disappointments, no questions for God: a low-risk, minimalist version of Christianity, safe from ever needing to have a difficult conversation with God. If we are to recover the voice of lament, we must dare to expect something from God—something that matters and something that will hurt us if God does not come through. We must run the risk of disappointment, a task made doubly difficult because we live in a wealthy, powerful society, not a third world subject to the whims of the wealthy. But my concern is that our loss of difficult questions for God is the result of our own apathy and the absence of a belief in a God who is at work in our lives and world. Without a correction of this basic faith issue, we will never rejoin our mentors on the other side of the canyon.

CHAPTER TWELVE

You Have Turned My Mourning into Dancing!

I waited patiently for the LORD;
he inclined to me and heard my cry. . . .
He put a new song in my mouth,
a song of praise to our God.
—PSALM 40:1, 3A

Give thanks with a grateful heart,
Give thanks to the Holy One. . . .
And now let the weak say, "I am strong."
Let the poor say, "I am rich"
because of what the Lord has done for me.
—HENRY SMITH ("Give Thanks")

I thank God for January 25, 2011, the day I entered the Comprehensive Pain Management Program at Baylor University Medical Center in Dallas, Texas. The prior year, 2010, had drained my soul, though its forerunners had reason to be proud of their contributions to the task. Between July 2007 and December 2009 I went through four surgeries on the nerves in my left foot and ankle, and another to implant a neurostimulator in my spine in an attempt to break up the pain signals still radiating up from my foot. But nothing took the pain away. During these years, pain became a daily companion, ranging from the sensation of putting my toes into a light socket, a burning ache coming up from my foot into my calf, or pressure that felt as if my foot would explode. It was present from the moment I got out of bed until I fell asleep at night.

As the new year began (2010), my marriage ended. I never imagined it possible to cry so many tears or to feel so alone. At the same time, my physical pain was slowly and inevitably wearing me down. Meanwhile, as the year started, I was growing more and more weary from pain. During the day, only drug-induced naps could give me a brief reprieve. At night, I began to wake to stabbing pain in my toes. I prayed that God would take away the pain (physical and psychological) and give me my life back. I gave thanks that I still had my good leg; I couldn't imagine facing pain in both. But I confess that silence was more and more replacing my voice in prayers; I had neither the language nor the energy for engaging God. If prayer was to carry the day, it would be because of others speaking words I could not muster.

My students began to call me "House"—I had the limp, the cane, the beard, and pills in my pocket—if not the surly attitude. I also had the depression that accompanies chronic pain. I took on every day as a battle with pain—and lost the fight every day. Sooner or later, the pain overwhelmed, took control, and all I could do was surrender to medication that rendered my mind impotent. I knew I was slowly losing the war. I had resigned as chair of my academic department. Students in my classes came to understand long pauses as moments of intense but passing pain. But now the pain was taking away my ability to read and think. An early edition of this manuscript, three-fourths complete, sat on the shelf for two years. I couldn't write. Yet somehow (and looking back I don't know how), I managed to complete the 2010 spring semester, exhausted.

In the summer, I set out on a quest to find help. I didn't know where to go, but I knew I couldn't keep going in the direction I was headed. At the time my diagnosis was RSD (Reflex Sympathetic Nerve Dystrophy) or CRPS (Chronic Regional Pain Syndrome), two different names for the same poorly understood neurological disorder. Desperate for anything that would take away the pain, I asked my doctors to amputate my left lower leg, even though I knew the odds for a successful outcome were slim at best. They considered the option and for a while it looked as if I would have a chance for pain-free living, but then they refused. A decision for which I give thanks now but at the time sent me into a tailspin.

I felt like a leper, an outcast shouting "unclean" in every medical office I visited. Chronic illness tends to fall between the cracks of a medical culture designed to diagnose and treat patients who get well or at least better. Complaints of chronic pain also raise suspicion of an addict looking for an unsuspecting physician who will prescribe more narcotics. I saw four more specialists over the next three months. One stated outright that there was nothing he could do to help me and referred me to a physician with a three- to four-month wait list. The others referred me back and forth among themselves like a tennis ball in a doubles match at Wimbledon; what they could do, they deferred or simply refused to do. By the end of summer, I had made no progress, and, while I was waiting, the same symptoms—the same burning, radiating pain—began in my right foot and lower leg.

I thank God that my original podiatrist, foot surgeon, and brother in Christ Dr. Corey Brown would not let me give up. He and my friends urged me to find someone at a research institution. I found Dr. Carl Noe, Professor and Medical Director at the Eugene McDermott Center for Pain Management at the University of Texas Southwestern Medical Center in Dallas. In October, after examining me, he spoke simple words: we can help you. We began to experiment with off-label usage of medications that had shown promise for the treatment of nerve pain. More important, he referred me to the Comprehensive Pain Management program at Baylor University Medical Center, a program he co-founded in the 1990s. And, with my employer's timely switch of insurance carriers, I was able to start the program on January 25, 2011. At my graduation four weeks later, Dr. Vujovich presented me with a top hat and a dancing cane inscribed with words from Psalm 30, "You have turned my mourning into dancing."

Thanksgiving Psalms

As we have seen, lament springs from the claims of praise. Taken seriously, the declaration that "the Lord reigns" leads to confusion and protest when life is not experienced as a well-ordered result of divine sovereignty. In the same way, thanksgiving psalms are born from the practice of lament and reflect the crisis that evoked lament. In these songs, the poets stress the Lord's role in bringing life out of the pit of death. For these writers, things do not just get better or work themselves out as if God had nothing to do with it. Rather, just as the psalmists held God accountable for negligence when life collapsed, they herald new life as nothing less than God's work. The same faith that informs praise and evokes lament requires an expression of gratitude when God intervenes.

Thanksgiving is not, however, a mere return to the cadence of praise—as if nothing had happened. Psalms of thanksgiving keep alive the memories of time spent in the pit, because what has happened has not only changed my life but has now become a part of my life—my story. How could Job ever be the same? How is he to answer the question, "How many children do you have?" The Lord may give him twice as much as he lost, but Job can no longer live with a naïve view of retribution theology; the memory of his experience on the ash heap reminds him that no matter how righteous he may be, no one has a guaranteed future. Faith does not require us to ignore the scars from our losses; even the resurrected Christ still had his wounds. Nor does faith promise memory erasure so that we can live and act as if nothing happened. Something has happened—death in all its forms: abuse, pain, grief, rape, aggression, divorce. Nonetheless, in the rhythm of resurrection, God's work in our lives becomes part of our faith story and integral to our new language of thanksgiving.

Psalm 30

Like the language of lament, thanksgiving also has its own grammar of discrete elements: an initial declaration of thanks to God, an invitation for others to join the poet in giving thanks, retelling my experience in the storm and God's intervention, and a statement of intention—what I will do now that God has answered my lament. As a case study in thanksgiving, Psalm 30 exemplifies the grammar of gratitude.

Declaration of Thanks

> I will extol you, O LORD, for you have drawn me up,
>> and did not let my foes rejoice over me.
> O LORD, my God, I cried to you for help,
>> and you have healed me.
> O LORD, you have brought up my soul from Sheol,
>> restored me to life from among those gone down to the Pit.
> (30:1–3)

This initial declaration of thanks emphasizes three themes. First, the psalm reflects a life-changing crisis. The poem refers to enemies that stood against the poet (v. 1) and his near-death experience—perhaps a literal brush with death but more likely an experience of life that is no more than living death (the terms "Sheol" and "the Pit" [v. 2)]). Second, during the crisis, the poet cried to the Lord for help—he used the grammar of lament (v. 2). And third, the writer attributes his change of fortune to the Lord. He did not just get better, pull himself up out of the grave, or work things out. In a style reminiscent of the accusations in lament, each verse asserts that "you" (the Lord) are responsible for the dramatic reversal from death to life: *you* have lifted me up, *you* did not let my foes win, *you* healed me, *you* brought me out of the grave, and *you* restored my life. It was *you*—not me or anything else that changed my life.

Other thanksgiving songs also open with declarations of gratitude, as if they have just experienced God's work and must express appreciation at this moment—now. Like lament's abbreviated address ("O God" or "O Lord"), the grateful poets are anxious to tell God how they feel:

> Praise is due to you,
>> O God, in Zion;
> And to you shall vows be performed,
>> O you who answers prayer! (65:1–2a)

> I love the LORD, because he has heard
>> my voice and my supplications.

> Because he inclined his ear to me,
>> therefore I will call on him as long as I live. (116:1–2)

The passionate faith that fueled lament now empowers bold and unabashed gratitude. These poets emerge from the storm with a common reflex response: Thank God! The Lord heard my prayer and rescued me! And these writers are not alone; other psalms of thanksgiving and confidence (another category of psalms on the other side of lament) begin with gratitude that cannot wait a second or syllable longer: 9:1–2, 18:1–2, 32:1–2, 34:1–2, 75:1, 107:1, 118:1.

Inviting Others to Gratitude

> Sing praises to the LORD, O you his faithful ones,
>> and give thanks to his holy name.
> For his anger is but for a moment;
>> his favor is for a lifetime.
> Weeping may linger for the night,
>> but joy comes with the morning. (30:4–5)

A second characteristic move of thanksgiving is to summon others to join the celebration. On the one hand, this invitation may be due to the use of these psalms to accompany thank-offerings in the temple (e.g., 66, 116); the poet explains why he has brought his gift and urges others nearby to offer thanks with him. On the other hand, the scope of the invitations often stretches well beyond the confines of the temple.

> Let the redeemed of the LORD say so,
>> those he redeemed from trouble
> And gathered in from the lands,
>> from the east and from the west,
>> from the north and from the south. (107:2–3)

> Let Israel say,
>> "His steadfast love endures forever."

Let the house of Aaron say,
>"His steadfast love endures forever."

Let those who fear the LORD say,
>"His steadfast love endures forever." (118:2–4)

Sing to God, O kingdoms of the earth;
>sing praises to the LORD. (68:32)

Make a joyful noise to God, all the earth. . . .
All the earth worships you;
>they sing praises to you,
>sing praises to your name. (66:1, 4)

In daring fashion, the poets extend invitations to all God's people, all who fear the Lord, every kingdom, and all the earth. What God has done in my life is cause for all creation to give thanks, not because I am the center of the universe but because I need help to express adequate gratitude. Just as I rely on others to speak for me when I am on the sea and have no words, I need others to come alongside and help me give thanks; or, as Paul put it, "Rejoice with those who rejoice and weep with those who weep" (Rom. 12:15).

Despite the exuberant invitation, however, Psalm 30 does not whitewash God's role during the time of disorientation: God was angry (v. 5). We may take fresh courage knowing that God's anger lasts only a moment before it is overtaken by God's favor, but the poet doesn't deny or cover up the divine anger that led to weeping through the night (v. 5). To take another example, Psalm 66 urges people to sing joyfully to God's name (vv. 1–2), to come and see what God has done (v. 5), and to bless the one "who has kept us among the living" (v. 9a). But the poet cannot and will not deny that their trouble was of God's making:

For you, O God, have tested us;
>you have tried us as silver is tried.
You brought us into the net;
>you laid burdens on our backs;
You let people ride over our heads;

we went through fire and through water;
yet you have brought us out to a spacious place. (vv. 10–12)

Thanksgiving is not a matter of denying what caused my distress or giving thanks for the trouble—whether it was my sin (41:4, 65:3, 66:10–12), the enemy (118:10, 123:2–3), or God. Nor does thanksgiving retract the harsh accusations of lament, issue an apology for words spoken in pain, or waffle about the meaning of what I said. Rather, gratitude builds on the same faith claims we find in lament. The God who reigns must be held accountable when chaos overwhelms order and must be thanked when he reestablishes order that reverses chaos. The poets do not hold God's reign to be an either/ or proposition, as if God can be disassociated from times of sorrow but acclaimed as the source of joy. They still believe what they said about God in their laments, and this belief becomes a point of acclamation in their new songs: We know God reigns and rescues those who cry to him because we prayed and God saved us.

Telling My Story

As for me, I said in my prosperity,
"I shall never be moved."
By your favor, O Lord,
you had established me as a strong mountain;
you hid your face;
I was dismayed.
To you, O Lord, I cried,
and to the Lord I made supplication:
"What profit is there in my death,
if I go down to the Pit?
Will the dust praise you?
Will it tell of your faithfulness?
Hear, O Lord, and be gracious to me!
O Lord, be my helper!"
You have turned my mourning into dancing;

> you have taken off my sackcloth and clothed me with joy.
>
> (30:6–11)

The most distinctive element of thanksgiving is telling my story—what happened, or nearly happened (without denial of God's role), and how God has changed my life. In Psalm 30, the writer admits that he once thought nothing bad would ever happen to him; he was secure because the Lord had made him as strong as a mountain (vv. 6–7a). But, in a heartbeat, God hid his face from the psalmist, and life fell apart (v. 7b). The writer was "dismayed" (NRSV), devastated, and confused by God's decision. If sin was the problem, the poet inexplicably doesn't mention it. Instead, he says the problem was God and so it was to God that the poet appealed—a prayer so fresh that he remembers the words and recites them in verses 7–10. What was once spoken in lament now serves as the crux of thanksgiving. The God to whom I appealed has responded and exchanged mourning for dancing, sackcloth for joy (v. 11).

The same movement, from "what I said then" to "my gratitude for God's response," is visible in several psalms:

> I cried aloud to him,
>> and he was extolled with my tongue. . . .
> But truly God has listened;
>> he has given heed to the words of my prayer. (66:17, 19)

> In my distress I called upon the LORD;
>> to my God I cried for help.
> From his temple he heard my voice,
>> and my cry to him reached his ears. (18:6)

> As for me, I said, "O LORD, be gracious to me;
>> heal me, for I have sinned against you." (41:4)

> I had said in my alarm,
>> "I am driven far from your sight."
> But you heard my supplications
>> when I cried out to you for help. (31:22; cf. 32:5)

In addition to mentioning a prior appeal, like Psalm 30, other songs of thanksgiving and trust include the past lament as part of the new song (e.g., 28, 40, 54).

What all this means is that thanksgiving—genuine and biblical—is not possible without the prior practice of lament. If we did not cry to God when the waters poured in and overwhelmed us, if we did not hold God accountable for the breach, there is no reason to thank God now. The God who is responsible for restraining the winds and waves is responsible for causing or allowing the storm to brew in the first place—or he is not the God who reigns. The faith of the psalmists cannot accept one God without the other, same God. Which brings me back to the concerns I raised in Chapter Two: Our loss of lament threatens authentic thanksgiving. Lament is the backbone of thanksgiving, without which our songs of gratitude are hollow and limp—sentimental platitudes without a faith spine. We may sing the vocabulary of thanksgiving, but, without the prior practice of lament, we are speaking a different language from what we find in Psalms. As Michael Jinkins explains, "There is no Promised Land apart from the experience of bondage. There is no Easter apart from the Passion. Only the congregation who inhabits the psalms of lament inhabits the full praise of God" (*In the House of the Lord*, 69).

Declaration of Intent

> . . . so that my soul may praise you and not be silent.
>
> O LORD my God, I will give thanks to you forever. (30:12)

The final movement of thanksgiving is the expression of resolutions as a result of God's saving intervention. While there are some experiences we want to forget, these psalmists want to remember what happened on the sea and what God has done to change the course of their lives. Memory of God's work prompts me to resolve to do something that recognizes and honors God's help. Occasionally, these resolutions have to do with vows or promises made to God during the storm. For example,

> I will come into your house with burnt offerings;

> I will pay you my vows,
> Those that my lips uttered
>> and my mouth promised when I was in trouble.
> (66:13–14)

> I will offer to you a thanksgiving sacrifice
>> and call on the name of the LORD.
> I will pay my vows to the LORD
>> in the presence of all his people. (116:17–18)

These poets promised thank-offerings when they cried out to God in lament, so now they resolve to keep their promises. In fact, it is likely that their songs accompanied their presentation of sacrifices. Other psalms, like Psalm 30, express new determination to praise or rejoice in the Lord (18:49, 30:12, 75:9, 118:28–29), assert confidence in God's present and future help (124:8, 138:7–8), or relax in the knowledge that God has set them safely in his presence (41:12, 65:4).

As time passes, with memory intact, our initial exuberant thanksgiving matures into tones of confidence and praise. As we look back on our experience in the storm, we can be confident that when we are on the sea again (and we will be), God will be with us, because we remember when God was with us and led us through other difficult times (Ps. 23, 121, 138). With the passage of even more time, the memories of what God has done provide new reasons for praise: Our God not only orders the world (the typical reason for praise) but reorders the world for those tossed about on the waves. So while Psalm 113 begins with an imperative common to the old songs ("Praise the LORD!"), the poet reflects on new causes for praise:

> He raises the poor from the dust,
>> And lifts the needy from the ash heap . . .
> He gives the barren woman a home,
>> Making her the joyous mother of children.
> Praise the LORD! (vv. 7, 9)

And Psalm 146 urges us to praise because

> The LORD sets the prisoners free;
>> the LORD opens the eyes of the blind.
> The LORD lifts up those who are bowed down;
>> the LORD loves the righteous.
> The LORD watches over the strangers;
>> he upholds the orphan and the widow
>> but the way of the wicked he brings to ruin. (vv. 7b–9)

These poets (and we) know these things to be true about God's way in the world because we have seen and experienced God's work in the middle of our own storms. So while times of lament do not exclude singing songs of praise, with faith they eventually lead back to reinvigorated and renewed praise.

Thanks for What?

Lament psalms set a trajectory toward gratitude by their final, sometimes abrupt, movement toward confidence and praise. As I mentioned earlier, researchers typically account for this fifth element of lament in three different ways: 1) The poet added the expression of confidence/praise after God intervened and answered his prayer (i.e., praise was not part of the original lament). 2) In response to the lament (spoken aloud in the temple), a priest or prophet spoke an oracle of reassurance on behalf of God to the psalmist: God has heard and will act as requested. A few texts retained such oracles (e.g., Ps. 12:6, 60:8–10, 108:1–10), but most laments did not include these words—creating what now appears to be an abrupt shift from complaint to praise. 3) Nothing has happened and no one has intervened. Instead, the psalmist reassures himself that, despite current circumstances, God is faithful and worthy of praise.

The question of how to account for the movement from lament to praise or thanksgiving is not a mere antiquarian interest. Quite the opposite, how we answer this question may contribute to our spiritual journeys or become an obstacle. It is easy to move from lament to thanksgiving when God changes my circumstances just as I want: My child recovers from leukemia. I didn't get a pink slip when the company reorganized. Unemployed, I land a job. Employed, I get the promotion. The doctor pronounces my spouse cancer free. The hurricane veers north and misses my hometown. Paralyzed, my friends carry me to the Lord, and he heals me (Matt 9:2–8). When God works in our lives according to our dreams, we are grateful—and our faith communities celebrate with us by rehearsing our stories (just as in the Psalms).

I am concerned, however, that we only know how to recognize and celebrate God's work when it corresponds to our desires. Our definition of "healing" (of any sort) is narrow and deeply flawed, limiting gratitude to a thin slice of God's work in the world. My experience has led me to think a lot about Paul and his mysterious ailment. Paul told the church at Corinth that he had a "thorn in the flesh" (whatever that might have been) and that he prayed multiple times that God would remove it. I expect many churches and individual believers also prayed on Paul's behalf. But God said no. Instead of getting what he wanted, Paul received God's grace to live with what he had—and what was not going to change. Paul learned to accept his limitations and to be grateful for grace that did not change his circumstances, but that taught and enabled him to live with his thorn (2 Cor. 12:7–10). From my perspective, most of us are more like Paul than like the paralytic who picks up his bed and walks. Nicholas Wolterstorff, reflecting on the death of his son, puts thorns and grace in terms of coping and overcoming:

> And I know now about helplessness—of what to do when there is nothing to do. I have learned coping. We live in a time and place where, over and over, when confronted with something unpleasant we pursue not coping but overcoming. Often we succeed. Most of humanity has not enjoyed and does not enjoy such luxury. Death shatters our illusion that we can make do without coping. When we have overcome absence with phone calls, winglessness with airplanes, summer heat with air-conditioning—when we have overcome all these and much

more besides, then there will abide two things with which we must cope: the evil in our hearts and death. (*Lament for a Son*, 72–73)

I thank God for the day I began the pain management program at Baylor University Medical Center, but I am not "healed." I still live with the same if not worse pain every day. I walk slowly with a distinct limp, usually with the aid of a cane—sometimes with my wheelchair. I only get so many steps a day, so I spend them with care. Three to four days a week, I work out in a local rehab pool or in the gym. Every day, I practice meditation techniques designed to keep my body relaxed and train my mind to focus and be calm. I stretch regularly, avoid caffeine, eat well, and take my medication. What I once did without thought now requires effort, and what I took for granted is beyond my grasp: working long hours, managing high stress, standing for more than just a few minutes, or traveling with ease. Of course I wish I didn't have my set of problems (along with everyone else). I prayed for a long time that God would take away the pain. But instead, in many ways and through many people, God is teaching me how to live well with what I have—and what is not going to change. And while that is not the answer I wanted, I am profoundly grateful for God's grace.

God answers our prayers for help, sometimes just as we hoped, other times not. But even when we get what we prayed for, we often emerge from the storm soaked to the bone and shivering for weeks from the experience. Doctors are not able to fix every birth defect or the damage caused by all those seizures in the first months of life. Some children are not going to get well—or get better. Severed nerve cells, as of yet, do not grow back together. God may grant remission from cancer or complete healing, but the scars do not go away—nor does the fear of relapse. Some grandparents face the challenges (and blessings) of parenting their grandchildren. For many at sea, their circumstances, their lives, are not going to get better—just more and more complicated and difficult.

My experience with chronic pain, learning to live well but not "getting better" (by the normal definition) has made me especially sensitive to the stories of people whose lives are defined by continuous storms on the sea. For these believers, the greatest act of faith may never come in a thanksgiving song for a God who finally did what I wanted, but in gratitude for a God and faith community who supply the grace to live well in storms that never let up. As long as our thanksgiving, however, only acknowledges instances when we get what we wanted, our gratitude is stunted and incredibly painful to those to whom God says no. Our vision of gratitude needs to recognize the faith stories of those to whom God has said, "My grace is sufficient for you" (2 Cor. 12:9). And, as a community of faith, we need to learn how to come alongside these believers with understanding, acceptance of God's answer and God's grace, and hospitality for thorns that keep growing and storms that cycle back over and over. We need gratitude for grace in all its forms.

CHAPTER THIRTEEN

Learning to Lament

Granting or withholding permission to lament is further determined
by what happens in the worship and liturgy of a congregation.
Congregations and their leaders who insist that the worship service
in all of its parts be "upbeat," even in the case of funeral or memorial
services, declare thereby their unwillingness to permit full and honest
expressions of loss, sorrow, and anger in the face of suffering and death.
—KATHLEEN D. BILLMAN AND DANIEL L. MIGLIORE (*Rachel's Cry*, 110)

When some people lament, they stand before the greatest of powers,
the fire-breathing dragons, the terrorizing empires, the despoilers of
communities, and, like slaughtered souls, like a slaughtered lamb on a
dragon-infested battlefield, they go out beyond their altars, and their
spacious sanctuaries, and their multiroom education wings, and their
inviting recreation centers, and cry out in their world, "We've had all we're
gonna take; we're not taking any more. We're at God's breaking point!"
That's what happens when you recapture lament. So, let me ask you one more
time, "Do you really, really want to recover it?"
BRIAN K. BLOUNT ("Breaking Point: A Sermon," 153)

I f I could revisit any one worship experience in my life, it would be
in Tulsa, Oklahoma, on a Sunday in 2002. I was the guest speaker, a
common role for me in those days, and, since it was my first time to be with
this church, I was especially attentive to how they conducted the assembly and where I fit into the plan. Wade, (not his real name) the worship
leader, reviewed the order of worship with me but could in no adequate

way explain what would happen midway through the assembly. As people started filtering into the auditorium after Bible classes, Wade extended a holy welcome and led out with a vibrant series of praise songs. His manner matched the words and evoked the melody of Spirit-filled hearts overflowing with joy in the Lord—exuberant, unashamed, daring worship. We greeted one another, prayed together, and read Scripture. Then like a long-married couple anticipating one another's moves, Wade and the church turned down another path.

Pastors of all types took positions throughout the auditorium and in the private recesses of the foyer. With only a few words, Wade extended the church's welcome to those who were not experiencing life as a well-ordered whole—those for whom the happy songs didn't ring true. He invited us to a time of prayer with pastors, with friends, or alone. For the next ten minutes, as Wade and his team sang quiet songs of hope and trust, the auditorium was transformed. Vibrant praise hosted hurting people. Everywhere I looked, believers were listening to each other, praying together, crying together. To conclude this time, one pastor came to the front with a stack of note cards recording the prayer requests. Holding the cards he led the congregation in prayer—without personal detail but with passion for believers whose lives were being overwhelmed by the seas. He finished, told us that he was handing off the cards to a group who would be praying throughout the week, and then, with instinctive strides, Wade took the church back to undeterred confidence and praise.

Over the next several months, I returned to preach many times, and every week the church followed the same liturgy—the same pattern of worship. I have little recollection of what I preached about that first Sunday, or the weeks later. What I do remember is how this church seamlessly practiced the integration of praise and lament and how the whole church moved together to a natural rhythm—even dialogue—between these languages.

Our study has led to the conclusion that somewhere along the way we lost our bearings in regard to lament. Strong winds pushed us off the course set by our spiritual ancestors: the wishful optimism of our culture, discomfort with ambiguity, impatient need for quick solutions, and most of all—well-intended but misguided theology. As a result, what most Protestant churches practice and view as "normal" is, in fact, abnormal for biblical faith. We have veered off line and are sailing on a ship listing heavily toward shallow praises, absent the faith conviction of lament. My hope is that we are not only beginning to recognize the danger of our position but to see there is a better way to navigate the swells and waves than sailing headlong into the storm singing our happy songs. Here, in this final chapter I want to plot out a few possible first steps in the right direction—practical ways in which we may begin to recover the practice of lament. First, however, I need to ensure that we are clear about where I am not trying to take us.

Corrective measures run the risk of a pendulum swing to the opposite extreme. Frustration with pastoral models of leadership lacking efficient decision making may swing to rigid models of top-down organization (or vice versa). Overemphasis on grace may slingshot to works-based salvation (or vice versa). So, concerns for an overreaction to the loss of lament merit some caution. Despite the necessity of a singular focus in this book to make the case for lament, I am not advocating that we become the First Christian Church of Moaning and Groaning, replace our worship leaders with dirge specialists, or exchange praise teams for lament teams. What I am advocating is a theologically sound practice of the biblical language of lament, alongside other tongues of faith: praise, thanksgiving, wisdom (songs that teach a lesson), encouragement, and others. An overrecovery that leads our assemblies to be characterized by lament would be no more healthy than our present overindulgence in praise songs—or our past fascination with hymns in which we encourage one another (also a type of psalm) but rarely address God. We need the healthy balance of faith languages modeled for us by the Psalms.

Charting a Course toward Lament

Practically, we need to chart a course between two navigation markers, realizing that at first any new practice will feel awkward and extreme because of its unfamiliarity. On one side, we need to exercise caution in selecting the appropriate time and place for lament. Just as the poet of Psalm 39 was concerned not to speak inflammatory words of lament in the presence of the wicked (v. 1), we also need to have concern for the effect of our lament on others. Since lament is controlled speech to God, not unrestrained ranting, we can and should discern when and where to engage the practice of lament. As the writer of Ecclesiastes later says, "The wise mind will know the time and way" (Eccles. 8:5b). Some seasons in the life of a church will more naturally lend themselves to lament, others not. On the other side, however, we need to avoid exercising such extreme caution that we effectively maintain the ban on lament from the public life of the church. As some will advocate, on occasions, lament may be best suited for the privacy of individuals and small groups. But we must not restrict lament to private prayer and small groups. The book of Psalms was first and foremost for communal, not private or individual, use. If we do not change what we do in our assemblies, we have failed to recover the language of lament and will continue to sail off course to our own detriment and that of the kingdom of God. With wisdom, we need to plot a course between appropriate caution and extreme caution that makes no real change.

1. Theological Reimagination

Although what follows is more a holistic guide than sequential steps, theological reimagination is the necessary starting point for the recovery of lament. As long as we continue to understand God and our relationship with God and the church in the same ways that fostered the loss of lament, its recovery will be mechanical or legalistic at best. The heart of lament resides in basic theological concepts—and it is here that the battle for lament is won or lost.

In a Wednesday night children's Bible class just after the devastating earthquake in Japan (2011), a young child raised the question (anticipated by a wise teacher), "Why did God do this?" The teacher turned the question back to the students, "Why did this happen?" Most answers may be summarized as retributionist theology: God was punishing them for disbelief or so that they would believe. To which another student replied, "That can't be right—there were some there who did believe. It's like with Brad and Cara (two young members of the class with cancer; not their real names). What about when bad things happen to good people?" The teacher took the cue to reshape the conversation. "I don't think God made this happen. Sometimes bad things just happen." Then she led in a new direction. "What do you think God was feeling when he saw this happen?" The children were unsure at first how to answer. They were quiet (an unusual occurrence for this group), so the teacher turned to adult volunteers in the class who planted seeds: "Jesus wept. I think God was weeping," "His heart was breaking"—at which point a child interrupted, "I think God was crying."

How we view God determines what we do with the language of lament. Do we envision a God who weeps over us as his heart breaks, suffering with us—as much like the divine friend described in Genesis 2, as the divine but distant king described in Genesis 1? Which biblical metaphors for God do we choose to emphasize: father, king, warrior—or mother, friend, shepherd? Do we worship a God incarnate in Jesus, the suffering man of sorrows who knows our grief, or only the Christ in triumphal entry? Do we imagine a God who prefers plain statement of what we think and how we feel or a God who likes an endless stream of compliments regardless of how we feel at the moment? Do we think God can handle difficult conversations and hard words or that God must be handled with kid gloves lest we offend a fragile divine ego? Do we trust God enough to entrust to him our truest feelings—allowing that God may correct me when needed (e.g., Job 38:1–2; 40:1–2; Jer. 12:1–6; 15:15–21) or disregard inappropriate requests? Describe what your God is like, and I can tell whether lament is likely to play any role in your relationship.

In the same way, how we view the church decides what faith languages will be spoken. If we view the church's assembly as a place to put on happy faces and answer every "how are you?" with "just fine," it is unlikely that any practice of lament will take root. If we continuously and restrictively call our time together "Praise and Worship," we may exclude lament from the outset. If we are intent on making the church a place where we encourage focus on God by leaving our cares and troubles at the front door, we have no need for lament. Or if our goal is to attract others to a place of enthusiastic positive worship, call it what we will, but it is a church that has lost its biblical moorings and is adrift on the tides of culture. I am far from convinced that nonbelievers or the unchurched are looking for another dysfunctional family unable or unwilling to acknowledge anything other than victory over the hardships of life.

After the death of his son, Nicholas Wolterstorff asked why we insist that men put on tearless faces:

> But why celebrate stoic tearlessness? Why insist on never outwarding the inward when that inward is bleeding? Does enduring while crying not require as much strength as never crying? Must we always mask our suffering? May we not some-times allow people to see and enter it? (*Lament for a Son*, 26)

I've found that, for those in pain, the most difficult place to go is church. I had to force myself to go to church the Sunday after my house burned and every Sunday during my divorce. And I hear the same confession from others who have buried spouses or struggled with serious illness. Nothing fits. In our rush to be positive and enthusiastic, we isolate even further those who are hurting. I don't need a church that ignores my pain or glibly tells me everything is going to be alright—I know better. If we really want to attract people to the gospel, we first need to practice the gospel in our assemblies—reaching out to the sinners, the outcasts, and the lepers instead of choreographing a command performance for those who experience life as whole (unless, of course, who we really want to attract are the wealthy young families with potential).

More, as Jinkins argues, to inhabit the psalms of lament "might mean that we—the Christian community—might have to place ourselves in a position to risk our favored position in society" (*In the House of the Lord*, 106–107). Rather than siding with the status quo through songs and prayers that celebrate the established order, we may need to side with those on the margins of society who need prayers of lament and protest against our own privilege. To be sure, how we imagine the body of Christ determines what the church will do when we come together and what the church will do, if anything, with lament.

Finally, our understanding of our relationship to God will lead us to or away from lament. The practice of lament hinges on two related relational risks: 1) am I prepared to risk everything in this relationship—including the risk of speaking the truth of my life and experience, and 2) am I ready to risk reliance on God—to expect something of God? The easiest way to avoid lament is to never expect anything from God in the first place; then we are never disappointed and have no need of truthful words for difficult conversations. I fear this may be at the heart of our loss. We have become so self-sufficient and self-reliant that whether God does anything is immaterial to our lives. We are in control, and, in control, I am disappointed with no one except myself and have no need to speak the truth of my life to anyone—including God. But lament comes from the lips of those who are not in control, those dependent on God's next move and disappointed by God's failure. These Christians, and there are many across the world, need and expect something of their God and risk everything in the relationship.

These core theological issues cannot be resolved with a series of sermons or classes, but only with persistent reimagination. Lament requires a change in culture, not just a change of mind or intellectual assent. We must do more than add a few exiled psalms to our liturgies; we must reinterpret our lives in terms of the theology of the psalms. To be sure, a study of the language of lament will be a necessary step or series of steps over months and years; this book was written for just such a purpose. But, just as the church did not lose the language of lament overnight, neither will we recover our spiritual inheritance quickly or easily. The task calls for patient endurance and casting a compelling theological vision.

2. Practices for the Church

As we lead the church to theological reimagination, we may also begin to introduce practices of lament. With care, we can help the church regain one of its native tongues, but if we are not careful—especially if we are impatient—our efforts may prompt knee-jerk reactions against lament that set us further back. So, slowly at first, at a pace parallel to the church's understanding and readiness (and prepared for inevitable push-back), we may reintroduce this faith language in several different ways.

1. *Read one lament psalm as a part of the assembly each week.* A preface of a few words will help the church transition into this time: "As we gather to celebrate the reign of Christ, we acknowledge that many gathered here and around the world are not experiencing life today as a well-ordered whole. We (or they) are hungry, in pain, in prisons of various types, frightened, alone, or in grief. Even if not for ourselves, in obedience to our Lord's instruction, we take up this prayer for them."

The selection should be made with care, again matching the church's readiness for this language with the appropriate psalm. To help with selections, Appendix IV provides a list of lament psalms and the focus of their lament. In addition, especially at first, who reads may be a decisive factor in the church's reception of lament. The church is more apt to follow a respected leader known for a shepherd's heart for the hurting than someone they do not know. At first, one lament psalm a month may sufficiently stretch the church. Good feedback loops and perhaps even focus groups with members representative of the church will be helpful guides. In time, the practice of reading a lament psalm will pave the way for gifted writers and poets to compose and read laments that especially relate to the church's life.

2. *Set aside time in the assembly for lament.* Instead of or along with the reading of a lament psalm, provide an organized way for believers to pray with pastors, friends, or alone. Resist the temptation to tack on time for lament after the assembly. Most important—separate this time from the altar call or invitation. These practices carry a good bit of baggage collected over the years; for example, fear of making a public response and assumptions of guilt when someone responds. While it may be possible to combine a time to lament with an altar call, it seems an especially difficult way to introduce the practice of lament to a church.

In addition to my experience in Tulsa that I described earlier, I have seen this type of practice modeled in other venues. The university where

I teach conducts daily chapel services with a variable routine: Monday, all-university gatherings with a speaker; Thursday, small groups; Praise Fridays; and once every three-to-four weeks, "Come to the Quiet." As the title suggests, this assembly takes a subdued tone. Faculty and staff host small tables around the coliseum where students may write prayer requests and/or pray with the hosts. The student response to these days still amazes me and tells me that their generation is hungry for ways to live and speak honestly with God. My home church in Abilene once kept a practice of lament on Wednesday evenings. Similar to what I've already described, each assembly provided a ten-minute time of prayer, primarily for lament, with host couples across the auditorium.

3. *Sing a song of lament each Sunday.* Again, I recommend words of transition prior to the song (see above). As we saw in Chapter Two, the greatest difficulty with this practice is the sparse number of songs available. Perhaps of some help, metrical Psalters are available in several different editions. These books provide the text of the Psalms and separate tunes/music by which each psalm may be sung or chanted (see Appendix VI).

Jinkins aptly points out, "We cannot expect a people's understanding of God to reach much higher than their hymn books" (*In the House of the Lord*, 34). Consequently, much of our recovery of lament depends on the development of new hymns and hymnals. Thankfully, work has begun. New songs of lament are making their way among us, and new hymnal projects are taking renewed interest in lament. One prominent example is a project led by Mark Shipp, a talented musician and professor of Old Testament at Austin Graduate School of Theology. Shipp's team of specialists is preparing fresh translations of the psalms and multiple new musical settings for each, including the laments: *Timeless: Ancient Psalms for the Church. Volume 1: In the Day of Distress*, covering the first book of the Psalms (1–41), was published in 2011 (ACU Press), with subsequent volumes for Psalms 42–89 and 90–150, scheduled to appear every two to three years. Another new hymnal, *Psalms for All Seasons: A Complete Psalter for Worship* copublished by the Calvin Institute of Christian Worship, Faith Alive Christian Resources, and Brazos Press (2012), presents new and well known hymns that derive from Psalms, as well as guides for responsive readings. Projects such as *Timeless* and *Psalms for All Seasons* merit our support for their efforts to return the full spectrum of faith language back to the church.

4. *Conduct an annual lament service.* For centuries, Jews have observed an annual day of mourning on the 9th of Av (in July or August) to commemorate the destruction of the first temple (586 BCE) and the second temple (70 CE), as well as other causes for lament. Taking a cue from our spiritual ancestors, we might also conduct an annual lament service in which we recognize our losses over the past year(s) and bring these to lament with the body of Christ. In past years, my home church held such a service on a Sunday evening in February. The advantage of an annual lament service is the "no surprise" factor. Those who attend know the purpose of the gathering and choose whether to participate. This choice, however, is also the disadvantage of an annual service. Unless the church engages in additional practices of lament, an annual service will continue to segregate lament from the corporate life of the church.

5. *Be ready with a contingency plan for lament.* The life of a church will have moments that call for a season of lament. Like "teachable moments" when students are especially ready to learn, we need to be ready when a church (for various reasons) may have special need for lament. In one way or another, I have been part of churches who found themselves in such a circumstance: youth groups traveling to special events involved in terrible and tragic accidents, beloved leaders or members unexpectedly dying late on a Saturday night or early Sunday morning, school shootings that involved the children of members and friends, not to mention our shared experience of 9–11. When events rock our churches, we need to be ready to jettison our Sunday order of worship and replace it with prepared liturgies and plans for lament. If we are not prepared, we will lose these moments when the church is most ready for and in its greatest need of the language of lament.

6. *Acknowledge the presence and need for lament on festive occasions.* Each Mother's Day when a friend of mine knew the church would draw

special attention to and praise mothers, she could not face the pain. Instead of coming to the assembly, she went into the mountains to pray—alone. She was single and more than anything wanted to be married and to be a mother, but she was not. The mountains are full of women on Mother's Day, women whose pregnancies ended in miscarriage, women unable to get pregnant, women who have buried children—and children without mothers. To take a quite different but related example, a move to a new sanctuary may be a day of great anticipation and joy, but, for those who were married in the old sanctuary, those who found faith there, and those who mourned spouses, parents, and children in the outdated and inadequate old building, the day is bittersweet with the loss of a space filled with memories.

Every festive celebration in the life of a church holds a palm branch in one hand and a dagger in the other—a means of praise and a cause of pain: a baby blessing, a marriage, a baptism, Father's Day, Christmas, Easter, and even national holidays. In the midst of our celebrations we need to ask, "Who is included and who is left out? Who may be caused pain by our praise?" The solution, however, is not to avoid any special event that might exclude—every act of praise excludes someone. Rather, a church that acknowledges the pain created by our praise and provides a space to lament alongside the praise is genuinely rejoicing with those who rejoice and weeping with those who weep (Rom. 12:15).

7. *Use lament in times of grief—funerals and memorials.* Walter Brueggemann, followed by many others, has compared the formal structure of lament to Elisabeth Kubler-Ross's analysis of the five stages of grief.

Lament	Grief (Kubler-Ross)
1. Address to God	1. Denial and Isolation
2. Complaint	2. Anger
3. Motivation	3. Bargaining
4. Petition	4. Depression
5. Praise	5. Acceptance

Kubler-Ross's elements correlate to the movement within biblical lament. She discerns four stages of plea prior to acceptance, just as Israel's laments contain four elements of appeal prior to praise. The parallels are remarkable; more significant, however, are the dissimilarities.

> (a) Israel practices covenantal address instead of denial; (b) Israel engages in expectant petition instead of depression; (c) in Israel, the form itself centers in intervention, whereas Kubler-Ross must treat the intervention ambiguously and gingerly because the context of modernity must by definition screen it out; and (d) in Israel, the form of the rhetoric, like the form of the event, is undeniably covenantal. As such, the form serves to set the experience of grief and suffering in a context of covenant. (*The Psalms and the Life of Faith*, 93–94)

What distinguishes Israel is her faith in a God with whom she shares covenant. As a result, the movement from appeal to confidence and praise in lament comes from God, whether through an assurance of divine presence or God's direct intervention. For Kubler-Ross, the move from depression to acceptance is achieved through the presence of someone who will sit quietly, listen, and be present until the end. The human experience of grief is the same, but Israel's laments provide a faith-filled form to deal with the chaotic formlessness of death (in all its forms) and reassert the presence of a God in the storm. Eugene Peterson further explains:

> The continuation of speech after the personal address is an assertion of created order. No matter how disordered our speech, no matter how disoriented our experience, the act of putting it into words puts it into form: order is worked back into our systems in the very act of praying our formlessness, our ugliness, our chaos. . . . Formlessness takes form. The poetic mind, which is a creative mind following creative patterns after the manner of its Creator, begins to display the forms of creation in the very speech that questions whether

> there is anything remotely resembling creation. (*Answering God*, 110–111)

Lament, then, can be a pastoral resource for guiding believers through the process of grief. Whether through the reading of lament psalms or structuring the funeral on the order of lament, Israel's laments enable us to grieve in a way different from the world—as those who have faith.

These seven mutually supportive practices are only suggestive of the ways in which we may begin to redeploy lament in the life of the church. As I have already argued, lament arises from theology—but it is important to note here that the practice or nonpractice of lament also shapes our theology. The loss of lament, as Brueggemann argues, costs us the ability to raise questions in heaven *and on earth*:

> A community of faith that negates laments soon concludes that the hard issues of justice are improper questions to pose at the throne, because the throne seems to be only a place of praise. I believe it thus follows that if justice questions are improper questions at the throne (which is a conclusion drawn through liturgical use), they soon appear to be improper questions in public places, in schools, in hospitals, with the government, and eventually in the courts. Justice questions disappear into civility and docility. (*The Psalms and the Life of Faith*, 107)

What we do in the assembly of the church matters because it shapes who we are and what we do outside of church. Our praise and thanksgiving shapes us to be a grateful people—and lament instills within us a sense of justice for those experiencing injustice. A church that has lost its nerve to lament before God will likely lack the nerve to confront oppression and be prone to support the status quo.

3. Preaching Lament

Preaching from Psalms is a complicated proposition: the psalms are our prayers and songs to God, how does our word to God become God's word to us? On this count, perhaps preachers should be excused for skipping over the Psalms. Space does not allow a full discussion of this issue; Psalms—including its laments—do provide a rich homiletical resource. In particular, Sally Brown suggests four ways in which lament can shape sermons: 1) lament "can provide a hermeneutical framework, or map, for a sermon that journeys deeply into suffering and its many-sided effects on our relationships"; 2) a pastoral lament can name and embrace a present experience of loss, stressing the cry of anguish and appeal for help in lament; 3) a critical-prophetic lament sermon will emphasize the ideas of protest, imprecation, and self-examination; and 4) a theological-interrogatory lament sermon will investigate the divine nature and raise questions about God's purpose. In her essay, Brown summarizes examples of each type of sermon, preached in different places on September 16, 2001, the Sunday after the attacks of 9–11 (see "When Lament Shapes the Sermon," 29). To give a glimpse of what such preaching might look like, the following are excerpts from these sermons. The first was preached by Brent Copeland in Tallahassee, Florida (a sermon employing lament as a hermeneutic lens), the second from Jeremiah Wright in Chicago (a critical-prophetic lament sermon). Both sermons come from the text of Psalm 137.

> We should never have placed our confidence in walls and towers and markets. They had no power to keep us safe. They were not proof of God's special blessings on us after all. Now those symbols, idols as much as icons, lie in ruins. . . . What shall we sing? [In response to the violent images of revenge in Psalm 137] . . . God invites us to sing these words so that we can offer them to God instead of putting them into practice. . . . As honest lament these words are sacred. As national policy they are the wrong road to follow.

> We took Africans from their country to build our way of ease. . . . We bombed Grenada. . . . We bombed the black civilian community of Panama. . . . We bombed Iraq, we killed

unarmed citizens. . . . We bombed Nagasaki. . . . [Now] we
are indignant because the stuff we have done overseas is now
brought right back into our own front yards. . . . Violence
begets violence. Hatred begets hatred, and terrorism begets
terrorism. ("When Lament Shapes the Sermon," 32, 34)

Context will determine how a preacher draws from the laments to proclaim a word from God when the unexpected and unthinkable occur. But,
I wonder, do we remember what we preached or heard the Sunday after
9–11? Did we continue on with church as usual and the planned sermon
series, or did we find in a lament from the Psalms a rich resource to guide
us in a new world of terrorism?

4. Recovery of Personal Lament

Throughout our study, I have focused on the communal aspect of lament
rather than individual or private practices. I've kept this focus for two reasons. First, despite its initial appearance (the prevalent "I" in the psalms),
the book of Psalms is first and foremost a communal book. Scott Ellington
explains,

> That biblical lament is offered to God is clear, but perhaps less
> obvious is the essential role that the community plays. The
> prayer of lament is not a private thing, but is offered "out loud,"
> "standing up," and "in church." Lament is not the property of
> the individual, but belongs to the community that presents
> itself before God. (*Risking Truth*, 7)

This is not to say our private prayers do not matter, but to assert that
our private practice is formed by public practice—and not the other way
around.

Second, I have focused on public practice because, in many ways, our
private prayers are the easiest to change.

To just do it, however, does not mean that it will be easy. It will not.
Our lamentless experience has taught us prayer scripts that will be difficult

to break. But, through praying the Psalms, we may not only pray but learn how to pray—acquire the language, the grammar, and the syntax of lament (and other languages) to guide us beyond the Psalms. At the beginning, it may be helpful to read/pray a psalm of lament twice, through two lenses: 1) Pray with attentiveness to the places in the psalm that intersect with my life and needs. 2) Pray a second time with attention to who in my life (and world) needs these words—on whose behalf do I need to pray this psalm? In this way, we may avoid what Peterson calls inebriated, selfish prayer ("Left to ourselves we are never more selfish than when we pray" [*Answering God*, 91]). We may alleviate the danger of prayer that wallows in our subjective feelings by praying the very Psalter that teaches us lament.

A Final Word

Years ago, I was part of a small group in Denver that read one of the harsh imprecatory psalms together, discussed it, and then asked, "Would it be appropriate to read or pray this psalm in church on Sunday?" The group custom was for everyone to answer the final question, no exceptions. Our answers were diverse—some yes, some no, some if the circumstances were right. Then a relative newcomer to our group responded. She had lived through years of a difficult journey, growing up in a faith community, leaving, and only making a return in the past few months. She only said, "I think that if I had grown up in a church like that I would have never left."

My journey over the past ten years has taught me that, as humans, we live much of our lives on the sea. As Peterson says, "The human condition teeters on the edge of disaster. Human beings are in trouble most of the time. Those who don't know they are in trouble are in the worst trouble" (*Answering God*, 36). No matter whom we meet, they are most likely living through a storm. The rains may let up for a time; God may clear the skies. Thank God! But often, like the pain in my left leg (when I began this book) and now in my right leg and left arm (as I write these last words), the issue is not how to solve the problem so that it goes away or how to get by until things get better—this side of heaven many storms never go away. Rather, the issue is how to live in the midst of a storm—to hurt with God instead of without God. The book of Psalms invite us into a world of dialogue in which authentic relationship with God in the downpour is possible.

APPENDIX I

Works Cited

The Baptist Hymnal. Nashville, TN: Lifeway Worship, 2008.

Billman, Kathleen D., and Daniel L. Migliore. *Rachel's Cry: Prayer of Lament and Rebirth of Hope.* Cleveland, OH: Pilgrim Press, 1999.

Black, C. Clifton. "The Persistence of Wounds." In *Lament: Reclaiming Practices in Pulpit, Pew, and Public Square,* edited by Sally A. Brown and Patrick D. Miller, 47–58. Louisville, KY: Westminster John Knox, 2005.

Blount, Brian K. "Breaking Point: A Sermon." *Lament: Reclaiming Practices in Pulpit, Pew, and Public Square,* edited by Sally A. Brown and Patrick D. Miller, 145–153. Louisville, KY: Westminster John Knox, 2005.

Brown, Sally A. "When Lament Shapes the Sermon." *Lament: Reclaiming Practices in Pulpit, Pew, and Public Square,* edited by Sally A. Brown and Patrick D. Miller, 27–37. Louisville, KY: Westminster John Knox, 2005.

Brueggemann, Walter. *The Message of the Psalms: A Theological Commentary.* Minneapolis, MN: Augsburg Fortress, 1984.

———. *Praying the Psalms: Engaging Scripture and the Life of the Spirit.* 2nd ed. Eugene, OR: Cascade Books, 2007.

———. *The Psalms and the Life of Faith.* Edited by Patrick D. Miller. Minneapolis, MN: Augsburg Fortress, 1995.

Clifford, Richard. *Psalms 1–72.* Abingdon Old Testament Commentaries. Nashville, TN: Abingdon, 2002.

Drake, Wiley. Interview on "The Allen Colmes Show," Fox News Radio, June 2, 2009 http://video.foxnews.com/v/3931975/prayer-of-death/

Duvall, Robert. *The Apostle*. October Films, 1997.

Elliot, Charlotte. "Just As I Am," originally published in the *Christian Remembrancer*, 1835.

Scott A. Ellington, *Risking Truth: Reshaping the World through Prayers of Lament*. Princeton Theological Monograph Series. Eugene, OR: Pickwick Publications, 2008.

Harris, Randy. *God Work: Confessions of a Standup Theologian*. Abilene, TX: Leafwood Publishers, 2009.

Hopkins, Denise Dombkowski. *Journey through the Psalms*. Revised and Expanded. St. Louis, MO: Chalice, 2002.

Howe, Julia Ward. "Battle Hymn of the Republic" originally published in *The Atlantic Monthly 9* (February 1862): 10.

Jinkins, Michael. *In the House of the Lord: Inhabiting the Psalms of Lament*. Collegeville, MN: Liturgical Press, 1998.

Kushner, Harold S. *When Bad Things Happen to Good People*. New York: Schocken Books, 1981.

Lewis, C. S. *Christian Reflections*. Grand Rapids, MI: Eerdmans, 1967.

———. *A Grief Observed*. London: Faber and Faber, 1961. (Originally published under the pseudonym N. W. Clerk)

———. *The Problem of Pain*. London: Whitefriars Press, 1940.

Mays, James. *The Lord Reigns: A Theological Handbook to the Psalms*. Louisville, KY: Westminster John Knox, 1994.

Mays, James. *Psalms*. Interpretation: A Bible Commentary for Teaching and Preaching. Louisville, KY: Westminster John Knox, 1994.

Miller, Patrick D. "Heaven's Prisoners: The Lament as Christian Prayer." *Lament: Reclaiming Practices in Pulpit, Pew, and Public Square*, edited by Sally A. Brown and Patrick D. Miller. Louisville, KY: Westminster John Knox, 2005.

Nestle, Eberhard, Erwin Nestle, Barbara Aland, and Kurt Aland, eds. *Novum Testamentum Graece*. 27th ed. Stuttgart: Deutsche Bibelgesellschaft, 1993.

Peterson, Eugene. *Answering God: The Psalms as Tools for Prayer*. New York: Harper & Row, 1989.

———. *The Message*. Colorado Springs, CO: NavPress, 2002.

The Presbyterian Hymnal. Louisville, KY: Westminster John Knox, 1990.

Psalms for All Seasons. Grand Rapids, MI: Faith Alive Christian Resources, 2012.

Robbins, Vernon K. *Exploring the Texture of Texts*. Norcross, GA: Trinity Press, 1996.

Songs of Faith and Praise (SOFP). Brentwood, TN: Howard Publishing, 1994.

Smith, Henry. "Give Thanks," *Hosanna! Music*. Colorado Springs, CO: Integrity, 1978.

Weiser, Artur. *The Psalms*. The Old Testament Library. Translated by Herbert Hartwell. Louisville, KY: Westminster John Knox, 1962.

Wiesel, Elie. *Night*. Translated by Stella Rodway. New York: Hill & Wang, 1960.

————. *The Trial of God*. Translated by Marion Wiesel. Introduction by Robert McAfee Brown. New York: Schocken Books, 1995.

Westermann, Claus. *Praise and Lament in the Psalms*. Translated by Keith R. Crim and Richard N. Soulen. Louisville, KY: Westminster John Knox, 1981.

Wolterstorff, Nicholas. *Lament for a Son*. Grand Rapids, MI: Eerdmans, 1987.

APPENDIX II

Discussion Guide

Chapter One
Life on the Sea

1. Outside of Job and Psalms, what other biblical texts use water or water imagery to describe chaotic forces that stand against life? Read or summarize these texts. What role does water play in the text? What does water represent? How does an awareness that water may represent more than H_2O change your understanding of the text? (You might also consider the use of water imagery in our hymns.)

2. In what ways is your present experience of life "on the sea"? How does God's speech to Job about the sea (Job 38:8–11) make you feel? How does the promise of Revelation (21:4) make you feel? In what ways do these texts encourage and/or discourage you?

3. Who do you know who is living through a storm that is unlikely to ever go away or get better? (It may be you.) Describe the storm or trouble. What is the future outlook? How can the body of Christ be most helpful in these specific cases?

4. Reread the citation from Walter Brueggemann on page 20–21. The author asserts a similar concern for "what passes these days as worship, that a faithful relationship with God requires endless platitudes and songs of joy when our world and our lives are in chaos" (20–21). Though we will return to this topic in detail in coming chapters, what is your initial reaction to these claims? Do you see a disconnection between what you read in the Sunday paper and what happens in Sunday worship? If so, describe the disconnection. If not, describe the ways in which Sunday worship responds to the chaos and turmoil in your community.

5. How do you think U.S. culture influences our attitudes toward hardship, illness, or other difficulties? In what ways is this influence good or helpful? In what ways is this influence unhealthy or harmful to us? How do you think U.S. cultural values have influenced the way the church views and responds to people living through storms?

Chapter Two
The Book of Praises

1. In what ways do the results of the author's analysis of the Psalms surprise you?

2. In what ways do the results of Holt's analysis of hymnals surprise you? Does your experience affirm or challenge the author's claim that "the prayers and songs in most churches today consist almost exclusively of praise and thanksgiving"?

3. Why do you think our hymnals and worship practices differ so much from the book of Psalms? What factors (cultural, theological, or other) influence hymnals and the types of songs we sings in our assemblies? What appears to be the guiding principles that determine the selection of songs and biblical readings each week where you worship?

4. What difference do you think it makes whether a church sings or prays laments on a regular basis? How does the presence or absence of this practice shape the attitudes and actions of the church outside worship? How might the practice of lament change us? In your discussion, respond to the following claim by Kathleen Billman and Daniel Migliore:

> A church that has forgotten or feels uncomfortable with this dimension of prayer is to that extent alienated from the biblical tradition, cut off from the cries of suffering people in our congregations, society, and around the world, and deaf to the groaning of the whole creation so gravely endangered today by human abuse and exploitation. (*Rachel's Cry*, 42)

5. Keep a log of hymns and biblical texts read in worship over a four-week period. Analyze and compare these results to the author's study of the Psalms and Holt's review of hymnals. What do you discover? Do the results alarm you in any way? In what ways do the results assure or comfort you?

6. Why do you think Israel regarded lament to be an essential faith language? Why do you think many Christians view lament with suspicion? How do you regard lament?

Chapter Three
My God, My God, Why?

1. What are the most common hardships, fears, and realities of life today? What do you think were the most common hardships for ancient Israelites? How do our lives differ from theirs? In what ways has the Christ event changed the challenges that we face from day to day? How does a belief in resurrection affect your response to hardship?

2. How do we most often recognize and bear one another's burdens? How does our practice of lament in worship help or hurt us in this task? In what ways might communal lament enable us to better recognize and bear one another's burdens?

3. Are you suspicious of the language of lament? Why? How does the presence of lament in the life of Jesus and the early church help allay your concerns? Explain.

4. Read Hebrews 5:7. What do we learn about Jesus' prayer life from this text? The author asserts that "the prayers at the garden and cross were not exceptions. The writer of Hebrews claims that a good portion of the prayer life of Jesus may best be characterized as lament" (42–43). To what extent does Hebrews 5:7 support this claim? After reading this chapter, how has your understanding of Jesus' prayer life changed?

5. Read Luke 18:1–8 and Mark 7:24–30. What prayer virtues do these texts assert? How do these stories envision prayer? How do these stories and their virtues support or question the concept of lament prayer?

6. Prior to reading this chapter, how did you imagine Paul and Silas singing in prison? How has your understanding of this event changed in light of this chapter? Explain.

7. Read Revelation 6:9–11. What request do the martyrs make? What is the response to their request? Are they reprimanded? Why or why not? To whom do they ascribe or give their desire for vengeance? Read Romans 12:19–21. How does the martyrs' prayer align with Paul's teaching in Romans? (see fuller discussion in Chapter Nine).

Chapter Four
The Contours of Lament

1. Recall a time in which you were suspended in liminal space or time (it could be now). Describe the situation. What state or status were you leaving? To what new state were you moving? Did you resist the movement? How did the experience of liminality make you feel? What helped you navigate this time? What made the experience more difficult?

2. How are the biblical laments similar to our public and private prayers? How do they differ from a typical Sunday morning prayer where you worship?

3. Identify a recent or current difficulty in your life. Analyze the problem through the three-fold lens of lament. After your analysis, write or speak a prayer that acknowledges and names these aspects of your struggle.

   - How did the difficulty affect you? How did you contribute to or cause the problem? How did you feel?

   - How did others contribute to your hardship? How did they help you? How did they cause trouble or make things worse?

   - What did God do or not do to help? How did God's actions (or inaction) make the problem worse or cause the hardship to continue without resolution?

4. Continue to reflect on your past or present experience of adversity. In view of your analysis of the problem, what do you specifically need God to do in regard to each person or factor in the struggle? Why should God do these things? Articulate specific reasons why God needs to do what you ask.

5. What do you think best explains the sudden movement from complaint and petition to confidence and praise in Psalm 13 and 54? Explain. What enables you to express praise and trust even when the storms of life are at their worst?

Chapter Five
Have Mercy on Me, O God, a Sinner

1. The author claims that telling the truth about ourselves is not easy, especially admitting that we don't have our act together and confessing our failures. Why do we want to appear better than we are? What fears or expectations cause us to "put on our Sunday best" before other believers and before God?

2. What factors contribute to our hesitancy to confess sins? What can we do to overcome these problems? What benefits might we experience if we spoke honestly and openly about our failures?

3. How are our public prayers for forgiveness similar to what we find in Psalms 130, 25, and 51? How do our prayers differ from these psalms? What do you think accounts for the differences? Do the differences concern you? Why or why not?

4. Study Psalms 130, 25, and 51. Identify the five typical elements of lament in each psalm. What metaphors or images do these psalms employ? Describe the images and the feelings they evoke. In what ways do these psalms express passion for forgiveness and God's redeeming work?

5. Compose a lament for sin. Include the five typical elements of lament (address, complaint, petition, motivation, and confidence/praise). Identify what effects sin has had or is having in your life, the lives of

others, and beyond. Share your lament with the class or discussion group.

6. Other laments for sin include Psalm 39 and Psalm 143. Read these psalms carefully and identify the five common elements of lament. What do these psalms ask of God? What struggles do they admit? What reasons do they give for why God should get involved?

Chapter Six
Why Are You Cast Down, O My Soul?

1. What evidence of God's reign do you see in your life and the world around you? How does this evidence evoke praise? Where is evidence of God's reign most lacking in your life and the world? In what ways does this lack of evidence stir up or require lament?

2. If Psalm 42–43 (or 27) were merely complaint, how would it be different? What would the psalm say that it does not mention? What would the psalm not express that it says? What is the difference between gossip and lament?

3. Have you ever felt homesick for God? Explain when and why you felt this way. What did you do? In what way might Psalm 42–43 have helped you through this time?

4. Experiment with different ways of reading the refrain of Psalm 42–23. In what different tones or moods may this refrain be read? Poll the class: How do you understand or read this refrain today? Discuss the results. Why do we hear different tones or moods in this refrain?

5. How do the two parts of Psalm 27 (vv. 1–6 and 7–14) reflect your life? Explain. What images from verses 1–6 most comfort or encourage you? What requests does the psalmist make in verses 7–14? Which of these requests most resonates with your life today? Why?

6. The author emphasizes that, in the life of faith, all experiences of life are the proper subject for prayer. What has been the most significant or overwhelming experience of your life this past week? What faith language (e.g., praise, lament, thanksgiving) is needed to express your experience to God? If lament, does Psalm 42–43 or Psalm 27 adequately express your experience? Explain where these psalms help and where they fall short.

Chapter Seven
There Is No Health in My Bones

1. Read Psalm 38 with special attention to the poet's description of his troubles. Identify the complaints in three categories: personal (how the writer feels or is suffering), social (what others have done), and theological (God's actions). How does the overwhelming description of suffering make you feel? What do you think has actually happened to this psalmist?

2. Weigh in on the ongoing debate between the author and his students regarding Psalm 71. How old do you think the writer is? Why? What are the unique challenges of growing old? What fears or concerns do you have about growing old? How does Psalm 71 speak for you?

3. Psalm 39 accuses God of brutally hitting or slapping the psalmist. Why is this an especially difficult image or metaphor? What clues in the psalm help identify what is actually happening in the writer's life? What do you think is the literal or actual problem?

4. Read Exodus 22:23; 23:9, 12 and Deuteronomy 24:17. What ethical obligations does God require of Israel in regard to sojourners? How does this teaching inform your reading of Psalm 39:12—the psalmist's claim to be a sojourner? What obligations does this status place on God?

5. How do pain, illness, and physical suffering take away a person's ability to speak or communicate with others? What social impact does prolonged illness or disability have on the person suffering? Why? How may the church best respond to those dealing with chronic physical problems? How might Psalm 38 provide help?

Chapter Eight
How Long, O God, Is the Foe to Scoff?

1. Recall an occasion when you experienced conflict with an enemy. What did you say to God in prayer about the situation? Did you specifically mention the person or group? Why or why not? What did you ask God to do? Did your request fall into one of the three plot points discussed in this chapter? Explain. If your request fell into groups two or three, did you consider the implicit or unspoken consequences of your prayer on their lives? Explain.

2. How do public prayers in your faith community most often speak of conflict? Identify three to five common approaches (including silence, if common). Reflect on the complex social, political, and economic implications of these prayers. If God does what we ask, what are the real-world consequences for others? How do you feel about asking God to do these things?

3. Who or what is the most frequent subject of your prayers? Why do you think this is so? Most of us spend the majority of our prayer time making requests for our families, our friends, our communities, and ourselves. How do the lament psalms regarding enemies challenge self-centered prayers?

4. Brainstorm: Who are the marginalized groups in your community? How might the psalms that speak about enemies be relevant for these groups? Read Psalm 13 or 17 as a prayer on behalf of one or more of these groups. How does the psalm fit their situation? In what ways does our prayer on their behalf compel us to action?

5. Reconsider the citations at the beginning of the chapter and the author's self-confessed unease with the psalms studied in this chapter. Are the "socio-economics of liturgy" at work in the church where you worship? If so, how? In what ways might we repel this tendency? If not, in what ways does your church intentionally avoid this pitfall?

6. Reflect on the plight of believers in Nazi Germany prior to and during World War II. At this time who were the enemies of the Jews? What would prayer on behalf of the Jews need to say about their enemies? What would prayer on behalf of the Jews risk?

Chapter Nine
Like a Snail Dissolves into Slime

1. When did you last hear one of the eight imprecatory psalms (35, 58, 59, 69, 79, 83, 109, 137) or another psalm that speaks against an enemy read in a worship assembly? Describe the situation and your reaction to the psalm. If you cannot remember such a time, why do you think we avoid these texts? Reconsider the citation from Eugene Peterson at the beginning of this chapter. How might a failure to pray these psalms cause the loss of an essential resource for doing battle with evil?

2. Read the lyrics of the "Battle Hymn of the Republic" (perhaps the closest hymn we have to a psalm about an enemy). To which of the five types of prayer regarding enemies does this song correspond? Why? What does it say about the enemy? How do you think this song related to the time period in which it was written (1861)? What do you think of when you sing this song?

3. Reflect on the author's three conclusions: If nothing else, the imprecatory psalms

  - teach us how to pray the ethic of Romans 12:17–21,
  - teach us the level of honesty God seeks in our prayers, and
  - prompt us to take our eyes off ourselves and see the world.

  In what ways do these psalms encourage these actions? Which of these ideas is most important for your own prayer life? Why?

4. Brueggemann encourages us when encountering an imprecatory psalm to ask "Whose psalm is this?" In other words, who needs this prayer spoken on their behalf? Read Psalm 35 and/or Psalm 58. Who needs us to speak these prayers? Why? With these people or groups in mind, pray one or both psalms.

5. Compare the situations in which Psalm 35, 58, 59, 69, 79, 83, 109, or 137 were written and Wiley Drake's prayer against President Barack Obama. How are the circumstances similar? How do they differ? What lessons or cautions can we learn from this comparison?

6. Do you recall an occasion when you observed someone confidently concluding that his or her position was God's position? Describe the situation. How did they arrive at their conclusion? What did they do as a result? Was it helpful or harmful? What are the greatest dangers in assuming we represent and act for God?

Chapter Ten
Will You Hide Yourself Forever?

1. What is the most difficult question you have ever asked or been asked? What made the question so difficult?

2. If you had the opportunity to ask God one question, what would you ask? Why? What does your question assume about God and your relationship to God?

3. Which of the eight questions or sets of questions discussed in this chapter most surprises or shocks you? Why? How would you feel if you heard someone ask God these questions?

4. Have you ever heard someone question God in a public prayer or song? If so, share your experience and describe how those present responded. How do you think the psalmists would have responded to the person praying? If not, why do you think we avoid asking God difficult questions? What do you think the psalmists might say to us?

5. Describe the closest friendship you have ever experienced. What made this person such a good friend? What did you talk about? How do your conversations with this friend compare to the psalmists' conversations with and questions for God?

6. Read each of the eight sets of questions discussed in this chapter. Identify the assumptions each question makes about God and/or the psalmist's relationship to God. What memories from Israel's experiences with God stand in the background of each question? How do we differ from the psalmists and their relationship to God?

7. What questions do you recall Jesus and the early church asking God? How do their questions compare to questions in the Psalms? What do their questions teach us about the relationship God seeks with us?

Chapter Eleven
Where Is Your Steadfast Love of Old?

1. Read Psalm 44, 88, and 89. Identify the specific expectations that these psalmists have of God. In what ways do they claim God has not kept his part of the covenant?

2. What specific expectations do you have of God in your relationship? Has God ever not met or broken your expectations? If so, explain when and how you were disappointed. What did you do? How did you pray? If not, in what ways might it be possible for God to let you down? What do you think you would do if this happened?

3. Have you ever experienced a time when it seemed that God was not present? How did you feel? How did you pray? What was it like to go to church during that time? What have you learned from

the Psalms that will help you the next time you experience loss or disappointment?

4. Psalm 88 expresses the common ancient Israelite understanding of death and the afterlife as a place separated from God's love and help (vv. 11–12). How do you think the New Testament ideas of resurrection and heaven might change the way this psalmist prayed? How might the idea of resurrection intensify or lessen his speech to God?

5. The author mentions an ongoing debate that he has with his students regarding the element of praise/confidence in Psalm 88. Do you see praise or confidence in Psalm 88? If so, where? If not, why do you think the psalmist omitted this common feature of lament?

6. How does Psalm 44 encourage the reader "to take a long view of faith and relationship with God that stands against the present disillusionment"? What difference does this perspective make when we face hardships? In what way or by what specific steps can we make the same move?

Chapter Twelve
You Have Turned My Mourning into Dancing!

1. Practice the art of thanksgiving by composing your own thanksgiving psalm. Be sure to include all four common elements: initial declaration of gratitude, invitation to others to join your thanksgiving,

retelling your story, and resolutions. Share your psalm and story with your discussion group or a friend.

2. What "thorns in the flesh" do you live with? In what ways has God said no and in what ways has God graced you to live with thorns?

3. Read other psalms of thanksgiving (Pss. 9, 18, 41, 65, 66, 68, 75, 107, 116, 118, 124, 138). Which of these psalms most resonates with your life and experience of God's grace? Why?

4. The author asserts, "Lament is the backbone of thanksgiving, without which our songs of gratitude are hollow and limp—sentimental platitudes without a faith spine. We may sing the vocabulary of thanksgiving, but, without the prior practice of lament, we are speaking a different language from what we find in the Psalms" (169). How do you think the absence of lament from our assemblies has affected our efforts to give thanks? What might we do to recover the biblical language of thanksgiving?

5. What do you think best accounts for the shift from complaint and appeal to confidence and praise in lament psalms? In the past, what has enabled you to move from prayers of appeal to thanksgiving?

6. The author claims that our truncated thanksgiving (only for prayers answered according to our wishes) is "incredibly painful to those to whom God says no. Our vision of gratitude needs to recognize the faith stories of those to whom God has said, 'My grace is sufficient for you' (2 Cor. 12:9)" (169). How might we include these faith stories in our communal practice of thanksgiving? Do you have a faith story in which God said no but provided new resources to cope with your loss? How might you share your story?

Chapter Thirteen
Learning to Lament

1. Do you agree or disagree with the author's claim that "the heart of lament resides in basic theological concepts—and it is here that the battle for lament is won or lost" (170)? What theological concepts (e.g., views of God, church, and our relationship to God) do you think most influence our prayers and the practice of lament? Which views are most exclusive of lament? Why? Which views most embrace lament? Why?

2. When have you found it most difficult to attend worship assemblies? Why was it difficult? What would have made it easier or more compelling for you to attend?

3. Identify the most recent special occasions recognized by the church you attend. For whom was the day an occasion for joy? Why? For whom might the day have been an occasion for grief? Why? What was or might have been done in the assembly to recognize and welcome both groups?

4. In what ways have you experienced a church that practiced lament? Share your experience. What did the church do? How did members participate? How did you feel or respond to their lament?

5. In addition to the lament practices mentioned in this chapter, in what other ways might a church integrate lament into its communal life?

6. If you regularly pray the Psalms or have done so in the past, share your experience. Why did you pray the Psalms? How did you pray them? In what ways did your practice influence your prayer life?

APPENDIX III

For Further Reading

Chapter One

- For further study of the metaphor of water and the idea of chaos in the Old Testament and the ancient Near East:
  - William P. Brown, "The Voice of Many Waters: From Chaos to Community," ch. 5 in *Seeing the Psalms: A Theology of Metaphor* (Louisville, KY: Westminster John Knox, 2002).
- Commentaries for teaching and preaching from Psalms:
  - Richard Clifford, *Psalms 1–72* and *Psalms 73–150*, Abingdon Old Testament Commentary (Nashville: Abingdon, 2002 and 2003).
  - James Limburg. *Psalms*, Westminster Bible Companion (Louisville, KY: Westminster John Knox, 2000).
  - James L. Mays. *Psalms*, Interpretation: A Bible Commentary for Teaching and Preaching (Louisville, KY: Westminster John Knox, 1994).

Chapter Two

- For a detailed discussion of the different types or genres of psalms see:
  - Hermann Gunkel, *An Introduction to the Psalms: The Genres of the Religious Lyric of Israel* (Macon, GA: Mercer University Press, 1998; German original, 1933).
  - Sigmund Mowinckel, *The Psalms in Israel's Worship* (Grand Rapids, MI: Eerdmans, 2004; German original, 1962).
- For less technical treatments of the different types of Psalms:

- o Bernhard W. Anderson, *Out of the Depths: The Psalms Speak for Us Today*, 3rd ed. (Louisville, KY: Westminster John Knox, 2000).
- o W. H. Bellinger Jr., *Psalms: Reading and Studying the Book of Praises* (Peabody, MA: Hendrickson, 1990).
- o Walter Brueggemann, *The Message of the Psalms: A Theological Commentary* (Minneapolis, MN: Augsburg Fortress, 1984).
- o Walter Brueggemann, "Psalms and the Life of Faith: A Suggested Typology of Function," ch. 1 in *The Psalms and the Life of Faith* (Minneapolis, MN: Augsburg Fortress, 1995).
- For discussion of the loss of lament in churches:
  - o Kathleen D. Billman and Daniel L. Migliore, "The Loss and Recovery of the Prayer of Lament," ch. 1 in *Rachel's Cry: Prayer of Lament and Rebirth of Hope* (Cleveland, OH: Pilgrim Press, 1999).
  - o Walter Brueggemann, "The Costly Loss of Lament," ch. 5 in *The Psalms and the Life of Faith* (Minneapolis, MN: Augsburg Fortress, 1995).
  - o Nancy J. Duff, "Recovering Lamentation as a Practice in the Church," ch. 1 in *Lament: Reclaiming Practices in Pulpit, Pew, and Public Square*, Sally A. Brown and Patrick D. Miller, eds. (Louisville, KY: Westminster John Knox, 2005).
  - o William L. Holladay, *The Psalms through Three Thousand Years* (Minneapolis, MN: Augsburg Fortress, 1993), 293–300.
  - o Denise Dombkowski Hopkins, "The Synagogue, the Church, and the Psalms," ch. 2 in *Journey Through the Psalms*, rev. and expanded ed. (St. Louis, MO: Chalice, 2002).
  - o Lester Meyer, "A Lack of Lament in the Church's Use of the Psalter," *Lutheran Quarterly* 7 (1993): 67–78.

Chapter Three

- On lament in the Bible:
  - o Kathleen D. Billman and Daniel L. Migliore, "The Prayer of Lament in the Bible," ch. 2 in *Rachel's Cry: Prayer of Lament and Rebirth of Hope* (Cleveland, OH: Pilgrim Press, 1999).

- C. Clifton Black, "The Persistence of the Wounds," ch. 5 in *Lament: Reclaiming Practices in Pulpit, Pew, and Public Square*, ed. Sally A. Brown and Patrick D. Miller (Louisville, KY: Westminster John Knox, 2005).
- Scott A. Ellington, "Risking the World in Job," "Jeremiah and the Vocation of Shared Suffering," "Can Messiah Come Without a Cry?: Lament in the New Testament," chs. 4–6 in *Risking Truth: Reshaping the World through Prayers of Lament* (Eugene, OR: Pickwick Publications, 2008).
- On the Qumran texts:
  - James C. VanderKam, *The Dead Sea Scrolls Today* (Grand Rapids, MI: Eerdmans, 1994).
- On the history of early Christian singing:
  - Everett Ferguson, *Early Christians Speak* (Austin, TX: Sweet, 1971).
  - William L. Holladay, *The Psalms through Three Thousand Years* (Minneapolis, MN: Augsburg Fortress, 1993), chs. 7–10.
  - James McKinnon, *Music in Early Christian Literature* (Cambridge: Cambridge University Press, 1987).

Chapter Four

- For short discussion on the psalms of lament:
  - Denise Dombkowski Hopkins, "Complaining in Faith to God," ch. 5 and "Life in the Meanwhile," ch. 6 in *Journey Through the Psalms*, rev. and expanded ed (St. Louis, MO: Chalice, 2002).
  - Walter Brueggemann, "From Hurt to Joy, From Death to Life," ch. 3 and "The Formfulness of Grief," ch. 4 in *The Psalms and the Life of Faith* (Minneapolis, MN: Augsburg Fortress, 1995).
- For extended discussion of lament:
  - Kathleen D. Billman and Daniel L. Migliore, *Rachel's Cry: Prayer of Lament and Rebirth of Hope* (Cleveland, OH: Pilgrim Press, 1999).

- ○ Sally A. Brown and Patrick D. Miller, eds., *Lament: Reclaiming Practices in Pulpit, Pew, and Public Square* (Louisville, KY: Westminster John Knox, 2005).
- ○ Scott A. Ellington, *Risking Truth: Reshaping the World through Prayers of Lament* (Eugene, OR: Pickwick Publications, 2008).
- ○ Michael Jinkins, *In the House of the Lord: Inhabiting the Psalms of Lament* (Collegeville, MN: Liturgical Press, 1998).

Chapter Five

- On lament for sin:
  - ○ Bernhard W. Anderson, with Steven Bishop, "Psalms of a Broken and Contrite Heart," ch. 5 in *Out of the Depths*, 3rd ed. (Louisville, KY: Westminster John Knox, 2000).
  - ○ Walter Brueggemann, *The Message of the Psalms* (Minneapolis, MN: Augsburg Fortress, 1984), 94–106.
  - ○ J. Clinton McCann, Jr. "Prayer and Identity: For I Know My Transgressions," ch. 6 in *A Theological Introduction to the Book of Psalms* (Nashville: Abingdon, 1993).
- On preaching about lament for sin:
  - ○ Tom A. Jones, "Create in Me a Pure Heart (Psalm 51)," ch. 12 in *An Honest Cry: Sermons from the Psalms in Honor of Prentice A. Meador, Jr.* (Abilene, TX: Leafwood Heritage, 2010).
  - ○ Colin Packer, "A Song for Sinners (Psalm 32)," ch. 13 in *An Honest Cry: Sermons from the Psalms in Honor of Prentice A. Meador, Jr.* (Abilene, TX: Leafwood Heritage, 2010).
- On reading the metaphors and images of the Psalms:
  - ○ William P. Brown, *Seeing the Psalms: A Theology of Metaphor* (Louisville, KY: Westminster John Knox Press, 2002).
  - ○ Walter Brueggemann, "The Liberation of Language," ch. 2 in *Praying the Psalms: Engaging Scripture and the Life of the Spirit*, 2nd ed. (Eugene, OR: Cascade Books, 2007).

Chapters Six-Seven

- On Preaching lament for personal pain and illness:

○ Harold Hazelip, "Lord, Give My Life Meaning (Psalm 90)," ch. 14 in *An Honest Cry: Sermons from the Psalms in Honor of Prentice A. Meador, Jr.* (Abilene, TX: Leafwood Heritage, 2010).

○ Jack Reese, "Living at the Seams (Psalm 89)," ch. 4 in *An Honest Cry: Sermons from the Psalms in Honor of Prentice A. Meador, Jr."* (Abilene, TX: Leafwood Heritage, 2010).

○ Landon Saunders, "Who Is My God? (Psalm 27)", ch. 6 in *An Honest Cry: Sermons from the Psalms in Honor of Prentice A. Meador, Jr."* (Abilene, TX: Leafwood Heritage, 2010).

Chapters Eight–Nine

- On enemies and the imprecatory psalms:
  ○ Walter Brueggemann, "Vengeance: Human and Divine," ch. 5 in *Praying the Psalms: Engaging Scripture and the Life of the Spirit*, 2nd ed. (Eugene, OR: Cascade Books, 2007).

  ○ Nancy L. DeClaisse-Walford, "The Theology of Imprecatory Psalms," ch. 5 in *Soundings in the Theology of Psalms: Perspectives and Methods in Contemporary Scholarship*, ed. Rolf A. Jacobsen (Minneapolis: Fortress Press, 2011).

  ○ Joel M. LeMon, "Saying Amen to Violent Psalms: Patterns of Prayer, Belief, and Action in the Psalter," ch. 6 in *Soundings in the Theology of Psalms: Perspectives and Methods in Contemporary Scholarship*, ed. Rolf A. Jacobsen (Minneapolis: Fortress Press, 2011).

  ○ Eugene Peterson, "Enemies," ch. 8 in *Answering God: The Psalms as Tools for Prayer* (New York: Harper & Row, 1989).

  ○ Larry Silva, "The Cursing Psalms as a Source of Blessing," ch. 13 in *Psalms and Practice: Worship, Virtue, and Authority*, ed. Stephen Breck Reid (Collegeville, MN: Liturgical Press, 2001).

  ○ Claus Westermann, *Praise and Lament in the Psalms*, trans. Keith R. Crim and Richard N. Soulen (Louisville, KY: Westminster John Knox, 1981), 188–196.

- On Preaching Imprecatory Psalms:
  ○ Mike Cope, "Entrusting God with our Hatreds (Psalm 137)," ch. 8 in *An Honest Cry: Sermons from the Psalms in Honor*

of Prentice A. Meador Jr., ed. Bob Chisholm and Dave Bland (Abilene, TX: Leafwood Heritage, 2010).

Chapters Ten-Eleven

- On God in the laments:
  - Scott A. Ellington, "Risking an Imperfect God," ch. 2 in *Risking Truth: Reshaping the World through Prayers of Lament* (Eugene, OR: Pickwick Publications, 2008).

Chapter Twelve

- On Psalms of thanksgiving:
  - Bernhard W. Anderson, with Steven Bishop, "Singing a New Song," ch. 6 in *Out of the Depths*, 3rd ed. (Louisville, KY: Westminster John Knox, 2000).
  - Walter Brueggemann, "Psalms of New Orientation," ch. 4 in *The Message of the Psalms* (Minneapolis, MN: Augsburg Fortress, 1984).
  - Denise Dombkowski Hopkins, "I'll Never be the Sam Again," ch. 7 in *Journey Through the Psalms*, rev. and expanded ed. (St. Louis, MO: Chalice, 2002).

Chapter Thirteen

- On the practice of lament and pastoral ministry:
  - Kathleen D. Billman and Daniel L. Migliore, "The Prayer of Lament in Recent Pastoral Theology," "Toward a Pastoral Theology of the Prayer of Lament," and "The Prayer of Lament and the Practice of Ministry," chs. 4–6 in *Rachel's Cry: Prayer of Lament and Rebirth of Hope* (Cleveland, OH: Pilgrim Press, 1999).
- On the practice of lament in African American tradition:
  - Peter J. Paris, "When Feeling like a Motherless Child," ch. 10 in *Lament: Reclaiming Practices in Pulpit, Pew, and Public Square*, ed. Sally A. Brown and Patrick D. Miller (Louisville, KY: Westminster John Knox, 2005).
- On praying the Psalms:
  - Walter Brueggemann, *Praying the Psalms: Engaging Scripture and the Life of the Spirit*, 2nd ed. (Eugene, OR: Cascade Books, 2007).

○ Eugene Peterson, *Answering God: The Psalms as Tools for Prayer* (New York: Harper & Row, 1989).

- On lament and preaching:
  ○ Sally A. Brown, "When Lament Shapes the Sermon," ch. 3 in *Lament: Reclaiming Practices in Pulpit, Pew, and Public Square*, ed. Sally A. Brown and Patrick D. Miller (Louisville, KY: Westminster John Knox, 2005).
  ○ John Mark Hicks, "Preaching Community Laments: Responding to Disillusionment with God and Injustice in the World," ch. 4 in *Performing the Psalms*, ed. Dave Bland and David Fleer (St. Louis, MO: Chalice Press, 2005).
  ○ J. Clinton McCann, Jr., and James C. Howell, "The Problem of Pain," ch. 7 in *Preaching the Psalms* (Nashville: Abingdon Press, 2001).

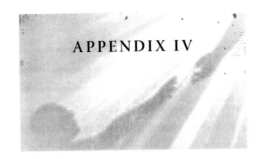

Psalms According to Type

The Psalms			
Praises	Laments	Thanksgiving & Trust	Other
41	60	27	22

Book 1			
Praises	Laments	Thanksgiving & Trust	Other
			1
	2		
	3		
	4		
	5		
	6		
	7		
8			
	9–10		
	9–10		
		11	
	12		
	13		
			14
			15
		16	
	17		

Praises	Laments	Thanksgiving & Trust	Other
		18	
			19
		20	
			21
	22		
		23	
			24
	25		
	26		
		27	
	28		
29			
		30	
	31		
		32	
33			
		34	
	35		
			36
		37	
	38		
	39		
		40	
		41	
3	19	12	7

Book 2			
Praises	Laments	Thanksgiving & Trust	Other
	42–43		
	42–43		
	44		
			45
		46	
47			

48			
			49
			50
	51		
	52		
			53
	54		
	55		
	56		
	57		
	58		
	59		
	60		
	61		
	62		
	63		
	64		
		65	
		66	
67			
		68	
	69		
	70		
	71		
			72
3	19	4	5

Book 3			
Praises	Laments	Thanksgiving & Trust	Other
			73
	74		
		75	
76			
	77		

Praises	Laments	Thanksgiving & Trust	Other
			78
	79		
	80		
			81
82			
	83		
84			
	85		
	86		
87			
	88		
	89		
4	9	1	3

Book 4			
Praises	Laments	Thanksgiving & Trust	Other
	90		
		91	
92			
93			
		94	
95			
96			
97			
98			
99			
100			
			101
	102		
103			
104			
105			
			106
11	2	2	2

Book 5			
Praises	**Laments**	**Thanksgiving & Trust**	**Other**
		107	
	108		
	109		
			110
111			
112			
113			
114			
115			
		116	
117			
		118	
			119
	120		
		121	
122			
	123		
		124	
		125	
126			
			127
128			
129			
	130		
		131	
132			
			133
134			
135			
136			
	137		
		138	

			139
	140		
	141		
	142		
	143		
	144		
145			
146			
147			
148			
149			
150			
20	11	8	5

Causes for Lament in the Psalms

Psalm	Enemy				Self							God			
	Attack	Speech	Wicked	Against God	Undefined or Other	Sorrow or Distress	Phys. Pain, Illness	Sin	Honor or Shame	Protests Innocence	Alone	Absent or Delayed	Anger	Sense of Separat.	Other
2	*	*		*											
3	*	*		*											
4		*				*			*						
5		*				*				*					
6					*	*	*					*	*		
9–10	*	*								*					
8	*	*										*			
12		*													
13					*	*						*			
17	*	*								*					
22	*	*				*	*			-		*			
25					*	*		*	*						
26										*					
28										*					
31	*	*				*	*								
35	*	*	*				-		-			-			
38	*	*	*			*	*	*			*	-		*	

Psalm	Enemy				Self							God			
	Attack	Speech	Wicked	Against God	Undefined or Other	Sorrow or Distress	Phys. Pain, Illness	Sin	Honor or Shame	Protests Innocence	Alone	Absent or Delayed	Anger	Sense of Separat.	Other
39						*		*	*						*
42–43	*	*	*	*		*				-		*		*	
44	*	*								*		*			
51								*						-	
52		*	*												
54	*		*												
55	*	*	*			*									
56	*					*									
57	*					*				-					
58		*	*	-											
59	*	*	*	-						*					
60	*											*	*		
61					*	*				*					
62	*	*	-							-					
63	*													*	
64	*	*	*												
69	*	*	*			*		*	*		*	*		-	
70	*	*													
71	*	-	*			-			*	*		-		-	
74	*	*	*	*		*			*			*	*	*	
77						*							*		
79	*	-		*		*	-	-				*	*		
80		*		*		*						*	*	-	*
83	*	*		*											
85								-					*		
86	*					*	-								
88						*	-				*	*	*	*	
89	-	-				-	*					*	*	-	
90						*		*				*	*		

Psalm	Enemy				Self							God			
	Attack	Speech	Wicked	Against God	Undefined or Other	Sorrow or Distress	Phys. Pain, Illness	Sin	Honor or Shame	Protests Innocence	Alone	Absent or Delayed	Anger	Sense of Separat.	Other
102		*				*	*						*		
108	*									*				*	
109		*	*			*	-			*					
120		*				*									
123		*	*			*									
130						-		*							
137		*				*									
140	*	*	*												
141	*		*						-						
142	*					*					*				
143	*					*			-		-	-			
144	*	*	-												

* denotes an explicit and/or primary cause of lament

- denotes an implied and/or secondary cause of lament

APPENDIX VI

Metrical Psalters, or Hymnals Containing Psalm Sections

Reprinted by permission from Mark Shipp, ed.
Timeless: Ancient Psalms for the Church Today,
Volume One: In the Day of Distress, Psalms 1–41
(Abilene, TX: ACU Press, 2014)

Ainsworth, Henry. *The Ainsworth Psalter.* Amsterdam: 1612.

The Board of Education and Publication, Reformed Presbyterian Church of North America. *The Book of Psalms for Singing.* Pittsburgh: Crown & Covenant, 1998.

Christ Church. *Cantus Christi.* Moscow, ID: Canon Press, 2002.

Christian Reformed Church in North America. *Psalter Hymnal.* Grand Rapids: CRC, 1988.

The Church of England. *Hymns Ancient and Modern: New Standard Edition.* Norwich: Canterbury, 1983.

The Commission on Worship of the Lutheran Church—Missouri Synod. *Lutheran Service Book.* St. Louis: Concordia, 2006.

Livingston, Neil. *The Scottish Metrical Psalter of 1835.* Glasgow: Maclure & Macdonald, 1864.

Mather, Richard, John Eliot, et. al. *The Whole Booke of Psalmes, Faithfully Translated into English Metre* ("*The Bay Psalm Book*"). Cambridge, MA: Stephen Daye, 1640.

Presbyterian Church of America, Reformed Presbyterian Church of North America. *Trinity Psalter.* Pittsburgh: Crown & Covenant, 2000.

The Standing Committee for the Publication of the Book of Praise. *The Book of Praise of the Canadian Reformed Church: Anglo-Genevan Psalter.* Winnipeg, MN: Canadian Reformed Church, 1984.

Sternhold, Thomas, John Hopkins, et. al. *The Whole Book of Psalms, Collected into English Metre.* Oxford: Clarendon, 1812.

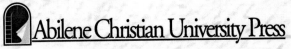

CPSIA information can be obtained
at www.ICGtesting.com
Printed in the USA
FSOW02n1412210415
6551FS